Domain Ontology Learning from the Web

David Sánchez

Domain Ontology Learning from the Web

An Unsupervised, Automatic and Domain Independent Approach

VDM Verlag Dr. Müller

Imprint

Bibliographic information by the German National Library: The German National Library lists this publication at the German National Bibliography; detailed bibliographic information is available on the Internet at http://dnb.d-nb.de.

Cover image: www.purestockx.com

Publisher:
VDM Verlag Dr. Müller Aktiengesellschaft & Co. KG , Dudweiler Landstr. 125 a, 66123 Saarbrücken, Germany,
Phone +49 681 9100-698, Fax +49 681 9100-988,
Email: info@vdm-verlag.de

Zugl.: Barcelona, UPC, Diss., 2007

Produced in USA and UK by:
Lightning Source Inc., La Vergne, Tennessee, USA
Lightning Source UK Ltd., Milton Keynes, UK
BookSurge LLC, 5341 Dorchester Road, Suite 16, North Charleston, SC 29418, USA

ISBN: 978-3-8364-7069-8

To my mother and my father

Acknowledgements

This work has been supported by the "Departament d'Innovació, Universitats i Empresa de la Generalitat de Catalunya i del Fons Social Europeu".

First of all, I would like to thank Toni Moreno for giving me the opportunity of beginning my research in Artificial Intelligence. I would also like to acknowledge the suggestions and comments of Ulises Cortés, Aida Valls, Horacio Rodríguez and Ioannis Katakis who have contributed to make this a better work.

These lines are also addressed to my colegues at the Rovira i Virgili University, place in which I have developed the major part of my work. I would also like to acknowledge specially David Isern who has been an unvaluable help.

Finally, I would like to thank very especially to my mother and my father, who have supported me every day of my life.

Contents

List of Figures

List of Tables

Chapter 1

Introduction

At the end of the 20th century and the beginning of the 21st, ontologies have emerged as an important research area in Computer Science. Their origins, from a philosophical point of view, are found in the ancient Greece. Ontology is a philosophical discipline dealing with the nature and the organization of reality. In essence, it tries to answers questions such as *What characterizes being?* and eventually, *what is being?*.

In the modern era, ontologies have been created to share and reuse knowledge across domains and tasks. Currently, they are widely used in knowledge engineering, artificial intelligence and computer science, in applications related to knowledge management, natural language processing, e-commerce, intelligent integration information, information retrieval, database design and integration, bio-informatics, education, *etc*. One of their goals is to reduce (or eliminate) the conceptual and terminological confusion among the members of a virtual community of users (humans or computer programs) that need to share electronic documents and information of various kinds. This is achieved by identifying and defining a set of relevant concepts that characterize a given application domain.

Some reasons for developing ontologies are:
-   To make domain assumptions explicit, easier to change and to understand.
-   To separate domain knowledge from operational knowledge.
-   To constitute a community reference for applications.
-   To share a consistent understanding of what information means.

1.1 Ontology basics

In [Studer *et al.*, 1998], an ontology is defined as a formal, explicit specification of a shared conceptualization. *Conceptualization* refers to an abstract model of some phenomenon in the world by having identified the relevant concepts of that phenomenon. *Explicit* means that the type of concepts used, and the constraints of their use, are explicitly defined. *Formal* refers to the fact that the ontology should be machine-readable. *Shared* reflects the notion that an ontology captures consensual knowledge, that is, it is not private of some individual, but accepted by a group.

In [Neches *et al.*, 1991] a definition focused on the form of an ontology is given. An ontology defines the basic terms and relations comprising the vocabulary of a topic area as well as the rules for combining terms and relations to define extensions to the vocabulary. Other approaches have defined ontologies as explicit specifications of a conceptualization [Gruber, 1993] or as shared understanding of some domain of interest [Uschold and Gruninger, 1996].

Different knowledge representation formalisms exist for the definition of ontologies. However, they share the following minimal set of components:
- *Classes*: represent concepts. Classes in the ontology are usually organised in taxonomies through which inheritance mechanisms can be applied.
- *Relations*: represent a type of association between concepts of the domain. Ontologies usually contain binary relations. The first argument is known as the domain of the relation, and the second argument is the range. Binary relations are sometimes used to express concept attributes. Attributes are usually distinguished from relations because their range is a data type, such as string, numeric, *etc.*, while the range of a relation is a concept.
- *Instances*: are used to represent elements or individuals in an ontology.

There exist several categorizations of ontologies in function of a particular aspect (such as expressiveness [Lassila and McGuinness, 2001] or subject and type of structure [Van Heijst *et al.*, 1997]). An interesting classification was proposed by [Guarino, 1998], who classified types of ontologies according to their level of dependence on a particular task or point of view (see Figure 1).
- *Top-level ontologies*: describe very general concepts like *space*, *time*, *event*, which are independent of a particular domain. It seems reasonable to have unified top-level ontologies for large communities of users. Some examples are Sowa's [Sowa, 1999], Cyc's [Lenat and Guha, 1990] and SUO [Pease and Niles, 2002].
- *Domain ontologies*: describe the vocabulary related to a generic domain by specializing the concepts introduced in the top-level ontology. There are several representative ontologies in the domains of e-commerce (UNSPSC[1], NAICS[2], SCTG[3], e-cl@ass[4], RosettaNet[5]), medicine (GALEN[6], UMLS[7], ON9[8]), engineering (EngMath [Gruber and Olsen, 1994], PhysSys [Borst, 1997]), enterprise (Enterprise Ontology [Uschold *et al.*, 1998], TOVE [Fox, 1992]), and knowledge management (KA [Decker *et al.* 1999]).
- *Task ontologies*: describe the vocabulary related to a generic task or activity by specializing the top-level ontologies.
- *Application ontologies*: they are the most specific ones. Concepts in application ontologies often correspond to roles played by domain entities.

---

[1] http://www.unspsc.org
[2] http://www.naics.com
[3] http://www.bts.gov/programs/cfs/sctg/welcome.htm
[4] http://www.eclass.de
[5] http://www.rosettanet.org
[6] http://opengalen.org
[7] http://nih.gov/research/umls
[8] http://saussure.irmkant.rm.cnr.it/ON9/index.html

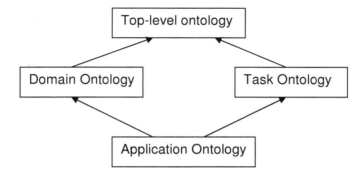

Figure 1. Ontology classification according to [Guarino, 1998].

The set of activities that concern the ontology development process, the ontology life cycle, the principles, methods and methodologies for building ontologies, and the tool suites and languages that support them, is called *Ontological engineering* [Gómez-Pérez and Fernández-López, 2004]. With regard to methodologies, several proposals have been reported for developing ontologies manually (more details in [Gómez-Pérez and Fernández-López, 2004]).

Considering Guarino's classification, philosophical ontologists and Artificial Intelligence logicians are usually involved in the task of defining the inalterable basic kinds and structures of concepts (objects, properties, relations, and axioms) that are applicable in every possible domain. Those basic principles are contained in the mentioned *Top-level ontologies* (also called *Foundational* or *Upper ontologies*).

On the contrary, *Application ontologies* have a very narrow context and limited reusability as they depend on the particular scope and requirements of a specific application. Those ontologies are typically developed *ad hoc* by the application designers.

At an intermediate point, *Task* and *Domain ontologies* are the most complex to develop: on one hand, they are general enough to be required for achieving consensus between a wide community of users and, on the other hand, they are concrete enough to present an enormous diversity with many different and dynamic domains of knowledge and millions of possible concepts to model.

A global initiative such as the Semantic Web relies heavily on domain ontologies. The Semantic Web [Berners-Lee *et al.*, 2001] tries to achieve a semantically annotated Web in which search engines could process the information contained on web resources from a semantic point of view, increasing drastically the quality of the information presented to the user. This approach requires a global consensus in defining the appropriate semantic structures (domain ontologies) for representing any possible domain of knowledge. In consequence, there is wide agreement that a critical mass of ontologies is needed for representing semantics on the Semantic Web [CACM, 2002; IEEE, 2001].

The construction of domain ontologies relies on domain modellers and knowledge engineers that are typically overwhelmed by the potential size, complexity and dynamicity of a specific domain. In consequence the construction of an exhaustive domain ontology is a barrier that very few projects can overcome.

It turns out that, although domain ontologies are recognized as crucial resources for the Semantic Web, in practice they are not available, and when available they are rarely used outside specific research environments.

Due to all these reasons, nowadays, there is a need of methods that can perform, or at least ease, the construction of domain ontologies. In this sense, *Ontology learning* is defined as the set of methods and techniques used for building from scratch, enriching, or adapting an existing ontology in a semi-automatic fashion using distributed and heterogeneous knowledge and information sources. This allows a reduction in the time and effort needed in the ontology development process. As will be presented in the state of the art chapter, several approaches have appeared during the last decade for the partial automatization of knowledge acquisition. To carry out this process, some of the following methods, techniques and tools can be used: natural language analyses, statistical methods, linguistic patterns, text mining, *etc*. This data-driven knowledge acquisition process uses text, electronic dictionaries, linguistic ontologies (like WordNet [Fellbaum, 1998]), and structured and semi-structured information and data as knowledge sources. Considering the nature of those learning corpus (reduced scope, noise-free, trusted, semi-structured), classical ontology learning methods have been designed accordingly [Gomez-Pérez and Manzano-Macho, 2003].

1.2 A new learning source: the Web

In the last years, with the enormous growth of the Information Society, the Web has become a valuable source of information for almost every possible domain of knowledge. This has motivated many researchers (introduced in chapter 2) to start considering the Web as a valid repository for Information Retrieval and Knowledge Acquisition tasks. However, the Web suffers from many problems that are not typically observed in the classical information repositories. Those sources, even written in natural language, are often quite structured in a meaningful organisation or carefully selected by information engineers and, in consequence, one can assume the trustiness and validity of the information contained in them. In contrast, the Web raises a series of new problems that should be tackled:

-   Web resources are presented in human oriented semantics (natural language) and mixed with a huge amount of information about visual representation. This adds a lot of noise over the really valuable information and makes difficult a machine-based processing approach. There have been several attempts to improve the machine interpretability of the web content like using a XML[9] notation to represent concepts and hierarchies, or the definition of some HTML extensions (like

---

[9] Extensive Mark-up Language: http://www.w3.org/XML

SHOE[10]) to include tags with semantic information, but none of them has been widely accepted.

- All kinds of documents for almost every possible domain coexist [Economist, 2005]. Some of them offer valuable up-to-date information from reliable sources; others are simply spam that even tries to confuse the user. Everyone can post any kind of information (fake or real) without any control and, in consequence, the Web becomes a completely untrustable environment.

- It presents a highly dynamic and uncontrolled changing nature. Web sites are rapidly modified, updated or deleted, making difficult and outdating any attempt of structuring the information (*e.g.* human-made Web directory services).

- The amount of available resources [Cameron, 2002], on one hand, can overwhelm the final user or information engineer that tries to search and access specific data; on the other hand, it makes nonviable a complex machine-based processing for extracting data in an automated way.

Due to all these facts, many of the methodologies for ontology learning that will be considered and described in the state of the art chapter of this document are not very suitable for working in such a particular environment.

Despite all these shortcomings, the Web also presents characteristics that can be interesting for knowledge acquisition: due to its *huge size* and *heterogeneity* it has been assumed that the Web approximates the *real* distribution of the information in humankind [Cilibrasi and Vitanyi, 2004]. Moreover, as will be justified in chapter 3, other facts such as its high degree of *redundancy* and the presence of publicly available *search engines*, can be useful for developing reliable learning methods.

Considering the massive need of domain ontologies and the invaluable source of information that can be the Web, the present work introduces a *novel approach to the ontology learning problem, presenting new techniques for knowledge acquisition specially adapted to the Web environment*. This last point is precisely the main differentiating characteristic of our approach against many classical ontology learning methods.

1.3 Goals and contributions

The main goals of the present work are:
- On the one hand, to acquire the relevant knowledge for a certain domain by analysing web resources, and represent it in an ontological fashion. This implies:
  - o To study the ontology building process and the main techniques used to learn ontological entities. Considering the basic ontological components described in the previous section, the learning process will be centred in the discovery of relevant concepts, taxonomic relationships and non-taxonomic ones.
  - o To study the web environment and the available web information retrieval tools in order to exploit their advantages and minimize their disadvantages in relation to ontology learning.

---

[10] Simple HTML Ontology Extensions: http://www.cs.umd.edu/projects/plus/SHOE

o To develop novel and especially adapted methodologies to perform knowledge acquisition tasks from the Web.

o To store and represent the obtained results using a standard ontological language in order to ease the reuse and interoperability.

o To evaluate the obtained results for several domains of knowledge in order to analyse the suitability and performance of the knowledge acquisition process.

- On the other hand, to perform the full learning process in the following way:

    o *Unsupervisedly*: this is especially important due to the amount of available resources in the Web and the potentially huge amount acquired knowledge, avoiding the need to request constantly the expert's opinion.

    o *Automatically*: this allows performing easily executions at any time in order to maintain the results updated. This characteristic fits very well with the dynamic nature of the Web.

    o *With independence of the domain*: this is especially interesting when dealing with technological domains where specific and non widely-used concepts may appear that typically have a poor coverage in electronic repositories. This implies that no domain related assumptions can be formulated and no predefined knowledge should be required to perform the learning process.

Considering these goals and our working environment, the learning process is based on two main ideas:

- *Incremental unsupervised learning*: as learning directly without any previous knowledge is a very difficult task, an incremental approach has been designed in which each learning step is enriched with the relevant knowledge acquired up to that moment. More concretely, once some basic knowledge for the desired domain has been acquired using a set of domain-independent learning patterns, it is used as a bootstrap to enrich, contextualize and adapt the learning process. This allows retrieving more domain related resources and discovering new domain specific knowledge. With several iterations of this procedure, it will potentially be able to perform a better and more efficient learning than with an individual, uninformed, unsupervised and exhaustive learning approach. As will be described in chapter 7, this iterative way of performing the learning process makes it suitable to be implemented in a distributed way, in which several analyses can be performed concurrently, improving the final throughput of the system.

- *Scalable learning approach*: the full learning process is divided in several simpler tasks that can be executed concurrently and, ideally, in parallel, taking profit from the computation power and hardware resources of a computer network. Each step is performed efficiently and in a scalable way taking profit of, as will be described in chapter 3, some of the peculiarities of the Web in which we base our proposal. In this sense, we prefer to perform, at the same time, a higher number of lightweight learning steps than a lower amount of more exhaustive ones. This approach is coherent with the fact that the Web is an untrustable, big and noisy environment in which exhaustive analytic procedures are not as suitable as more general lightweight ones [Pasca, 2004].

In summary, the main contributions of the present work to the ontology learning area are:

- A study of the Web environment. After identifying which are the main characteristics that define the Web and how they can represent problems to be solved or aids that can be exploited, an especially adapted learning methodology has been developed.
- A study of how several well known knowledge acquisition techniques (linguistic patterns and statistical analyses) can be applied to perform learning tasks from the Web environment. The features offered by Web search engines and how they can aid the learning process have been carefully considered.
- Considering the presented background and the ontology building cycle, the following learning methods have been developed:
  o An unsupervised, automatic, domain-independent approach for extracting and selecting domain related terms and organising them in a taxonomic way.
  o An unsupervised, automatic, domain-independent approach for discovering non-taxonomic relationships between concepts, composing a multi-dimensional semantic structure.
  o Additional methods for potentially improving the final structure, including the detection of named entities, class features, multiple inheritance and also a certain degree of semantic disambiguation.
- An integration and implementation of the developed learning methods in an incremental, scalable and distributed agent-based approach, providing an integral solution for learning domain ontologies from the Web. In this sense, feedback mechanisms for self-controlling the learning process (execution flow and finalisation), dynamic adaptation of the analysed corpus according to the concrete domain's nature and bootstrapping of the steps of the learning process have been applied. Final results have been mapped over the formal structures provided by a state-of-the-art ontology language (OWL).
- Design of different manual, semi-automatic, and automatic evaluation procedures for checking the quality of the results obtained for each of the designed learning methodologies. The evaluation process has been especially adapted to the availability of gold standards, electronic repositories and the particular nature of each learning step. An evaluation of each one for several well distinguished domains and a study on how the different parameters and learning alternatives influence the final results are also offered.
- Several direct applications of the developed learning methodologies and their potential results are presented. Those include the automatic structuring of digital libraries and web resources, and ontology-based Web Information Retrieval.

In summary, it can be argued that the main contributions of this work represent a novel approach for learning domain ontologies from the Web, covering the main steps of the ontology building process. The particular adaptation of several well known learning techniques to the considered corpus (web resources) and the exploitation of particular characteristics of the Web environment composing an automatic, unsupervised and domain independent approach distinguish the present proposal from previous works.

1.4 Overview of this document

The rest of the document is organised as follows:

- **Chapter 2** presents an extensive survey of the state of the art, where relevant approaches that have been proposed for performing knowledge related learning tasks are presented. On the one hand, we have summarized several *information extraction* techniques that use the Web as corpus. Part of this survey has been extracted from [Flesca *et al.*, 2004], [Laender *et al.*, 2002] and [Cimiano, 2006]. Even though their goals are certainly less ambitious than those of the knowledge acquisition approaches, they share some of the techniques employed for analysing resources and extracting valuable information. On the other hand, *knowledge acquisition* techniques (covering one or several steps of the ontology building process) are presented. Due to the enormous amount of approaches developed in this area in function of the learning corpus, we have centred the analysis in *knowledge acquisition from text* (as web resources are mainly presented in textual form). Part of this survey has been extracted from [Maedche and Staab, 2001], [Gómez-Pérez and Manzano-Macho, 2003] and [Buitelaar *et al.*, 2005b].
- **Chapter 3** presents our working environment: the Web. It discuses its main characteristics and features, discussing its advantages and disadvantages from the knowledge acquisition point of view. It justifies the viability of the Web as a learning corpus and it describes techniques that can be applied for extracting knowledge and how Web search engines can be used as an aid of the learning process. Concerning this last point, a survey of widely used search engines is presented and a discussion of their characteristics and their suitability for our purposes is introduced.
- **Chapter 4** introduces, from the ontological engineering point of view, the main ontological components (classes, relationships and instances) and the steps that should be followed in order to construct a domain ontology. For each one, a brief state of the art including some of the most widely used techniques and well known approaches are presented. As a conclusion of the analysis of each step, a justification of which techniques are used in the present proposal and the most novel aspects of our approach are commented.
- **Chapter 5** describes in detail, from a methodological point of view, each novel approach developed to deal with each ontology construction step. Concretely, methods for extracting domain related terms, constructing taxonomies and discovering non-taxonomic relationships from the Web are introduced. In addition to the method itself, for the taxonomic case, a discussion on how several well known linguistic patterns and statistical measures behave in extracting and selection domain terms is described. For the non-taxonomic case, a method for learning domain related patterns and a post-processing step for bringing semantic content to relation labels are presented. Moreover, additional methods to detect named entities, discover domain features and deal with semantic ambiguity are also introduced. Questions regarding the feedback mechanisms used to control the execution and finalisation of the learning process and the bootstrap techniques used to contextualize the analysis are introduced.

- **Chapter 6** introduces the evaluation of the results, defining the measures used to quantify their quality and several manual, semi-automatic and fully automatic approaches. Concretely, for each learning method designed, its specific evaluation procedure is described in detail, including the evaluation criteria and the results obtained for several well distinguished domains. Evaluation procedures have also been presented in the papers introduced for the previous chapter.
- **Chapter 7** discusses the computational complexity of the designed algorithms, describes the implementation of the proposed methods using the agent paradigm. Commentaries about the system's scalability and the performance improvements achieved by using a parallel approach are presented. The tools and libraries employed during the development, and the visualization and formal representation of the final results are also addressed in this chapter. Finally, several direct applications of the learning methodologies and the obtained results are detailed, including the structuring of digital libraries and web resources and the ontology-based information retrieval.
- **Chapter 8** contains a summary of the present work and presents some lines of future research.

Chapter 2

State of the art

In this chapter, a state of the art on techniques related to our proposal are presented. On the one hand, approaches for *information extraction* (mainly from the Web) are described in §2.1. Their main task consists on filling certain given target knowledge structures with instances through the analysis of textual information resources. Despite their limited results in comparison to an ontology learning methodology –information *vs.* knowledge-, some of them share important characteristics with the present work and are based in similar analytical techniques. On the other hand, a survey of the main approaches on *knowledge acquisition* (applied to ontology learning) is presented in §2.2. As many of them have been developed depending on the type of learning corpus, we will focus on *knowledge acquisition from text*, as the major part of web resources are presented in this form.

2.1 Information extraction

Classical methods on Information Extraction (IE) have focused on the use of supervised learning techniques such as hidden Markov models [Freitag and MacCallun, 1999; Skounakis *et al.*, 2003], Rule Learning [Soderland, 1999], or Conditional Random Fields [McCallum, 2003]. These techniques learn a language model or a set of rules from a set of hand-tagged training documents and then apply the model or rules to new texts. Models learned in this manner are effective on documents similar to the set of training documents, but extract quite poorly when applied to documents with a different genre or style. As a result, this approach has difficulty scaling to the Web due to the diversity of text styles and genres on the Web and the prohibitive cost of creating an equally diverse set of hand tagged documents.

In the context of web resources, a set of extraction rules suitable to extract information from a web site is called a *wrapper*. Two main approaches for wrapper generation tools have been proposed during the last years: the knowledge engineering –classical IE- and the automatic training approach –adaptive IE-. In the former approach, the extraction rules are designed by a domain expert, according to his background knowledge. Clearly, in such an approach the user skills play a crucial role in the successful identification and extraction of relevant information.

The adaptive IE instead exploits AI techniques to induce extraction rules starting from a set of information patterns that are marked for extraction by a user. In Table 1, as stated in [Cimiano, 2006] the main advantages and disadvantages of both approaches are summarised.

Table 1. Comparison of classical and adaptive Information Extraction.

Classical IE	Adaptive IE
+ very precise (hand-coded rules)	+ reasonable precision (rule induction)
+ handles domain-independent phenomena	+ higher recall
(to some extent)	+ no need for developing grammars
- need to develop grammars	- provide training data (expensive)
- expensive development & test cycle	- typically "overfitted" to the domain
- develop lexicons, gazetteers, *etc*	- rules can be hard to interpret

Research on learning extraction rules has occurred mainly in two contexts: creating wrappers for information agents and developing general purpose information extraction systems for natural language text. The former are primarily used for semi-structured information sources, and their extraction rules rely heavily on the regularities of the documents; the latter are applied to free text documents and use extraction patterns that are based on linguistic constraints.

Regarding the first type of systems (wrappers), in [Flesca *et al.*, 2004], a survey of the most important approaches is presented. The evaluated systems are:
-   ShopBot [Doorenbos *et al.*, 1997]: is an agent devoted to extract information from pages related to Web Services (*e.g.* e-commerce). Combines heuristic, pattern matching and inductive learning techniques.
-   WIEN [Kusmerick, 2000]: operates on structured texts containing information organized in a tabular fashion.
-   SoftMealy [Hsu and Dung, 1998]: is based on non-deterministic state automata and it was mainly conceived to induce wrappers from semi-structured pages.
-   STALKER [Muslea *et al.*, 2001]: is a system for learning supervised wrappers. It yields an Embedded Catalog Tree, representing the structure of the page as a tree.
-   Amilcare [Ciravegna, 2001]: it learns patterns to extract values of a slot to be filled in a template. It relies on a set of training data in which the values to be extracted are marked with XML-tags.

In contrast to wrappers, general purpose information extraction systems are focused on unstructured text using techniques based on linguistic constraints:
-   RAPIER [Califf and Mooney. 1999]: it takes as input a document and as template indication the data to be extracted and outputs pattern matching rules according to a given template.
-   SRV [Freitag, 2000]: is a top-down relational learning algorithm. It works on a given set of labelled pages and uses some features to generate first-order logic extraction rules.
-   WHISK [Soderland, 1999]: can deal with all kinds of text, since it exploits a syntactic analyzer and a semantic classifier. Given a training set of pages, it generates regular expressions which are used to recognize the context of relevant instances and their delimiters.

As some conclusions, also mentioned in [Etzioni *et al.*, 2004], the described systems are able to learn extraction patterns but either require a certain amount of training and/or operate only on structured documents and cannot handle unstructured text.

In order to overcome limitations related to data sparseness, in the last few years some authors have been using the whole Web (and not only a reduced corpus of resources) as a corpus. Those approaches take advantage of the available web search engines and the possibility of accessing massive amounts of up-to-date information (more details in chapter 3). Some relevant approaches based in those premises are:
-   PANKOW [Cimiano and Staab, 2005]: exploits the implicit knowledge available in the Web together with statistical information to propose formal annotations. If offers unsupervised instance categorization but presents a low recall.
-   KnowItAll [Etzioni *et al.* 2005]: its main aim is to discover all the members belonging to a certain class (*e.g.* all actors in the world). It uses discriminators to train a classifier which then predicts membership to a class.
-   TextRunner [Banko *et al.*, 2007]: it represents a state of the art IE system that is able to retrieve, in a very efficient way, domain independent relationships.

The presented approaches aim to extract information of textual or semi structured resources. In consequence, they operate at a different level of abstraction in comparison to ontology learning methods. The former results are lists of facts used to populate pre-defined structured. The later, including the present work, aim a higher level of comprehension, acquiring relevant knowledge (concepts, relations, instances) for a domain. However, as will be discussed in chapters 3 and 5 our approach for ontology learning exploits similar techniques (web search queries, statistical analyses) as the presented Web-based IE systems, but applying them to knowledge acquisition tasks.

2.2   Knowledge acquisition from texts

As stated in [Maedche and Staab, 2001], there are several approaches for ontology learning depending on the type of input:
-   *Knowledge acquisition methods from texts*: consist of extracting knowledge by applying natural language analysis techniques to texts. The most well-known approaches from this group are:
    o   *Pattern-based extraction* [Hearst, 1992; Morin, 1999]: a relation is recognized when a sequence of words in the text matches a pattern. For instance, a pattern can establish that if a sequence of N names is detected, then the N-1 first names are hyponyms of the Nth. This technique will be further discussed in chapter 4 as it is one of the bases of our methodology.
    o   *Association rules*: they were initially defined on the database field. Given a set of transactions, where each transaction is a set of literals, an association rule is an expression of the form X implies Y, where X and Y are sets of items. [Agrawal *et al.*, 1993]. Using association rules to achieve an automatic construction of concept hierarchies is derived from the idea that association rules with stronger support, confidence and more extensive conceptual relationships can be placed on the upper level of the ontology [Maedche and Staab, 2000].

Association rules have been used [Maedche and Staab, 2001] to discover non-taxonomic relationss, using a concept hierarchy as background knowledge.

o *Conceptual clustering* [Faure and Poibeau, 2000]: concepts are grouped according to the semantic distance between each other to make up hierarchies. Right now, there are still several problems in using this method which restrict its usability [Hotho *et al.*, 2001] as its inefficiency in high dimensional spaces.

o *Ontology pruning* [Kietz *et al.*, 2000]: the objective is to build a domain-ontology-based on different heterogeneous sources. It has the following steps. First, a generic core ontology is used as a top level structure for the domain-specific ontology. Second, a dictionary which contains important domain terms described in natural language is used to acquire domain concepts. These concepts are classified into the generic core ontology. Third, domain-specific and general corpora of text are used to remove concepts that were not domain specific. Concept removal follows the heuristic that domain-specific concepts should be more frequent in a domain-specific corpus than in generic texts.

o *Concept learning* [Hahn and Schulz, 2000]. A given taxonomy is incrementally updated as new concepts are acquired from real-world texts.

- *Knowledge acquisition methods from dictionary*: base its performance on the use of a machine readable dictionary to extract relevant concepts and relations among them. Traditional dictionaries present entries together with their synonyms, root words, etymology, *etc*. The definitions and relationships presented in the dictionary are used to determine the hierarchy relationships of concepts [Kietz *et al.*, 2000; Khan and Luo, 2002]. The dictionary-based construction method normally is the groundwork of other construction methods. The dictionary-based method has the following limitations:

1) An ontology formed using the dictionary-based method has a general scope and is not at all domain specific. Only when it is combined with another method does it provide a more significant and valuable ontological framework.

2) Its dependency to the particular dictionary makes the method incapable of adapting to an incessantly changing environment as the Web.

- *Knowledge acquisition methods from a knowledge base*: use knowledge bases as the sources for learning. The knowledge base must include basic rules and simple examples. The rules are used to assemble related ontology [Alani *et al.*, 2003].

- *Knowledge acquisition methods from semi-structured data*: the input is documents with a predefined structure, such as XML schemas.

As our proposal is based exclusively in the analysis of the Web and the major part of web documents are presented in unstructured natural language text, in the rest of this section only those methods that use text as input (sometimes the Web itself) will be analysed. For each method and tool, a summary of its relevant characteristics (methods of analysis, previous knowledge used or sources of information) is presented in Table 2 and Table 3. More detailed information about many of these methods can be found in [Gómez-Perez and Manzano-Macho, 2003; Buitelaar *et al.*, 2005] and in the listed references.

Methods and tools related to the present research are commented in chapter 4 where the main techniques used in the ontology learning process are presented.

Analysing the main characteristics of these methodologies and tools, in [Gómez-Pérez and Manzano-Macho, 2003], the following conclusions are presented.

From the methodological perspective, it can be concluded that:
- The presented methods are mainly based on natural language analysis techniques and use a corpus that guides the overall process. Only Maedche *et al.* work uses domain and general corpora to remove unspecific domain concepts from an existing ontology. The other ones only use domain documents to learn new concepts and relations.
- The most common semantic repository used by these methods is WordNet (more details in §6.2). This dependency is manifested by limitations presented by several methods when the searched information is not contained in WordNet [Navigli and Velardi, 2004].
- All these methods require the participation of a human being to evaluate the results and the accuracy of the learning process.

From a technological perspective, it can be concluded that:
- Most of these tools perform NLP (linguistic analyses, lexical-syntactic patterns, *etc*) to extract linguistic and semantic knowledge from the corpus used for learning.
- The tools can be classified in three main groups according to the technique followed to learn: conceptual clustering, statistical approaches, and linguistic and/or semantic approaches.
- It does not exist a fully automatic tool that carries out the whole learning process. Some tools are focused to help in the acquisition of lexical-semantic knowledge, others help to elicit concepts or relations from a pre-processed corpus with the help the user, *etc*.
- There are neither tools to evaluate the accuracy of the learning process nor to compare different results obtained using different learning techniques.

Table 2. Summary of knowledge acquisition methods from text.

Main reference	Main goal	Main techniques used	Reuse Ontol.	Learning sources	Associated tool	Evaluat.
[Agirre *et al.*, 2000]	Acquire concepts for an existing ontologies	Statistics Clustering Topic signatures	Yes	Domain text (web resources) WordNet	N/A	User
[Alfonseca and Man-andhar, 2002]	Acquire concepts for an existing ontologies	Topic signatures Semantic distance	Yes	Domain text WordNet	Welkin	Expert
[Aussenac-Gilles *et al.*, 2000]	Learn concepts and relations	Linguistic patterns Clustering	Yes	Domain Text Domain ontologies	GEDITERM TERMINAE	User
[Bachimont *et al.*, 2002]	Build a taxonomy	Linguistic techniques	No	Domain Text	DOE	Expert
[Faatz and Steinmetz, 2002]	Acquire concepts for an existing ontologies	Statistics Semantic distance	Yes	Domain corpus Domain ontology	Any ontology workbench	Expert
[Gupta *et al.*, 2002]	Build sublanguages in WordNet	Shallow text processing Term-extraction tech-niques	Yes	Domain text WordNet	SubWordNet Engineering tool	Expert
[Hahn and Schnattiger, 1998]	Learn new con-cepts	Linguistic and concep-tual quality labels Statistics	No	Domain text	N/A	Empiric measures Expert
[Hearst, 1998]	Acquire concepts for an existing ontology	Linguistic patterns	Yes	Domain Text WordNet	Welkin	Expert
[Hwang, 1999]	Elicit a taxonomy	Term-extraction ML techniques Statistics	No	Domain Text	N/A	Expert
[Khan and Luo, 2002]	Learn concepts	Clustering Statistics	Yes	Domain Text WordNet	N/A	Expert
[Kietz *et al.*, 2000]	Learn concepts and relations to enrich an ontology	Statistics	Yes	Domain and non-domain text Domain ontologies WordNet	Text-To-Onto	User
[Lee *et al.* 2003]	Acquire concepts for an existing ontologies	Association rules	Yes	Domain corpus (medical research abstracts), UMLS	N/A	Expert
[Lonsdale *et al.*, 2002]	Discover new relationships in an existing ontology	Mappings Linguistic techniques Graph theory	Yes	Terminological databases Domain ontology WordNet Domain text	N/A	User/ Expert
[Missikoff *et al.*, 2002]	Build taxonomies and fuse with an existing ontology	Term-extraction Statistics ML techniques	Yes	Domain text WordNet	OntoLearn	Expert
[Moldovan and Girju, 2001]	Acquire concepts for an existing ontology	Lexical-syntactic patterns Term extraction	Yes	Domain Text Lexical resources WordNet	N/A	Expert
[Nobécourt, 2000]	Learn concepts and relations	Linguistic analysis	No	Domain text	TERMINAE	User/ Expert
[Reinberger *et al.*, 2004]	Extract semantic relationships from text	Concept Formation Relation Extraction Shallow Linguistics Clustering	No	Domain text	N/A	Expert

[Rinaldi *et al.*, 2005]	Term and Taxonomy Extraction	Shallow Linguistics Patterns	No	Domain text	N/A	Expert
[Roux *et al.*, 2000]	Acquire new concepts for an existing taxonomy	Verb-patterns	Yes	Domain text Domain ontology	N/A	Expert
[Sabou, 2005]	Term and Taxonomy Extraction	Shallow Linguistic Analysis Patterns	No	Textual documentations attached to Web services	N/A	Expert
[Weng *et al.*, 2006]	Ontology learning for supporting information classification	Formal Concept Analysis	No	Documents from different data sources Libraries	N/A	Expert
[Wagner, 2000]	Learn new relationships for an existing ontology	Statistics	Yes	WordNet	N/A	Expert
[Xu *et al.*, 2002]	Learn concepts and relations among them	Lexical-syntactic patterns Statistics Text-mining	Yes	Annotated text corpus WordNet	TFIDF-based term classification system	Expert
This work	**Domain ontology learning: concepts and named entities, taxonomic and non-taxonomic relations**	**Statistics Linguistic patterns**	**No**	**Domain text (web resources)**	**Distributed knowledge acquisition platform**	**Semi-automatic Expert**

Table 3. Summary of knowledge acquisition tools from text.

Name	Goal and scope	Learning techniques	Method followed	Sources	User intervention	Interoper-ability
ASIUM [Faure and Poibeau, 2000]	Learn taxonomic Relations	Conceptual clustering	Own	Text syntactically analysed	Whole process	Any ontology development tool
Caméléon [Aussenac-Gilles and Seguela, 2000]	Tune generic patterns or build new ones. Find taxonomic and non taxonomic relations to enrich a conceptual model.	Reuse and tuning of generic patterns, Heart's proposal, pattern indication in text.	Own	Texts processed by taggers. Its own base of generic patterns.	Validates, adapts, or defines new domain specific patterns and relations.	Imports lists of terms from any text extractor.
Corporum-Ontobuilder [Engels, 2001]	Extract initial taxonomy	Linguistic and semantic techniques	Own	Text	Not necessary	OntoWrapper OntoExtract
DOE [Bachimont, 2000]	Help the ontologist in the ontology construction	Linguistic techniques	Own	NL text	Whole process	None
DOODLE/2 DOODLE-OWL [Morita et al., 2004]	Semi-automatic generation of ontologies	Statistics	Own	Machine readable dictionaries Domain text	Select relations and validate results	OWL
HASTI [Shamsfard and Bar-foroush, 2002]	Learn words, concepts and relations	Linguistic based Template driven	Own	Persian written texts	Not necessary	N/A
JATKE http://jatke.opendfki.de	A framework for ontology learning	Statistics-based Structure-based NLP-based	Various	Ontologies, documents, user feedback	Ontology changes	Protégé
KEA [Jones and Paynter, 2002]	Keyphrase extraction Algorithm	Statistics ML techniques Lexical processing	Own	NL text	Evaluation	WEKA ML Workbench
LTG [Mikheev and Finch, 1997]	Discover internal relations of texts in NL	Statistic inference Linguistic techniques	Own	NL text	Whole process	Any ontology development tool
MO'K Workbench [Bisson et al., 2000]	Learn concept taxonomy	Conceptual clustering	Own	Tagged text	Whole process	Any ontology development tool
Ontobuilder [Gal et al., 2004]	Compose ontologies from search formularies	Extraction rules	Own	Web forms	Supervision and validation	None
Ontogen [Fortuna et al., 2006]	Semi-automatic ontology construction	Statistical Analysis Clustering	Own	Text collections	Evaluation	N/A
OntoLearn [Navigli and Velardi, 2004]	Extract domain ontologies from virtual organizations	Linguistic analysis ML Statistics	Missikoff et al.	NL text (web resources) WordNet	Evaluation	None
OntoLT [Sintek et al., 2004]	Extract classes and properties form linguistically annotated text	Mapping rules Statistics	Own	Linguistically annotated text	Selection and validation	Protégé
Prométhée [Morin, 1999]	Extraction and refinement of patterns	Learning from examples	Own	Pattern-based	Whole process	N/A
RelExt [Schutz and Buitelaar, 2005]	Relation Extraction in Ontology Extension	Shallow Linguistic Parsing Statistical Analysis	Own	Domain specific text collection	Evaluation	N/A
SOAT [Wu and Hsu, 2002]	Acquisition of relationships	Phrase-patterns	Own	NL text	N/A	N/A
SubWordNet [Gupta et al., 2002]	Build a Sub WordNet	Several NL techniques and statistics	Own	NL text	Whole process	N/A
SVETLAN [Chaelandar and Grau, 2000]	Build a concept hierarchy	Conceptual clustering	Own	NL text	Validation	N/A

TERMINAE [Szulman et al., 2002]	Build an initial ontology	Conceptual clustering	Own	NL text	Validation	N/A
TextStorm and Clouds [Oliveira et al., 2001]	Build a taxonomy	Inductive Logic Programming Linguistic hypothesis	Own	NL text	Whole process	N/A
Text-To-Onto Text2Onto [Maedche and Staab, 2003]	Find taxonomic and non-taxonomic r elations	Statistics Pruning Association rules	Kietz et al.	NL text Dictionaries Ontologies	Validation	KAON tool suite
TFIDF-based term classification system [Xu et al., 2002]	Learn new concepts and relations among them	Text-mining Statistics	Hybrid text-mining to acquire domain terms	NL text	Evaluation	SPPC NLP tool
Welkin [Alfonseca and Rodríguez, 2002]	Enrich automatically existing general purpose ontologies	Semantic similarity	Alfonseca and Manandahar	Domain corpus WordNet	Not necessary	None
WOLFIE [Thompson and Mooney, 1997]	Learn a semantic lexicon	Statistics	Own	Pre-processed corpus examples	Validation	CHILL
This work	**Domain ontology learning: concepts and named entities, taxonomic and non-taxonomic relations**	**Statistics Linguistic patterns**	**Own**	**The Web**	**Evaluation**	**Web search engines OWL editors**

2.3 Summary and relation with our proposal

Once we have described the main approaches for information extraction and knowledge acquisition from natural language text resources and the Web in particular, several important aspects can be remarked in relation to the present work:

- Many AI techniques are involved in information extraction systems and in the different steps of the learning process, such as Natural Language Processing, Clustering, Association Rules, Pattern-based Learning, *etc*. Some of these techniques (mainly linguistic patterns) will be applied in the present work, adapting them to the Web environment.
- Most of the presented ontology learning techniques use as a corpus a reduced and pre-selected set of relevant documents for the covered domain. This approach solves some problems about untrustworthiness, noise and size that arise when developing an unsupervised, domain-independent Web-based approach but may suffer from data sparseness. Recently, some authors are starting to use the Web as a learning corpus, but many lack a full integration between the learning methodology and the Web environment.
- Most of the presented information extraction systems from the Web rely on documents that present a certain degree of structure. This fact limits their performance as scalable general-purpose solutions as the majority of web resources do not present any meaningful structure. Our approach is more related to the latest attempts of IR by using the Web as a massive corpus.
- Most of the knowledge acquisition methodologies and information extraction techniques presented use predefined knowledge to some degree, like training examples, previous ontologies, semantic repositories (WordNet) or even the supervision of a human expert. This fact makes difficult the development of domain independent solutions, impacting the scalability and versatility of those systems in wide and heterogeneous environments like the Web.
- Most of the ontology learning methods are focused on the acquisition of taxonomic relationships and often neglect the importance of interlinkage between concepts. Even though taxonomic knowledge is certainly of utmost importance, major efforts must be dedicated to the definition of *non-taxonomic conceptual relationships* between concepts in order to bring the higher degree of semantic content that ontologies require.
- Most of the learning techniques are only focused on a particular aspect of the ontology learning process. In consequence, usable results in the form of domain ontologies with good coverage can only be obtained by the non trivial combination of several approaches [Iria *et al.*, 2006].
- Most evaluation procedures are performed in a completely manual way, requiring the intervention of a user or a domain expert. Even though a fully automatic evaluation is a very difficult task due to the lack of electronic repositories or gold standards with which to compare the results, some ways for easing or semi-automating the evaluation process should be considered.

In order to make a novel contribution in the area of domain ontology learning from the Web, we present a proposal with the following main features:

- Unsupervised operation during the Web analysis and the learning process. This is especially important due to the amount of available resources, avoiding the need of a human domain expert. Optionally, the evaluation of the results could be performed manually by the user or a domain expert; however, automatic partial evaluation procedures are also presented (see chapter 6).

- Automatic operation that allows performing easily executions at any time in order to retrieve updated results. This characteristic fits very well with the dynamic nature of the Web.

- Domain independent solution, because domain independent techniques are employed, no domain related assumptions are formulated and no domain predefined knowledge (previous ontologies, lexicons, thesaurus, *etc*) is needed. This is especially interesting when dealing with technological domains where specific and non widely-used concepts may appear. In [Turney, 2001], an experiment is performed considering a large collection of scientific and technical journals in which only about 70% of the authors' keywords were found in WordNet (*e.g.* the word *Biosensor* [Sánchez and Moreno, 2006a] is not considered). On the other hand, 100% were indexed by AltaVista. The only restriction here is that our approach can only be applied to English written resources, due to the dependency of certain basic rules about word morphology, linguistic patterns and syntactic constructions.

- Lightweight analysis of web content. This fact, in conjunction with the exploitation of certain peculiarities of the Web (described in chapter 3), results in a scalable learning approach that can be applied both in general and concrete domains with good performance and domain coverage.

- Incremental learning method with dynamic adaptation of the evaluated corpus as new knowledge is acquired (as a bootstrap). Moreover, the system has continuous feedback about the productivity of the learning task performed at each moment (more details in chapter 5). This information is used to detect which are the most productive concepts on the ontology and decide dynamically the amount of analysis that is applied to the available corpus. This approach results in a good compromise between computational cost and domain coverage of the results, as only the concrete web resources for the most productive parts of the ontology are retrieved at each moment. Moreover, thanks to the decomposition of the learning process in several tasks, a distributed implementation is adequate (see chapter 7).

Chapter 3

Environment description

As mentioned in the introduction, the Web presents some characteristics which make it not very suitable the application of classical methodologies of knowledge acquisition. For that reason, we propose a new methodology that can fit better into the Web environment with the goals described in §1.1. In order to achieve them, a study of the characteristics presented by the working environment and a set of initial working hypothesis are needed as the point of departure. In this chapter a detailed description of the Web's features in relation to knowledge acquisition processes and an introduction and justification of the hypothesis and techniques employed to perform learning tasks are presented. More concretely:

- In §3.1, it will be argued that the Web can be a valid knowledge learning repository thanks to the huge amount of information available for every possible domain and its high redundancy. In this sense, the amount and heterogeneity of information is so high that it can be assumed that the Web approximates the real distribution of information [Cilibrasi and Vitanyi, 2004].
- The redundancy of information in such a wide environment can represent a measure of relevance and trustiness of the information. As will be introduced in §3.2, this redundancy may allow lightweight analytic approaches to obtain good quality results maintaining scalability and efficiency in this enormous and noisy environment [Pasca, 2005].
- The enormous size of the Web and the unsupervised nature of our approach make suitable the application of statistical analyses in order to infer information's relevance for a particular domain. As will be discussed in §3.3, statistical analyses applied over knowledge acquisition tasks is a good deal if enough information is available to obtain relevant measures. The case of the Web is especially adequate as it represents the hugest repository of information available.
- Web search engines do a great job in indexing and retrieving web resources if the queries are specific enough. In consequence, if appropriate queries are performed, they can be eventually used for retrieving domain related web resources. Moreover, they can provide web-scale statistics about information distribution in a scalable and efficient way. In general, as will be justified in §3.4, they can be used as an aid in the knowledge acquisition process.

3.1 The Web as a learning corpus

Many classical knowledge acquisition techniques present performance limitations due to the typically reduced used corpus used [Brill, 2003]. This idea is supported by current social studies as [Surowiecky, 2004], in which it is argued that collective knowledge is much more powerful than individual knowledge. The Web is the biggest repository of information available [Brill, 2003] with near 20,000 million web resources indexed by Google. This fact can represent a great deal when using it as a corpus for knowledge acquisition.

Apart from the huge amount of information available, another feature that characterizes the Web is its high redundancy. This fact has been mentioned by several authors and it is especially important because the amount of repetition of information can represent a measure of its relevance [Brill, 2003; Ciravegna *et al.*, 2003; Etzioni *et al.*, 2004; Rosso *et al.*, 2005]. This can be a good approach to tackle the problem of untrustworthiness of the resources: we cannot trust the information contained in an individual website, but we can give more confidence to a fact that is enounced by a considerable amount of possibly independent sources. This fact is also related to the consensus that the extracted knowledge should present: implicit consensus can be achieved as concepts are selected among the terms that are frequently employed in documents produced by the virtual community of users [Navigli and Velardi, 2004].

Thanks to those characteristics, the Web has demonstrated its validity as a corpus for research [Resnik and Smith, 2003; Volk, 2002] with successful results in many areas: question answering [Brill *et al.*, 2001; Kwok *et al.*, 2001], question classification [Solorio *et al.*, 2004], machine translation [Greffenstette, 1999], anaphora resolution [Bunescu, 2003; Markert *et al.*, 2003], Prepositional Phrase treatment [Calvo and Gelbukh, 2003; Volk, 2001], and ontology enrichment [Agirre *et al.*, 2000].

3.2 Lightweight analytical approach and NLP tools

In general, the use of complex text processing tools as a step towards accessing the knowledge within a huge repository as the Web is impractical [Pasca, 2005]. On the other hand, lightweight analyses can miss important information. However, if that information is relevant, sooner or later it will be contained in another resource, even expressed in another formal way. Thus, one can take profit of the amount of resources available and its high redundancy to perform lightweight analyses over a large amount of resources, achieving good scalability and competent results. This is one of the basic theses that, at the end of this document, we want to proof.

Our knowledge acquisition methodology will be based premise. In general, we will perform a lightweight evaluation of a reduced corpus of resources obtained from the Web to retrieve candidates for a final fact (concepts, relations…). Then, their relevance will be checked against a large amount of resources (the whole Web). Note that to check that relevance (through a statistical analysis), it will not be necessary to analyse the whole corpus of web sites that cover a certain fact, as it will be described in chapter 5. The more relevant discovered knowledge will be incorporated into the learning procedure as a bootstrap, allowing to repeat the process but with a higher degree of background knowledge and contextualization. This will allow retrieving new domain-dependent resources, performing more specific analyses and acquiring new concrete knowledge in a completely unsupervised way.

Even if it is lightweight, a certain degree of natural language processing of the web content is needed to interpret the text and extract relations. Lightweight natural language techniques have been applied successfully over unrestricted text [Pantel and Ravichandran, 2004; Phillips and Riloff, 2002; Ravichandran and Hovy, 2002].

In order to perform an efficient analysis, the amount of processed information from each web site will be reduced to the minimum. Concretely, only the nearest context of the analysed concept at each moment will be evaluated. Those pieces of relevant information are known as "text nuggets" and their analysis allows obtaining relevant results without an exhaustive processing of the whole text [Pasca, 2005].

Concerning the analysis of text itself, our proposal only considers English written resources and exploits some peculiarities of that language to extract knowledge. Therefore, a set of tools and algorithms for analysing English natural language is used for that purpose. Concretely:

- Stemming algorithm: allows obtaining the morphological root of a word for the English language. It is fundamental to avoid the redundancy of extracting the different equivalent morphological forms in which a word can be presented.
- Stop words analysis: finite list of domain independent words with very general meaning that can be omitted during the analysis. Determinants, prepositions or adverbs are typically contained in this category.
- Text processing tools for detecting sentences, tokens and parts of speech: in our approach the longest context considered for a particular concept will be the sentence in which it is contained.
- Syntactic analyser: it will be used to perform basic morphological and syntactical analyses of particular pieces of text that can contain valuable information. This will allow us to interpret and extract potentially interesting concepts and relationships. Even though their precision is not perfect and, in consequence, some useful information may be omitted, this is not an important problem thanks to the high redundancy of information in the Web.

3.3 Statistical analysis

In general, the use of statistical measures (*e.g.* co-occurrence measures) in knowledge related tasks for inferring the degree of relationship between concepts is a very common technique when processing unstructured text [Grefenstette, 1992; Lin, 1998; Schütze, 1993]. However, statistical techniques typically suffer from the *sparse data problem* (*i.e.* the fact that data available on words of interest may not be indicative of their meaning). So, they perform poorly when the words are relatively rare, due to the scarcity of data. This problem can be addressed by using lexical databases [Lee *et al.*, 1993; Richardson *et al.*, 1994] or with a combination of statistics and lexical information, in hybrid approaches [Jiang and Conrath, 1997; Resnik, 1998]. In this sense, some authors [Brill, 2003] have demonstrated the convenience of using a wide corpus in order to improve the quality of classical statistical methods. Concretely, in [Keller *et al.*, 2002; Turney, 2001] methods to address the sparse data problem are proposed by using the hugest data source: the Web.

However, the analysis of such an enormous repository for extracting candidate concepts and/or statistics is, in most cases, impracticable. Here is where the use of lightweight techniques that can scale well with high amounts of information, in combination with the statistical information obtained directly from the Web, can represent a good deal. In fact, on the one hand, some authors [Pasca, 2004] have enounced the need of using simple processing analysis when dealing with such a huge and noise repository like the Web; on the other hand, other authors [Cilibrasi and Vitanyi, 2006; Cimiano and Staab, 2004; Etzioni *et al.*, 2005] have demonstrated the convenience of using web search engines to obtain good quality and relevant statistics.

Regarding this last point, one of the most important precedents can be found in [Turney, 2001]. In this work, several heuristics for exploiting the statistics provided by web search engines are presented. Those measures, known as "web scale statistics" have been further discussed in [Etzioni *et al.*, 2004]. They use a form of *pointwise mutual information* (PMI) [Church *et al*, 1991] between words and phrases that is estimated from Web search engine hit counts for specifically formulated queries.

The conclusion is that the degree of relationship between a pair of concepts can be measured through a combination of queries made to a Web search engine (involving those concepts and, optionally, their context). Queries are constructed using the logical query language (AND, OR, NOT...) provided by the search engine. As an example, a typical score measure of co-occurrence between an initial word (*problem*) and a related candidate concept (*choice*) presented in [Turney, 2001] is (1).

$$Score(choice, problem) = \frac{hits(problem \ AND \ choice)}{hits(choice)} \qquad (1)$$

This score is derived from probability theory. Here, p(*problem* AND *choice*) is the probability that *problem* and *choice* co-occur. If *problem* and *choice* are statistically independent, then the probability that they co-occur is given by the product p(*problem*)p(*choice*). If they are not independent, and they have a tendency to co-occur, then p(*problem* AND *choice*) will be greater than p(*problem*)p(*choice*). Therefore the ratio between p(*problem* AND *choice*) and p(*problem*)p(*choice*) is a measure of the degree of statistical dependence between *problem* and *choice*. Since we are looking for the maximum score among a set of *choices* –or *candidates*-, we can drop p(*problem*) because it has the same value for all choices, for a given problem word, obtaining the final expression.

Those measures have been extensively used to evaluate the relevance of a set of candidates [Cimiano and Staab, 2004]. However, the problem of obtaining those candidates remains open. In consequence, a certain degree of knowledge (*e.g.* synsets from WordNet [Turney 2001]) or a previous analysis is still necessary in order to at least discover a representative set of candidates.

In our case, we base our proposal in the lightweight and incremental analysis of a corpus obtained from the search engine to retrieve a representative set of candidates (new concepts or relationships between them). In order to provide and scalable solution, candidate's relevance will be then evaluated against the whole Web through carefully designed queries into the search engine. As will be presented in chapter 5, in order to achieve the good quality results, we have designed and studied several Web scale statistical measures (using searcher's query language) for inferring information distribution. Different measures will be associated to each of the defined knowledge acquisition tasks (*e.g.* taxonomic and non-taxonomic learning).

3.4 Web search engines

The base of a knowledge acquisition methodology is the extraction of concepts and relationships from a corpus of documents that covers a certain domain. Ideally, that corpus should contain the most relevant and reliable documents for the specific domain. However, that premise requires that a certain pre-processing should be made by an expert to compile the initial set of resources.

As we intend to develop a domain independent and unsupervised methodology, the corpus of documents has to be obtained in other manners. More concretely, a reliable way of obtaining web resources is to use a search engine to retrieve lists of web sites matching with a specific query. In addition, as stated in §3.3, robust web-scale statistics can be obtained directly and efficiently from queries performed into a web search engine. As a result, one may realize about the important role that a web search engine can play in the knowledge acquisition process from the Web.

In this section, we describe in detail the behaviour and possibilities that currently available Web search engines offer. The objective is to analyse the ways in which a search engine can be exploited to perform knowledge learning tasks and which is the concrete search engine that fits better with our purposes.

Concretely, in §3.4.1, an overview of the main types of search engines is presented (*keyword-based* and *taxonomic* approaches). Next, in §3.4.2, we justify the type of search engine that fits well with our purposes (*keyword-based* engines) and we discuss the different aspects and features that can be exploited to aid the knowledge acquisition process. Finally, in §3.4.3, a comparison of keyword-based search engines is introduced, considering several parameters and functionalities that are important in our knowledge acquisition approach. As a conclusion, we state which the most reliable search engines to implement our ontology learning methodology are.

3.4.1 Web search engines classification

There are two main types of search engines [Yeol and Hoffman, 2003]:

- *Keyword-based search engines* (*e.g.* Google, Altavista, MSN Search, Yahoo): by far the most successful way for accessing available web resources. They apply simple but effective automatic keyword-based algorithms in order to retrieve web sites that match with a specific query. Moreover, they try to rank the list of returned web sites according to their relevance using several heuristics (*e.g.* Pagerank [Ridings and Shishigin, 2002]). They offer quite complete and up-to-date lists of web sites, but their accuracy depends extremely on the adequacy and concreteness of the user's query. Moreover, it is difficult to construct the most appropriate query due to the translation between the semantic concept searched (topic) to the

logic keyword-based notation used. In other words, their performance is limited
due to their lack of semantic analysis. So, in many situations, they return a huge
amount of resources, which have to be manually evaluated. The consequence is
that, usually, only the first resources are evaluated by the user [Jans, 2000].

- *Taxonomic approaches*: their goal is to solve the information-overload problem,
caused by a usually long list of retrieved documents in a keyword-based approach,
by providing a set of document clusters (or categories) and organising them in a
hierarchical structure. Clusters are determined by a term taxonomy that is provided
by human experts or dynamically defined in function of the retrieved documents.
There are two important approaches:

  o Web catalogues or directories, such as Yahoo, consist of a huge human-
  classified catalogue of documents which can be browsed by following a predefined hierarchical structure (see an example in Figure 2). The assignment of
  documents to the appropriate category is accurate only in the context that the
  human classifier has assumed. However, the manual updating is not appropriate
  to match the World-Wide Web's dynamic nature.

Figure 2. Manually defined categories presented by Yahoo for the *Cancer* domain.

  o Another approach consists on automatically creating a structured view of a
  ranked list: the idea is to group similar web resources into sets by applying
  clustering techniques. Some search engines are summarized in Table 4 and several examples of the results presented by some of those systems are presented
  in Figure 3 and Figure 4. Their goals are: 1) to create a hierarchical view automatically for each query, 2) to assign only relevant documents for a query into
  each category at runtime, and 3) to provide a user interface which allows iterative and hierarchical refinement of the search process. However, on the one
  hand, they offer a limited and reduced amount of web resources in comparison

to term-based search engines; on the other hand, the obtained categories present poor semantics and lack of a good structure. This hampers the comprehension of the domain structure and the browsing of the available resources. Moreover, if the domain is concrete (*e.g.* a query with two keywords), in most cases, no classification will be obtained. In other cases, they only cover a certain domain of knowledge (*e.g.* scientific or technical domains) and depend on manual construction of the presented categories (even with an automatic classification of web resources). In this sense, we can offer a potential contribution in the area of structuring web resources into a meaningful representation using our automatically acquired knowledge for the domain. As will be discussed later, this can be considered as an improvement over current systems.

Table 4. Overview of several cluster-based search engines.

Cluster search engine	URL	Description

Scatter/Gather System [Cutting *et al.*, 1992]	http://www.sims.berkeley.edu/~hearst/sg-overview.html	- Designed for browsing
		- Based on two novel clustering algorithms
		  · *Buckshot* – fast for online clustering
		  · *Fractionation* – accurate for offline initial clustering of the entire set

Carrot2 [Stefanowski and Weiss, 2003]	http://demo.carrot2.org/demo-stable/main	- Component framework - Allows substituting components
WiseNut	http://www.wisenut.com	- Query refinements - Online; Commercial
Vivisimo/ Clusty	http://www.vivisimo.com http://www.clusty.com	- Online; Commercial - Hierarchical - Conceptual
NorthernLight	http://www.northernlight.com	- Business research content only - Online; Commercial
Grouper [Zamir and Etzioni, 1999]	http://www.cs.washington.edu/research/projects/WebWare1/www/metacrawler	- Online - Operates on query result snippets - Clusters together documents with large common subphrases - Suffix Tree Clustering (STC) - STC induces labelling
Mapuccino [Maarek *et al.*, 2000]	N/A	- Relatively efficient - Similarity-based on vector-space model
SHOC [Zhang and Dong, 2004]	N/A	- Grouper-like - Key phrase discovery

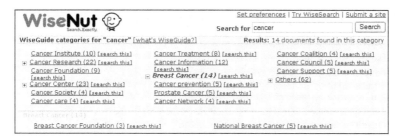

Figure 3. Clusters of web resources proposed by WiseNut for the *Cancer* domain.

Figure 4. Clusters of web resources proposed by Clusty and Vivisimo for the *Cancer* and *Sensor* domains respectively.

3.4.2   Web search engines as learning tools

Taking into consideration our corpus requirements (obtain a representative and up-to-date set of web resources from which to acquire knowledge) and the independency from the searched domain, we have opted for using keyword-based web search engines as the tool for obtaining the necessary corpus of web documents. They are very useful when the query is representative and concrete enough. The ranked list of web resources is quite updated and accurate thanks to the continually evolving scores obtained by the ranking methodology (*e.g.* Pagerank for Google). Moreover, the lack of any semantic analysis makes them suitable for any kind of possible domain of knowledge regardless of its generality. They will be considered as our particular experts for corpus selection with the advantage that they are experts in all types of domains. Even though the offered ranking of web sites is an added value, our proposal does not depend directly on the scoring algorithm. In other words, even without any sorting of web resources we are potentially able to obtain results, but the ranked list can improve the throughput of the learning process (less amount of useless resources analysed).

It is also interesting to note that web search engines are able to index content from resources presented in different formats (mainly *html*, but also *doc*, *pdf*, *ppt* or *rtf*) that in many situations store lots of valuable information. For that purpose, they store an html-based text representation of the resource content as cache. In this manner we can access in a uniform and transparent way to every resource with a unique html parser with independence of the particular original format.

In more detail, there are several aspects of web search engines that may result in a valuable aid in the knowledge acquisition process:

- The key point to obtain the maximum profit of keyword-based search engines is to construct the queries that will result in an adequate set of web resources at a certain moment of the analysis. As will be described in chapter 5, these queries will be created dynamically in function of the knowledge acquired up to a certain moment. Each new query will update the corpus of analysed documents, maximizing the throughput of the learning process. So, the more knowledge we have acquired, the more concrete and domain related set of web resources will be considered for evaluation. Query issues are closely related to the problems presented by the Web against traditional information retrieval systems. Typical IR queries involve long queries [Hearst, 1996] that can contextualize enough to obtain a suitable and reduced set of results. However, most Web queries are only two words long [Spink, 2001] and that is insufficient to identify the context [de Lima, 1999; Voorhees, 1994], resulting in an overwhelming set of results. In relation to our proposal, at the beginning, when no knowledge has been discovered, very simple queries are performed and high amount of noisy results are obtained. Analysing a representative set of those results will provide new knowledge that can be used to construct more concrete queries, and to obtain a reduced but less noisy and more contextualised corpus of documents to analyse.

- In addition to the list of web sites for a certain query, search engines will be also used to obtain previews of the information contained in the Web. Those are presented in the form of the context in which the queried keyword(s) is(are) presented (see Figure 5). These previews, typically called *snippets*, even offering a narrow context, are informative enough to extract related knowledge without accessing the web's content.

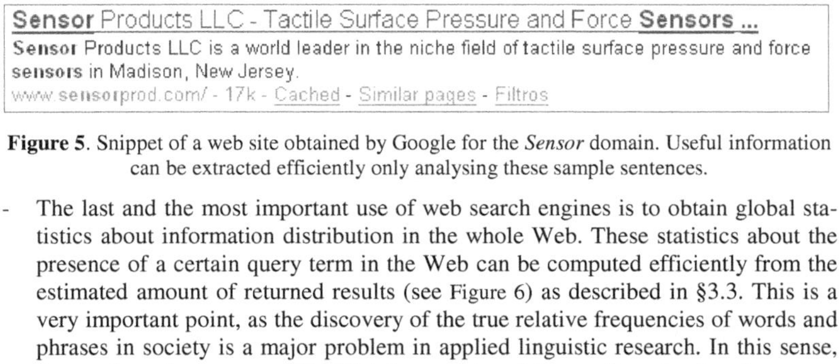

Sensor Products LLC - Tactile Surface Pressure and Force **Sensors** ...
Sensor Products LLC is a world leader in the niche field of tactile surface pressure and force sensors in Madison, New Jersey.
www.sensorprod.com/ - 17k - Cached - Similar pages - Filtros

Figure 5. Snippet of a web site obtained by Google for the *Sensor* domain. Useful information can be extracted efficiently only analysing these sample sentences.

- The last and the most important use of web search engines is to obtain global statistics about information distribution in the whole Web. These statistics about the presence of a certain query term in the Web can be computed efficiently from the estimated amount of returned results (see Figure 6) as described in §3.3. This is a very important point, as the discovery of the true relative frequencies of words and phrases in society is a major problem in applied linguistic research. In this sense, the number of resources of the Web is so vast, and the number of web authors generating web pages is so enormous (and can be assumed to be a truly representative very large sample from humankind) that the probabilities of web search engine terms, conceived as the frequencies of page counts returned by the search engine divided by the number of indexed pages, approximate the actual relative frequencies of those search terms as actually used in society [Cilibrasi and Vitanyi, 2004]. Based on this premise, some authors [Economist, 2005] have mentioned that the *relative page counts* of a web search engine can approximate the true societal words and phrases usage. This measure is very interesting if the adequate queries are formulated (introduced in §3.3) as it can give us an idea of the generality of a discovered concept or relation. Those measures, even estimated, can save us from analysing a large quantity of resources in order to obtain representative statistics, improving the scalability and the performance of the learning process with independence of the generality of the searched domain. The use of web search engines for obtaining valuable statistics for information retrieval and knowledge acquisition has been applied previously by several authors [Cilibrasi and Vitanyi, 2006; Cimiano and Staab, 2004; Etzioni *et al.*, 2004; Turney, 2001] obtaining good quality results in relation to classical statistical approaches.

Figure 6. Statistics about query terms presence in the Web returned by Google.

Even presenting all those advantages, the best keyword-based search engines available (like Google or Altavista) have some limitations that can influence negatively in web-based information retrieval tasks [Etzioni *et al.*, 2004]:

- Assuming that with very general results (*e.g.* millions of available web resources), most users will only evaluate the first ones, which are considered the most relevant, only the first 1000 web sites are presented. So, even with a very general query we will only be able to access the first 1000 web resources. This is an assumption derived again from the redundancy of information hypothesis and the premise that web search engines are able to rank the webs according to their importance: it will be possible to find the desired information without having to analyse the whole set of web resources. However, this restriction[11] does not represent a limitation for our approach. Thanks to the incremental learning process, the knowledge acquired from the analysis of a reduced set of web resources returned

---

[11] To overcome this restriction, a simple algorithm like Recursive Query Expansion (RQE) [Etzioni et al., 2004] can coax a search engine to return most if not all of its results. In essence, the algorithm constructs recursively different queries from an initial one by adding new key terms from a repository of common words. This forces the searcher to return a different set of results but without altering the initial meaning of the word. The result is a wider set of final results with a much higher amount of web sites.

for a specific query will allow to construct new more contextualized queries, updating the corpus of documents. In this sense, 1000 web sites is a more than
enough quantity, in our case, to advance to the next level of contextualisation in
the learning process.
- Another possible drawback can be the overhead introduced in the learning process
  by the response time of those web search engines for a specific query (in addition
  to the online accessing to the individual resources themselves). However, comparing this delay with the runtime required to obtain the same robust statistics from
  the analysis of a wide corpus, the benefits are clear.

3.4.3 Keyword-based search engine comparison

From the discussion presented in the previous section, it is clear the importance of the
search engine for our knowledge acquisition methodology. This is why we have studied the available alternatives in order to select the most adequate search engine for our
purposes.

Publicly available widely used keyword-based search engines have been considered. This will ensure that the search engine will be available and the quality of service maintained during the development. Concretely, Google, Yahoo and MSNSearch
have been considered. Other widely used searchers such as Altavista and AlltheWeb
use the database provided by Yahoo, offering very similar results.

Each analysed search engine has been evaluated from different points of view:
- *Access*: some search engines (such as Google) offer only access for programmers
  through calls to a specific API. Others only allow querying the web interface and
  parsing the results page. The first option is preferred as it is independent of the
  graphical representation of the results.
- *Limitations*: most search engines include access limitations in order to avoid
  hacker attacks and maintain the quality of service. Those are referred to a certain
  amount of queries performed per day or consecutively from a particular IP address.
- *Response time*: this is referred to the amount of time in which the results for a
  particular query are presented. Some search engines (such as Google) offer low
  priority access to API-based queries or introduce courtesy waits between consecutive queries.
- *Coverage*: the amount of web resources that a particular search engine is able to
  index for a particular query. In our case, the web coverage for general terms is not
  as important as the number of results presented for very concrete queries. This is
  because we do not intend to analyse millions of web resources for a very general
  query (that will correspond to the firsts steps of the learning process); on the contrary we desire that a very concrete query (*e.g.* with less than 100 results) returns
  the biggest amount of resources. In this last case, the higher degree of contextualization of the learning process will allow to obtain valuable domain information. In
  relation to the computation of web scale statistics, the absolute measure returned is
  not that important, as our main statistical employed measures are *relative*.

The results of the analysis performed for each search engine are summarised in Table 5, Table 6 and Table 7. The first two are referred to the coverage of each one, presenting some results obtained for different example queries of typical domains considered during the development.

Table 5. Number of estimated results obtained by several key-based web search engines for general domains.

Concept	Google	Yahoo	MSN Search
Cancer	295.000.000	247.000.000	28.431.256
Sensor	111.000.000	57.600.000	8.552.025
Biosensor	1.690.000	575.000	132.896
Mammal	12.300.000	8.440.000	1.028.376
Disease	343.000.000	242.000.000	36.217.421

In Table 5, general queries are performed, obtaining an enormous amount of potential results. Google is offering the largest amount of web resources in all cases, Yahoo is in the middle, and MSNSearch returns an amount that is almost one order of magnitude lower. However, it should be considered that MSNSearch does not count redundant web sites as the other search engines do by default.

Table 6. Number of estimated results obtained by several keyword-based web search engines for specific queries.

Search engine	Google	Yahoo	MSNSearch
"inoperable metastatic breast cancer"	50	22	1
"glucose amperometric biosensor"	106	26	9
"aquatic mammals especially"	115	76	28
"renal hypertension is caused by"	13	5	1
"capacitive sensor" "oscillation circuit"	99	7	1

In Table 6, very specific queries are performed in order to test the effective coverage for very narrow domains. In this case it is quite evident that Google offers the highest numbers, followed by Yahoo and, to considerable distance, MSNSearch.

Table 7. Summary of the main characteristics of each Web search engine.

Search engine	Access	Limitations	Coverage	Response time
Google	API Web access not allowed	1000 queries per day and account. Several accounts per IP allowed	**Highest**	*Slowest*
Yahoo	API Web access	5000 queries per day, account and IP	Medium	Medium
MSNSearch	Web access	**No limits**	*Lowest*	**Fastest**

Taking those facts into consideration, Table 7 shows summary of the analysed features of each search engine. Google has the best Web coverage but its very limited access and extremely slow response times through the search API, introducing courtesy waits of several seconds for consecutive queries really hampers its usefulness. On the other hand, MSNSearch offers a really good performance through the web interface with no limitations (even performing thousands of consecutive queries) at the cost of a reduced coverage especially for the most concrete queries. Yahoo stays at an intermediate point with slightly lower response and better coverage time than MSNSearch, but introducing access limitations.

The results of this empirical study are quite similar to those presented in [Dujmovic and Bai, 2006], in which the three search engines are exhaustively compared in relation to their *functionality*, *usability*, *IR performance* and *IR quality*. The main difference is that we evaluate Google from the API-based point of view, which results in considerable differences against the web interface access in relation to response time. Unfortunately, direct access to the Google's the web interface by program calls is not allowed.

The conclusion is that there does not exist a perfect search engine for our purposes. However, Google potentially offers the best recall for concrete domains with limited resources at the cost of a very limited access (not enough for medium sized domains). MSNSearch behaves in a complementary way, making it adequate for wide domains. This is because, due to the high redundancy of the Web, once a significant amount of web resources has been retrieved, the extracted knowledge using different search engines tends to be the same (further discussion in chapter 5). With respect to the web scale statistics, although the absolute values for a specific query may be quite different (as observed in Table 5 and Table 6), due to the particular estimation algorithm employed by each web searcher, the final score computed from those values tends to be very similar as they are *relative* measures.

3.5 Summary and conclusion

In this section we have presented and justified the characteristics (size, heterogeneity, redundancy) that define the WWW as a valid repository for performing learning and knowledge related tasks.

In addition we have also introduced the techniques (lightweight analyses, statistical measures) that are especially adequate to exploit those characteristics in order to develop knowledge acquisition methodologies.

Finally we have included a study of several types of available Web search engines and how they can be used to aid the learning process (retrieve web resources and compute statistical measures). On the one hand we have selected keyword-based search engines as the Information Retrieval paradigm that fits better with our learning requirements. On the other hand, we have empirically studied the behaviour and characteristics of some of the most used keyword-based search engines. As a result, we have not obtained a clear winner, even though several characteristics (such as coverage or performance) of some search engines can be suitable enough to be used in our knowledge acquisition process.

As it will be shown in the next chapters, the main point that influences on the suitability of a particular search engine is the access limitations. Certainly, when performing the full learning process of a domain, we will need to execute thousands of queries to the search engine to obtain resources and compute statistics. These last ones are especially important as we have extensively based our learning process in those measures; they are almost the only guidance that we use to infer information distribution and, at the end, define ontological classes and relationships. So, in consequence, our main search engine should be able to admit the high requirements about number of queries performed per day.

Considering the situation presented in the previous section, we have selected MSNSearch as our primary search engine, as it does not introduce access limitations. However, its main problem is the reduced coverage offered for very concrete domains. In consequence, we have also introduced the possibility of using an additional search engine during the search process in order to maximize the quality of the final results in those cases. Concretely, we have designed the following framework:

- MSNSearch is used as the main search engine, receiving all the queries when searching for general domains. A maximum of 50 web URLs can be retrieved with one query.
- For concrete domains, we have included Google as the engine from which to retrieve web resources to analyse as it has the highest coverage for much contextualized queries. Considering than up to 10 web URLs can be retrieved in one query through the Google API, the number of calls can be limited to a reasonable amount. This mechanism is combined with MSNSearch that will receive all the queries constructed to compute web scale statistics (the most common ones).
- Yahoo and other similar search engines (e.g. Altavista, AlltheWeb) powered by the same competent database are included as backup alternatives when the Google API service fails or MSNSearch introduces changes in the web interface (that require an adaptation of the implemented web parser).

Chapter 4

Ontology learning overview

In this chapter we analyse approaches employed for ontology learning from text that are related with the present research. First, we formally present the ontological components and which are the steps that should be followed in order to build an ontology.

As introduced in the first chapter, ontologies are composed at least by *classes* (concepts of the domain), *relations* (different types of binary associations between concepts or data values) and *instances* (real world individuals). Formally, in applications like [Abecker *et al.*, 1999; Resnik, 1993; Schurr and Staab, 2000], an ontology often boils down to an object model represented by a set of concepts or classes C, which are *taxonomically* related by the transitive *IS-A* relation H ∈ C x C and *non-taxonomically* related by named object relations R* ∈ C x C x String. On the basis of the object model, a set of logical axioms, A, enforce semantic constraints.

From the *Ontology engineering* point of view, there are several methodologies for constructing ontologies from scratch. In [Gómez-Pérez *et al.*, 2004] an overview of the methods is presented. Although they are employed mainly for manual creation of semantic structures, the major steps and guidelines can be applied in an automatic construction process. As mentioned by several authors [Brewster *et al.*, 2001; Lamparter *et al.*, 2004; Maedche, 2002; Buitelaar *et al.*, 2005], the main steps and knowledge acquisition techniques employed for building ontologies are (see Figure 7):

- Extraction of terms that represent domain concepts, building a lexicon. The main techniques employed to perform this task are:
  - o Statistical analyses, based on:
    - ▪ Co-occurrence (collocation) analysis for term extraction within the corpus.
    - ▪ Comparison of frequencies between domain and general corpora.
  - o Linguistic patterns: rules over linguistically analyzed text.
  - o Shallow linguistic parsing.
- Construction of an initial taxonomy of concepts using *is-a* relations. Some typical approaches use the following techniques:
  - o Statistical analysis.
  - o Clustering (*e.g.* FCA).
  - o Lexico-syntactic patterns.
  - o Shallow linguistic parsing.
  - o Document-subsumption.

o   WordNet-based approaches.
o   Taxonomy extension/refinement.
-   Identification and labelling of non-taxonomic relations (such as *part-of, related-to, similar-to, cause/effect*, but also other domain dependent relations). The following techniques are typically considered:
o   Anonymous relation extraction with association rules.
o   Named relation extraction by linguistic parsing.
-   Ontology population by the detection of instances for the discovered concepts. This is typically based on the discovery of named-entities.
-   Optionally, we can also treat semantic ambiguity (mainly polysemy and synonymy) in order to improve the quality of the results.
-   Evaluation of the obtained results (concepts, instances and relationships).

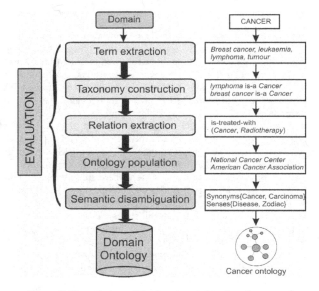

Figure 7. General steps of the domain ontology learning process.

In this chapter, different approaches for dealing with each step of the described ontology learning process are presented. In each case, the approach selected for the present work is introduced and justified taking into consideration our premises and goals and the state of the art of the technology.

Concretely, in the present work, we have centred the research in the discovery of domain concepts, taxonomies (described in §4.1) and labelled non-taxonomic relationships (covered in §4.2). In addition, as in any automatic learning process, the manual or automatic evaluation of the results has also been considered (summarized in §4.5). The detection of instances and the ontology population (detailed in §4.3) has been slightly covered during the extraction of domain concepts and only in the sense of distinguishing between normal words and named entities.

Semantic ambiguity treatment (introduced in §4.4) is a very hard task that is being exhaustively researched. Due to its complexity, it is beyond the coverage of our work. However, a pair of initial attempts for disambiguation adapted and derived from our learning methodology are presented in chapter 5.

4.1 Discovering concepts and taxonomic relationships

In order to perform the domain ontology construction process from scratch, the first step should be to retrieve an initial base of knowledge for the desired domain. This knowledge, then, can be used as a bootstrap in further and more complex learning steps. A lexicon and, more suitably, an initial taxonomy of the most important domain concepts is the common point of departure of many learning methodologies. So, our first objective should be to retrieve terms that are related to a domain -defined by a specific keyword-, building a hierarchy.

As summarized in §2.2 and at the beginning of this chapter, there exist many approaches for performing this task. However, as we intend to define an unsupervised, domain independent approach, appropriate techniques should be employed. As stated in [Cimiano et al., 2004], three different learning paradigms can be exploited. First, some approaches rely on the document-based notion of term subsumption [Sanderson and Croft, 1999]. Secondly, some researchers claim that words or terms are semantically similar to the extent to which they share similar syntactic contexts [Bisson et al., 2000; Caraballo, 1999]. Finally, several researches have attempted to find taxonomic relations expressed in texts by matching certain patterns associated to the language in which documents are presented [Ahmad et al., 2003; Charniak and Berland, 1999].

Pattern-based approaches are heuristic methods using regular expressions that have been successfully applied in information extraction. The text is scanned for instances of distinguished lexical-syntactic patterns that indicate a relation of interest. This is especially useful for detecting specialisations of concepts that can represent *is-a* (taxonomic) relations [Hearst, 1992] or individual facts [Etzioni et al., 2005]. The most important precedent is [Hearst, 1992], in which a set of basic domain independent patterns for hyponymy discovery and a methodology for obtaining new patterns are described (see some examples in Table 8).

Table 8. Examples Hearst linguistic patterns (NP=Noun Phrase).

Pattern	Example	Relation
NP {,} including {NP ,}* {or │ and} NP	… countries including Spain, or France.	hyponym("Spain", "countries"), hyponym("France", "countries")
such NP as {NP ,}* {(or │ and)} NP	… such mammals as dogs, cats, and whales.	hyponym("dogs", "mammals"), hyponym("cats", "mammals"), hyponym("whales", "mammals")
NP {,} such as {NP ,}* {or │ and} NP	… cancers such as breast cancer, and leukaemia.	hyponym("breast cancer", "cancers"), hyponym("leukaemia", "cancers")
NP {,} especially {NP ,}* {or│ and} NP	… insects, especially bees, and wasps.	hyponym("bees", "insects"), hyponym("wasps", "insects")

Those patterns summarize the most common ways of expressing specializations in English. As a consequence, many authors [Agichtein and Gravano, 2000; Iwanska *et al.*, 2000; Pasca, 2004; Snow *et al.*, 2004] have refined or used them as the base for their taxonomy learning methodologies.

However, the quality of pattern-based extractions can be compromised by the problems of *decontextualisations* and *ellipsis*. In the first case, for example, we can easily find a sentence like *"There are several treatments for dealing with cancer such as radiotherapy and chemotherapy"*; without a more exhaustive linguistic analysis we might erroneously extract *"radiotherapy"* and *"chemotherapy"* as subtypes of "cancer". For the second case, due to language conventions, we can find a sentence like *"cancers such as breast and lung"*; in this case, the ellipsis of the word *"cancer"* in both subtypes could result in the incorrect conclusion that *"breast"* and *"lung"* (and not *"breast cancer"* and *"lung cancer"*) are subtypes of *"cancer"*.

Another pattern-based approach for detecting specialisations is the use of noun phrases (*e.g. credit card*) and adjective noun phrases (*e.g. local tourist information office*). Concretely, in the English language, the immediate anterior word for a keyword is frequently *classifying* it (expressing a semantic specialization of the meaning), whereas the immediate posterior one represents the *domain* where it is applied [Grefenstette, 1997]. So, on the one hand, the *previous word* for a specific *keyword* can be used to obtain the taxonomic hierarchy of terms (*e.g. pressure sensor* is a subclass of *sensor*). If the process is repeated recursively we can create deeper-level subclasses (*e.g. air pressure sensor* is a subclass of *pressure sensor*). On the other hand, the *posterior word* for the specific *keyword* can be used to obtain the context in which the immediate anterior concept is applied (*e.g. colorectal cancer research* will be a domain of application of *colorectal cancer*). One can see that this heuristic results in much simpler extractions than Hearst's ones. However, unlike Hearst's ones, they are not able to detect all possible taxonomic relationships, but only those expressed by the concatenation of nouns and/or adjectives. In other words, using this pattern, we cannot discover that *"dog"* is a kind of *"mammal"*, but using Hearst's ones we can detect that *"breast cancer"* and *"leukaemia"* are both types of *"cancer"*.

As one can see, both patterns have advantages and shortcomings in relation to the degree of analysis required to perform extractions, the expected quality of the results and the potential coverage of the extracted set of results for a particular domain.

As a final note, pattern-based approaches present a relatively high precision but typically suffer from low recall due to the fact that the patterns are rare in corpora [Cimiano *et al.*, 2004]. Fortunately, as stated in §3.3, this data sparseness problem can be tackled by exploiting the Web [Buitelaar *et al.*, 2003; Velardi *et al.*, 2005].

Unsupervised pattern-based learning is one of the bases of our approach. As will be presented in chapter 5, pattern's regular expressions can be used to construct web search engine queries to retrieve documents and compute statistics. In order to present a novel contribution over existing approaches, we have combined those that we believe are the best characteristics of the two presented approaches (Heart's and noun phrase patterns) in order to improve the overall performance of the learning process. Concretely, in chapter 5, a study of how different linguistic patterns for hyponymy detection behave and a method for combining different linguistic patterns into an integrated, domain independent approach are presented.

4.2 Discovering non-taxonomic relationships

Even though, as shown in §2.2, many ontology learning techniques have been developed, most of these approaches focus on the automatic acquisition of classes and taxonomic relationships, and often neglect the importance of interlinkage between concepts. Even though taxonomic knowledge is certainly of utmost importance, major efforts must be dedicated to the definition of *non-taxonomic conceptual relationships*.

The discovery of non–taxonomic relations is considered as the least tackled problem within ontology learning [Kavalec *et al.*, 2004]. It appears to be the more intricate task as, in general, it is less known how many and what type of conceptual relationships should be modelled in a particular ontology.

In general, two tasks have to be performed. First, we have to detect which concepts are related. Second, and neglected in many situations, we have to figure out *how* these concepts are related; thus, a name for the relation has to be found. This is typically specified by a verb. In fact, the role of the verb as a central connecting element between concepts is undeniable. Verbs specify the interaction between the participants of some action or event by expressing relations between them. In parallel, it can be argued, from an ontology engineering point of view, that verbs express a relation between two classes that specify the domain and range of some action or event.

There are several trends in learning relationships from text depending on the degree of generality of the extracted relations.

Some authors have developed approaches for learning specific relationships such as part-of [Charniak and Berland, 1999], Qualia [Cimiano and Wenderoth, 2005] or Causation [Girju and Moldovan, 2002], by using specific language related linguistic patterns (*e.g. X consists of Y, X is used for Y, X leads to Y*). Even though those approaches may have interest for developing or enriching general purpose semantic networks (such as WordNet), they are not able to retrieve specific relationships that are crucial for constructing domain ontologies.

There have been other domain dependant approaches addressed primarily within the biomedical field as there are very large text collections available (*e.g.* PubMed). The goal of this work is to discover new relationships between known concepts (i.e. *symptoms, diseases*) by analyzing large quantities of biomedical scientific articles [Pustejovsky et al., 2002] [Vintar *et al.*, 2003].

Another stream, more firmly grounded in ontology engineering, systematically seeks new unnamed relations in text. Co-occurrence analysis between terms is used to infer relations with little attention to sentence structure. In those approaches the labelling problem is left upon the ontology designed (Text-to-onto [Maedche and Staab, 2000]) or WordNet mappings are used to automatically assign relations from a small predefined set (Ontolearn [Missikoff *et al.*, 2002]). The ASIUM system [Faure and Nedellec, 1998] hierarchically clusters nouns based on the verbs that they co-occur with. There is however no formal support for named relations.

The labelling problem is tackled in other approaches by relying on 'default' ones, under the assumption that, for example, the relation between a *Company* and a *Product* is always '*produce*' [Finkelstein and Morin, 1999]. [Byrd and Rabin, 1999] assign the label to a relation based on sentence patterns (*e.g. location* relation for the '-based' construction). They derive unnamed relations from concepts that co-occur by calculating the measure for mutual information [Church *et al.,* 1991] between terms. The Adaptiva system [Brewster *et al.,* 2002] allows the user to choose a relation from the ontology and interactively learns its recognition patterns. Such massive interaction however, does not pay off if the goal is to find important domain-specific relations, as in our case.

Other approaches aim to learn more general relations by exploiting the linguistic structure of text similarly to the present work. Relation extraction is therefore related to the problem of acquiring selection restrictions for verb arguments. In this sense, [Reinberger and Spyns, 2004] employ statistical methods based on frequency information over linguistic dependencies in order to establish relations between entities from a corpus of the biomedical domain. However, they are not concerned with labelling the discovered relations, which results in a similar approach to [Maedche and Staab, 2002] and [Kavalec *et al.*, 2004]. [Sabou, 2004] conducts her research on a corpus of controlled language from Web Service descriptions, which consists of simple sentence constructions from which ontology fragments can be extracted easily. Unfortunately, it needs a lot of manual interference. More recently, [Schutz and Buitelaar, 2005] developed a system (RelExt) that is capable of automatically identifying highly relevant triples (pairs of concepts connected by a relation) over concepts from an existing ontology. RelExt works by extracting relevant verbs and their grammatical arguments (*i.e.* terms) from a domain-specific text collection and computing corresponding relations through a combination of linguistic and statistical processing.

Our approach, as will be described in chapter 5, also works by studying the sentence structure (subject, verb, object). Concretely, we exploit verbs as the central point for discovering non-taxonomic relationships. On the contrary to the presented approaches, in our case, we start from domain-related verbs that we have learned automatically and unsupervisedly in a previous stage. We consider specific verb phrases as domain dependant semantic patterns that express non-taxonomic relations for a domain. So, they will be used as the seeds for retrieving domain related relationships and they will allow us to label them accordingly. This is very interesting as most of the previous works do not appropriately address the labelling problem. Lightweight analytic procedures and statistics compiled from querying a web search engine complete a scalable procedure to learn, extract and evaluate non taxonomic relationships for a particular domain.

4.3   Discovering named entities for ontology population

Ontology population commonly refers to the extraction of instances of ontological concepts from text. From the philosophical point of view, the distinguishing between a specialisation of a certain concept (*subclass*) or a particular individual (*instance*) can represent a matter of discussion. In general, one has to define specifically *which* the instances –real world entities- in a particular ontology are (*e.g.* persons, organisations, events, *etc.*). In any case, there is a wide agreement in considering *named entities* as instances. In most cases, this information is not contained in classical repositories as WordNet due to its potential size and its evolvable nature.

In general, the recognition of named entities and their associated categories within unstructured text traditionally relies on semantic lexicons and gazetteers. The amount of effort required to assemble large lexicons confines the recognition to either a limited domain (*e.g. medical imaging*), or a small set of predefined, broad categories of interest (*e.g. persons, countries, organizations, products*). This constitutes a serious limitation in an information seeking context [Pasca, 2004].

Many named entity recognizers traditionally rely on lists of names [Krupka and Hausman, 1998; Mikheev *et al.*, 1999]. The lists are compiled by humans, or assembled from authoritative sources. It is also possible to build recognizers that identify names automatically in text [Collins and Singer, 1999; Cucerzan and Yarowsky, 1999; Stevenson and Gaizauskas, 2000]. Such approaches usually attempt to learn general categories such as *organizations* or *persons* rather than refined categories. Even considering fine-grained categories [Fleischman and Hovy, 2002], they use a closed, pre-specified set of categories of interest, resulting in both explicit and implicit restrictions. In the first case, the training data introduces explicit restrictions. In the second case, it is the set of seed names, typically used in previous approaches, which introduces implicit restrictions on the acquired categories. Other authors [Fernández-López *et al.*, 1997; Lamparter *et al.*, 2004] are using a thesaurus like WordNet to perform this detection: if the word is not found in the dictionary, it is assumed to be a named entity. However, sometimes, a named entity can be composed by common words, so the use of a thesaurus is not enough.

Instead of depending on predefined categories, thesaurus or selected examples, other approaches take into consideration the way in which named entities are presented in the specific language. Concretely, languages such as English distinguish proper names from other nouns through capitalization. This simple but effective idea, combined with linguistic pattern analysis, has been applied by several authors [Cimiano and Staab, 2004; Grefenstette, 1997; Hahn and Schnattinger, 1998; Pasca, 2004; Downey *et al.*, 2007], obtaining good results without depending on manually annotated examples or specific categories.

In our case, once hyponym candidates have been discovered through pattern-based methods as described in §4.3, using the capitalization heuristics we are able to distinguish specializations (subclasses) from particular real world entities (named entities). As the extraction rules for candidates can be simple, this approach can be efficient enough to scale well within a large scale repository like the Web.

As will be described in §5.2, even though the retrieval of instances (in our case, only named entities) is not our priority, we will use those last assumptions to distinguish between candidates for classes and instances in a domain independent and unsupervised way. Again, the degree of confidence associated to each instance candidate will be computed from statistical analyses. However, our goal is not to propose a new general method for the recognition of named entities, but to present an additional fully integrated procedure to our ontology learning method that can improve the quality of the final result. Due to its unsupervised nature, it will present some limitations due to the lack of knowledge about the entity's semantics (e.g. we can detect that *American Cancer Society* and *British Childhood Cancer Survivor Study* are both named entities related to *Cancer* in some way, but we cannot infer that the first is an *organisation* and the second is a *report*).

4.4 Natural language ambiguity

An important problem in IR is semantic disambiguation: a word may have multiple meanings (polysemy), yet several words can have the same meaning (synonymy) [Ide and Veronis, 1998; Miller, 1996]. In general, solving polysemy increases the quality of the returned results (precision) by eliminating results of the wrong word-sense; treating synonymy increases the proportion of correct results (recall) by including terms that have the same meaning [Burton-Jones *et al.*, 2003].

In this section we are going to describe several classical approaches for those both important and complex problems.

4.4.1 Word sense disambiguation

The problem of the resolution of the lexical ambiguity that appears when a given word in a context has several different meanings is commonly called Word Sense Disambiguation (WSD). As shown in [Mihalcea and Edmonds, 2004], the supervised paradigm is the most efficient. However, due to the lack of big sense tagged corpora (and the difficulty of manually creating them), the unsupervised paradigm tries to avoid, or at least to reduce, the knowledge acquisition problem the supervised methods have to deal with. In fact, unsupervised methods do not need any learning process and they use only a lexical resource (*e.g.* WordNet) to carry out the word sense disambiguation task [Agirre and Rigau, 1995; Montoyo, 2000; Rosso *et al.*, 2003; Sidorov and Gelbukh, 2001].

In [Ide and Veronis, 1998] different approaches to unsupervised word sense disambiguation are described. On the one hand there are global, *context-independent* approaches, which assign meanings retrieved from an external dictionary by applying special heuristics. For example, a frequency based approach where always the most frequently applied sense is used. On the other hand there are *context-sensitive* approaches. This kind of methods uses the context of a word to disambiguate it. Recently, some authors [Rosso *et al.*, 2005] have been using the Web to disambiguate, analyzing text contexts in comparison to WordNet definitions or hyponym sets. However, in any case, attempting a general solution for complete disambiguation (*i.e.* for a given word, detect which of its, sometime very subtly distinguished, senses contained in a thesaurus like WordNet is the most suitable) is a very hard task. This is reflected in the less than impressive precision (around 60-70%) presented by the current state of the art approaches [Senseval, 2004].

In our knowledge acquisition process, the problem of polysemy can arise when a certain selected class has more than one sense or it is used in different contexts (*e.g. organ*). The direct consequence can be that the immediate subclasses and related concepts (*e.g. liver, heart, pipe_organ, internal_organ, symphonic_organ, lung*) will cover different domains corresponding to their specific sense (*e.g. specialised structural animal unit* or *musical instrument*). The ideal situation would be to group those classes according to the specific sense to which they belong (*e.g. liver, heart, internal_organ* and *lung*; *pipe_organ* and *symphonic_organ*) or to select only a specific subset (if the user is only interested in a concrete one).

Attempting to minimize that problem, we have considered the possibility of performing automatic polysemy disambiguation of taxonomical results as an additional step of our learning procedure. Following the same paradigm described previously, it will be unsupervised. Our approach shares some characteristics of general unsupervised methods such as context assumptions and the use of Web-based similarity metrics [Cilibrasi and Vitanyi, 2006]. It is described in detail in §5.7.1; in a nut shell, it consists on performing a clusterization of classes, using as a similarity measure the amount of co-occurrences of discovered terms within the available web resources.

4.4.2 Synonymy treatment

A very common problem of keyword-based web search is the use of different names to refer to the same entity. The goal of a web search engine is to retrieve relevant pages for a given topic determined by a keyword but, if a text does not contain this word with the same spelling as specified, it will be ignored. So, when using a search engine, in some cases, a considerable amount of relevant resources are omitted due to the strict word matching. In this sense, not only the different morphological forms of a given keyword are important (a task that is typically covered by stemming analysis), but also synonyms and aliases.

There are several well-known domain independent lexical database systems that include synonym information, such as WordNet [Fellbaum, 1998], BRICO [Haase, 2000], and EuroWordNet [Vossen, 1998]. These systems ensure a certain level of quality, at the cost of a substantial amount of human labour. A major limitation of such lexicons is the relatively poor coverage of technical and scientific terms. Specialised lexicons of concrete and individual technological domains with a higher coverage are not adequate for a general domain independent solution.

From a computer-based point of view, there are several methodologies that try to find synonyms for a given keyword. Statistical approaches to synonym recognition are based on co-occurrence of synonyms contexts [Manning and Schütze, 1999]. A classical technique based on this idea is *Latent Semantic Analysis*. The underlying idea is that the aggregate of all the word contexts in which a given word appears provides a set of mutual constraints that largely determines the similarity of meaning of words [Berry *et al.*, 1995; Deerwester *et al.*, 1990; Landauer and Dumais, 1997]. However, these techniques tend to return closely related words but, sometimes, not truly "equivalent" ones [Bhat *et al.*, 2004] (*e.g. Alcaeda* and *Alcaida*, but also *Cell* and *Bin Laden*).

Other techniques [Valarakos *et al.*, 2004] identify different lexicalizations based on the assumption that they use a common set of 'core' characters. These techniques can be useful to detect alternative spellings or abbreviations (*e.g. Pentium III, Pentium 3, Pent. 3*), but not for discovering synonyms (*e.g. sensor* and *transducer*).

Recent approaches for synonymy detection [Turney, 2001] use the Web, and more concretely web search engines, to perform the selection of synonyms. Given a list of candidates for synonyms previously selected, they perform the appropriate queries into a web search engine to obtain statistics that measure word's co-occurrence.

We have considered the possibility of discovering sets of synonyms that can be used to overcome some limitations of the keyword-based web searchers as an additional step of the learning methodology that can help to improve the recall of the final results. Our proposal obtains synonyms from the analysis of the Web in an unsupervised way. As will be described in §5.7.2, we use the knowledge achieved during the learning process (taxonomically related terms) as a bootstrap. In this manner we can create queries that contextualize enough the search to obtain web sites that cover the same topic (*e.g. cancer*) but without necessarily using the same lexicalization for the initial keyword (*e.g. carcinoma* or *tumour*). This method not only allows us to obtain synonyms and derivative morphological forms of an initial one, but also to check their representativeness, obtaining a ranked list of candidates.

4.5 Evaluation of the results

In order to prove the quality of the results obtained by the ontology learning process, an evaluation phase is mandatory. A properly evaluated structure will not guarantee the absence of problems, but it will make its use more reliable.

The evaluation of automatically obtained ontologies is recognized to be an open problem [OntoWeb, 2002]. Ontologies are fundamental data structures for conceptualizing knowledge which in many situations is non-uniquely expressible. As a consequence, we can build many different ontologies conceptualizing the same body of knowledge. This lack of consensus makes very difficult the comparison or the comparative evaluation of different approaches.

Recent efforts are being made on the area of evaluation tools and methods, but available results are on the methodological [Gómez-Pérez *et al.*, 2004] rather than on the experimental side [Brewster *et al.*, 2004; Dellschaft and Staab, 2006]. Analysing the proposals presented in different works (described in §2.2) for evaluating their learning methodologies, several conclusions can be extracted:

- Most of the evaluations of knowledge acquisition methods are developed *ad hoc* for the concrete learning methodology. There are not general purpose domain independent evaluation methods, only some guidelines.
- Authors that extract knowledge from specific and standard corpus (*e.g.* TREC[12] ones), typically compare their results with the ones obtained by previous works applied over the same data [Stokoe *et al*, 2003].
- Authors [Widdows, 2003] that develop methodologies for enriching or extending other semantic structures (*e.g.* domain ontologies, WordNet), typically perform the evaluation by analysing areas of knowledge already known (contained in the semantic structure) and comparing the obtained results.
- A common way of performing automatic evaluations is to apply different learning methods over the same corpus and compare their results [Agirre *et al.*, 2000; Navigli and Velardi, 2004]. However, none of those automatic methods is perfect and, in consequence, the obtained evaluation measures are not very accurate.

---

[12] http://trec.nist.gov

- In general, the most common way for evaluating automatic learning methodologies is manually, in which a human expert checks the obtained results and evaluates them according to his knowledge in the domain (some examples in [Cimiano and Staab, 2005; Velardi *et al.*, 2005]).

Concerning our proposal, as the quality of the final result will depend on the performance of every step of the learning process specific evaluation methods for each of them have been designed. In chapter 6, aspects of their concrete evaluation are introduced. Whenever a standard is available (as for the taxonomic case), evaluations have been performed manually analysing both the quantitative aspect (using IR standard measures of *precision* and *recall*) and the qualitative aspect (subjective evaluation of the results by a human expert) [Sabou, 2006]. In other cases (as for the non taxonomic relationships), evaluations are designed and performed by comparing the results against an available machine interpretable semantic repository like WordNet.

4.6 Summary

In this chapter we have introduced the main phases of the ontology construction process. For each one, we have presented the main learning techniques used to tackle them in an automated fashion. In our proposal, we have adapted some of them to the especial characteristics of the Web environment (as stated in chapter 3) in order to define a novel ontology learning methodology. More concretely:

- *Concept learning* and *taxonomy construction*: we have opted by an unsupervised approach based on a novel combination of several linguistic patterns for hyponymy detection. They configure a domain independent learning technique simple enough to be used within Web IR tools (web search engines). Moreover, their basic syntactic nature allows us to extract pattern instances from text without requiring exhaustive linguistic analyses.
- *Non-taxonomic relationships*: as general relationships are typically expressed by verb phrases linking sentence components, we centre the learning process in their detection and analysis. Concretely, contrarily to many of the previous approaches, we take verb phrases as the base for retrieving resources (by querying a web search engine), containing potentially interesting sentences. Those are then further analysed using lightweight techniques in order to extract verb labelled domain related concepts.
- *Named entities*: the discovery of particular domain individuals is considered during the learning process using capitalization heuristics in order to detect named entities. They are used to populate the domain ontology and to improve the final structure by distinguishing between domain concepts that become ontological classes and real world entities.
- *Semantic ambiguity*: some domains of knowledge can be affected by semantic ambiguity, mainly polysemy and synonymy. We have tackled those problems by proposing preliminary methods based on clustering techniques (for dealing with polysemy) and the web queries constructed according to the already acquired knowledge (for retrieving domain synonyms).

All the methodologies designed for dealing with all those ontology learning stages are carefully described and illustrated with examples in chapter 5. In addition, the evaluation issues will be discussed in chapter 6, including the approaches designed to check the quality of the results.

Chapter 5

Domain ontology learning methods

In this chapter, a detailed description of the developed ontology learning methods is presented. The core of our novel approach covers the acquisition of domain terms and the definition of taxonomic and non taxonomic relationships. The main advantage is the automatic and unsupervised operation, allowing to create domain ontologies from scratch. However, as learning without a base of knowledge is difficult, as will be described in §5.1, we propose an incremental learning process in which several learning steps are performed and each one is enriched (bootstrapped) with relevant knowledge acquired during the previous one. This allows us to perform a more specific analysis and learn new domain related knowledge.

The learning process is divided in several tasks. As contributions, we have developed methods and obtained results for the following aspects of the learning process:

- In §5.2, the discovery of related concepts for the domain and the construction of an initial taxonomy using a combination of domain independent linguistic patterns and web scale statistics are presented. In order to perform this process, a detailed discussion of the behaviour and performance of different pattern-based approaches (introduced in §4.1) and several statistical scores is also included.
- For the acquired terms of the hierarchy, a method for distinguishing between *domain concepts* and *named entities* is introduced in §5.3.
- For each class of the taxonomy, a method for acquiring related verbs and construct domain specific patterns is detailed in §5.4. Using them, we are able to retrieve non-taxonomically related terms and label relations using verb phrases.
- As a final step, a post-processing stage described in §5.5 is applied over the results in order to present a more compact and coherent structure.

In §5.6, we discuss some relevant aspects of the automatic and unsupervised process, regarding the feedback mechanism applied to control the execution and finalisation, and the bootstrapping techniques used to contextualize the analysis. Moreover, even though this aspect is beyond our primary goals, we have developed additional methodologies adapted to our learning procedure for treating ambiguity (polysemy and synonymy). They are shown in §5.7.

Summarizing, in this chapter, each contribution to domain ontology learning is described and illustrated with examples for different knowledge domains.

Evaluation issues for every learning step are addressed in chapter 6. The study of the computational complexity of the developed methods and their implementation is discussed in chapter 7.

5.1 Incremental learning process

Ontology learning from the Web is a complex process, involving the analysis of thousands of web sites and the evaluation of hundreds of ontological candidate components. In consequence, we have divided the full process in several simpler tasks that deal, iteratively, with each learning step. In addition, each step can be executed as many times as required in function of the amount of knowledge already acquired (more details in §5.6).

Even though each methodology developed for dealing with each learning task can be executed independently, they have been designed to be executed in an integrated and iterative way. In this manner, the knowledge already acquired in one step can be used to constrain the analytical process, constructing more specific queries. In addition, the concepts and relationships retrieved can be used as seeds for further analyses. At the end, through several iterations of the learning process, the system incrementally constructs the semantic network of concepts that composes the domain ontology.

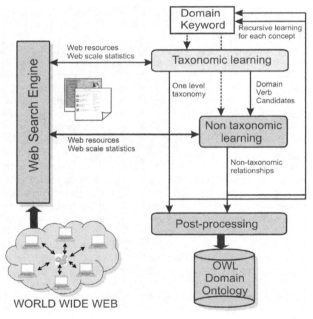

Figure 8. Ontology learning methodology.

As shown in Figure 8, the learning process is divided in the following phases:
- *Taxonomic learning*: it starts from a user specified keyword that indicates the domain for which the ontology should be constructed. This term is used as a seed for the learning process. As no background knowledge is available, at this initial stage of the analysis, only general queries using domain independent patterns can be performed into the search engine. Instead of developing complex analyses with a large amount of those resources, which may result in questionable results due to the lack of knowledge, only subtle and lightweight analytic procedures are executed over a reduced amount of resources. This allows detecting the most directly related knowledge and composing an initial taxonomy. This process is described in detail in §5.2. A procedure for detecting named entities and include them as instances of the taxonomy is also performed (see §5.3). The output of this process is a one-level taxonomy with general terms and a set of verbs that have appeared in the same context as the searched domain keyword during the analysis. This taxonomy configures an initial knowledge base from which further develop the learning process.
- *Non-taxonomic learning*: the verb list compiled in the previous phase and the initial keyword are used as the base of knowledge for the non-taxonomic learning process. They are used as a bootstrap for constructing domain related patterns and perform specific queries into the search engine. The result is that we are able to obtain additional domain knowledge in the form of non-taxonomically related concepts. This process is detailed in §5.4.
- *Recursive learning*: the two previous learning stages are recursively executed for each obtained concept (taxonomically and non-taxonomically related). Each one becomes an individual seed for a particular set of further analyses. As the learning evolves, queries are longer, the search is more contextualized, web resources are more domain related and, in consequence, the throughput of the methodologies and the quality of the results are potentially higher. The finalisation of this recursive process is controlled by the algorithm itself considering, as described in §5.6, the learning throughput of the already executed steps. At the end, we obtain a multi-level taxonomy in which each concept can be non-taxonomically related to other ones that, at the same time, can be the object of new taxonomic and non-taxonomic analyses. An illustrative example of a part of the structure that we are able to obtain is presented in Figure 9.
- *Post-processing*: the final structure is post-processed in order to detect implicit relationships, avoid redundancies and obtain a more compact structure that will become the final domain ontology. This phase is described in §5.5.

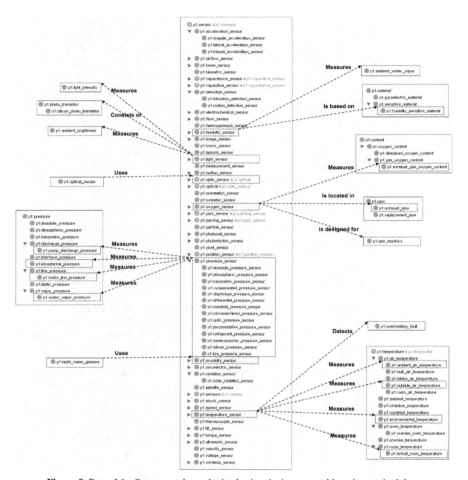

Figure 9. Part of the *Sensor* ontology obtained using the incremental learning methodology.

5.2 Taxonomic learning

As mentioned in the previous section, the first step of the learning process is the creation of an initial basic taxonomy of terms that will relate with *is-a* relationships the concepts that are representative for the searched domain. Moreover, if individualities (concretely, named entities) for a specific concept are found, they will be considered as instances of the corresponding classes as will be described in §5.3.

As presented in chapter 4, the process is based in general *linguistic patterns* for detecting hyponymy in a particular language (English), allowing the development of an unsupervised and domain independent methodology. The extraction of *hyponym candidates* is followed by a *selection* of the most related ones, involving web-scale statistical analyses about co-occurrence of terms. Web information distribution, as presented in §3.3, is considered at this stage in order to infer basic semantics unsupervisedly and in a highly scalable way (considering the corpus size and the amount of candidates to evaluate). The selected candidates are finally used to construct the taxonomy.

In the past, we developed a basic methodology for constructing taxonomies based on those premises [Sánchez and Moreno, 2006a]. However, we realized that the performance of that method could be improved in several ways by considering carefully the possibilities that different *linguistic patterns* and *web statistics* offered to us.

So, the approach presented in this document is an evolution of the previous one, which uses a *combination of linguistic patterns for hyponymy detection and statistical measures especially adapted to the Web environment*.

So, the *main contributions* of the developed methodology are:

1. A study (as shown in §5.2.1) of how different linguistic patterns for hyponymy detection behave in extracting terms for constructing taxonomies.
2. A study of Web scale statistical measures for inferring concepts relevance for the domain and selecting the most related terms.
3. A method for combining different linguistic patterns within an integrated, domain independent, automatic and unsupervised taxonomy learning process, using an incremental learning approach.

5.2.1 Linguistic patterns for hyponymy detection

In this section we offer a study of the behaviour and performance of the linguistic patterns described in §4.1 in the extraction of hyponym candidates. The objective is to decide which can be an adequate way to use those patterns in order to develop the taxonomy construction methodology that will be described in §5.2.2.

The hyponymy detection patterns considered are the ones defined by Hearst [Hearst, 1992] and those based on noun phrases [Grefenstette, 1997], as stated in §4.1. We have conducted several tests in order to discover which results (different kinds of hyponym candidates) we can potentially obtain. Then, we have defined a set of extraction cases for each one and proposed a way in which both kinds of patterns can be combined in order to improve the individual performance of each pattern.

5.2.1.1 Hearst's patterns

Starting with Hearst's patterns (using the set presented in Table 8, in §4.1), we have conducted several experiments for different domains in the following way:

- Consider a keyword that represents the domain of knowledge to be explored (*e.g. Cancer*).

- Construct a query for a web search engine using each pattern and the specified domain (*e.g. "cancer such as"*).
- Retrieve the first N web sites for each query and extract the clear text (without information about the visual representation).
- Find matchings of the corresponding pattern in the text and extract candidates (noun phrases) using the pattern's regular expression and a syntactic analyzer.

Evaluating the set of extracted hyponym candidates, we have distinguished several situations according to the number of meaningful words (nouns and adjectives) that compose the noun phrase candidate for hyponym.

For noun phrases containing only one word, we have identified the following three cases:

1. One word valid hyponyms (*e.g. "cancer such as* **leukaemia**"): those terms express correct specialisations of the meaning of the initial keyword and can be added to the domain taxonomy.
2. One word incorrect hyponyms (*e.g. "cancer such as* **radiotherapy**"; *"cancers such as* **the following**"): they are typically referred to concepts that are related in some way (but not taxonomically) to the main concept; in the worst situations, candidates may not have any kind of relationship with the domain. Those cases typically result from the fact that we are considering a very narrow context during the extraction. Analysing the whole sentence we may realize the specific sense of this extraction (*e.g. "treatments for cancer such as* **radiotherapy**"; *"different types of cancers such as* **the following** *: breast cancer, lung cancer"*). However, this kind of analysis requires, in general, much more effort and semantic background that the one we would expect from an unsupervised, automatic and web scalable methodology.
3. One word hyponym with ellipsis (*e.g. "cancer such as* **lung**"): those terms express a specialisation by adding new terms (nouns or adjectives) to the main concept. However, in this case, the ambiguity inherent to natural texts arises: in order to avoid redundancy the writer omits the main concept. The extracted term can be a correct one if we are able to realize that it needs to be concatenated to the main concept in order to express the correct specialisation.

When dealing with noun phrases composed by two meaningful words, we can distinguish between the situation in which the word on the right side is the same as the main concept or not. For the first situation, we can distinguish the following two cases:

4. Multiple word valid hyponyms (*e.g. "cancer such as* **breast cancer**"): similarly to Case #3, those terms express a specialisation by adding new words (nouns or adjectives) to the main concept n an explicit way, and can be added to the domain taxonomy.
5. Multiple word incorrect hyponyms (*e.g. "cancer especially* **dangerous cancer**"): this case is quite rare for this type of patterns and it represents a specialisation of the main concept that cannot be considered as a correct subtype in a taxonomy. The most common situations are the use of general purpose adjectives to qualify the main concept.

When none of both words of the noun phrase is the main concept (*e.g. "cancer including* **follicular lymphoma**") and with noun phrases composed by more than two meaningful words (*e.g. "cancer including* **invasive breast cancer**"), multiple levels of hyponym relationships are represented. In this situation, several relations of any of the mentioned cases may arise (*e.g. lymphoma* is a subtype of *cancer* and *follicular lymphoma* is a subtype of *lymphoma;* or *breast cancer* is a subtype of *cancer* and *invasive breast cancer* is a subtype of *breast cancer*). In consequence, it can be considered as a composition of the mentioned cases and can be partitioned in simpler relationships that should be analyzed individually.

Finally, as Hearst's patterns typically define lists of terms, we can find cases that mix features from different identified cases (*e.g. "cancers, including* **sarcomas, certain hematologic malignancies, breast, colon** *and* **prostate cancers**"). In this situation, each noun phrase should be extracted, identified and analyzed according to its particular nature.

In addition to these identified cases (that can be considered as "ideal"), the scenario is more complex if problems inherent to natural language are considered. The most common problematic situations are the following:

- The use of synonyms in order to avoid repetition of terms (*e.g. "cancer such as* **colon tumours**") may add confusion in the identification of the particular hyponymy case. This situation can be corrected if we are able to detect synonyms (more details in §5.7.2). However, true synonyms are actually very hard to find and, in most cases, there may be subtle differences of meaning that can be also correctly considered as specialisations.
- Misspellings (*e.g. "cancer such as* **brest cancer**") are very common in open environments like the Web. They should be treated adequately in order to avoid them.
- Proper names (*e.g. "centers related with cancer such as* **National Cancer**") are referred to individuals more than to specialisations of the domain. They should be distinguished from normal words in order to present a correct taxonomy.
- Polysemy (*e.g. "cancer such as* **zodiac cancer**") is another problem derived from natural language ambiguity that can be considered (see §5.7.1). It is hardly solved even in supervised approaches [Mihalcea and Edmonds, 2004].

Summarizing, Hearst's patterns allow to find a wide spectrum of taxonomic relationships for the specific domain (good recall) but problems about ellipsis, decontextualisations and natural language ambiguity can affect seriously their quality (compromised precision). These intuitions will be proved with results obtained for several well distinguished domains in §6.3.

5.2.1.2 Noun phrase-based pattern

On the other hand, we have those hyponymy relationships expressed by a noun phrase that includes the main concept as its last word (*e.g. breast cancer*). In this case, the extraction experiments have been performed in a slightly different way:

- Consider a keyword that represents the domain of knowledge that we want to explore (*e.g. Cancer*) and use it as the query for the search engine.

- Retrieve the first N web sites for each query and extract the useful text.
- Find matchings of this term in the text as a noun phrase and extract candidates for hyponymy by analysing morphologically the immediate previous words (nouns or adjectives).

For this pattern, the extraction cases are very simple (and also the queries and extractions), as they can be reduced to the mentioned correct Case #4 (*e.g. breast cancer* is a subtype of *cancer*), the incorrect Case #5 (*e.g. world cancer*), and more generally, the recursive case (*e.g. invasive breast cancer* is a subtype of *breast cancer* and *breast cancer* is a subtype of *cancer*).

Ambiguity in the form of polysemy and misspellings may also appear in the retrieved subtypes. However, in this case, we are not able to detect all possible relationships, because only some hyponyms of the full potential set are normally expressed in this way (*e.g. lymphoma* is not usually expressed as "*lymphoma cancer*").

Summarizing, and comparing them to the Hearst's patterns, with this approach we only are able to obtain a reduced subset of the possible hyponyms for a domain (lower recall) but its simplicity results in a higher robustness to decontextualizations and ellipsis (higher precision). Again, these intuitions will be illustrated with results for several well distinguished domains in §6.3.

5.2.1.3   Combining linguistic patterns to improve taxonomy learning

As one can see from the extraction cases presented above, both approaches behave in a quite complementary way (in relation to precision and recall). A combination of both may compensate their behaviours (as summarised in Table 9) and result in an increase of the global learning performance. This is one hypothesis of the present work.

Table 9. Types of hyponym candidate extractions (valid or incorrect) according to the type of linguistic pattern employed.

Extraction case	Example	Hearst	Noun phrase
#1. One word **valid** hyponyms	*leukaemia*	X	-
#2. One word **incorrect** hyponyms	*radiotherapy*	X	-
#3. One word hyponym **with ellipsis**	*lung*	X	-
#4. Multiple word **valid** hyponyms	*breast cancer*	X	X
#5. Multiple word **incorrect** hyponyms	*dangerous cancer*	X	X

Concretely, the following aspects for the mentioned cases may be taken into consideration:
- Cases #1 (the correct one) and #2 (the incorrect one) are exclusively obtained through Hearst's patterns. In order to maximize the learning performance, both cases should be distinguished. As Case #2 is incorrectly obtained due to a non-contextualized extraction, we will try to contextualize the analysis as much as possible in order to reject these hyponymy candidates.

- Case #3 (the not so correct one due to ellipsis) is only extracted through Hearst's patterns. However, on the correct form, with explicit inclusion of the main concept, it corresponds to a multiple word hyponym that can be easily detected with the noun phrase-based pattern. In consequence, this potentially incorrect extraction can be compensated by using the second pattern type.
- Cases #4 (the correct one) and #5 (the incorrect one) may appear from both pattern approaches. However, they are more easily extracted, analyzed and distinguished through the noun phrase-based pattern approach.

In order to simplify the analysis, the more general situation, in which several hyponym levels appear in the same noun phrase, will be considered by treating each relation individually. In other words, following the incremental philosophy, only the most general one will be considered at each moment and the specializations will be treated individually in new iterations of the learning process.

Additional problems such as misspellings or the presence of proper names are also treated as will be introduced in the following sections. More complex situations involving ambiguity may require additional effort to be solved. As will be shown in §5.7, we have developed techniques that can be a first step for dealing with them.

5.2.2 Taxonomy learning methodology

In this section, our learning methodology for constructing taxonomies using a combination of linguistic patterns and web scale statistics is presented.

The most novel idea is to define a method that maximizes the performance of the learning process by taking into consideration the behaviour of the different linguistic patterns (considering the conclusions presented in the previous section) and a set of specifically designed statistical scores to measure the relevance of extracted terms and relationships.

5.2.2.1 Hearst-based extraction

As shown in Figure 10, the method starts from a single concept specified by the user that represents the domain to be explored (*e.g. cancer*). It is worth noting that the initial concept could be composed by several words (*e.g. breast cancer*) providing a higher degree of concreteness if desired. As we have defined an iterative learning process, further analyses will involve concepts composed by several words.

The first step is to use linguistic patterns to extract candidates for hyponymy from the text. In this case, Hearst's patterns (the set introduced in Table 8, in §4.1) are applied first as they have a potentially higher recall and their lower precision will be compensated later through the use of noun phrase-based patterns (for Cases #3, #4 and #5). Concretely, using each Hearst pattern (*e.g. NP such as NP*) and the initial keyword (*e.g. cancer*), we compose several queries (*e.g. "cancer(s) such as"*) for a web search engine. Different queries for each pattern are composed using the pattern's regular expressions (*i.e.* using singular and plural keyword forms and optional colons).

They allow to obtain a first set of web resources that contain matchings of those patterns. The web content is parsed in order to remove visual information and the final clear text is obtained. This text is parsed and, using the appropriate pattern regular expression, candidate concepts for hyponymy (covering Cases #1 to #5) are obtained. In order to extract only valid candidates (noun or adjectives) a morphologic and syntactic analyser is employed only over the corresponding pieces of text. Candidates that are a single word (such as *leukaemia*) and those composed by a noun phrase (such as *breast cancer*) are distinguished. Moreover, candidates are analysed by an English stemming algorithm to detect different morphological forms of the same concept.

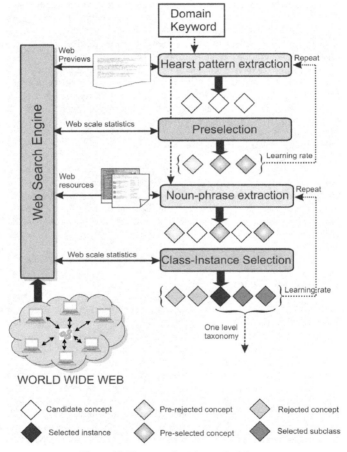

Figure 10. Taxonomy learning methodology.

The next step is to figure out, from the list of candidates, which are the correct and most related ones to the specific domain. In order to define an unsupervised method, we use an approach based on statistical measures computed from Web information distribution to perform the selection of candidates. As introduced in §3.3, we use web scale statistics obtained directly from a web search engine to obtain robust web scale measures in an efficient way. As this approach requires creating queries involving the extracted candidates and the initial keyword, the suitability of the statistical values about candidate relevance will depend on the specific formulated queries. In this case, we focus the process in the distinction between Case #1 (correct) and #2 (incorrect), as both are exclusive of Hearst's approach. As the last one appears due to non-contextual extractions, we will need queries as contextualised as possible. In this case, derived from the score (1) presented in §3.3, we have designed several queries and formulated different scores.

$$Score\_A(candidate) = \frac{hits("candidate" \ AND \ "keyword")}{hits("candidate")} \qquad (2)$$

This is the typical way of obtaining measures about co-occurrence and to infer the degree of relationship between terms [Turney, 2001; Cimiano and Staab, 2004; Etzioni *et al.*, 2005]. However, it does not ensure that the relationship between *candidate* and *keyword* is taxonomic. It only measures whether they co-occur or not in the text and, in consequence, an incorrect extraction of Case #2 may be selected.

$$Score\_B(candidate) = \frac{hits("candidate \ keyword")}{hits("candidate")} \qquad (3)$$

This second approach tries to bound the context by joining both terms using double quotes. This measure can be useful for hyponyms based on noun phrases as Cases #4 and #5 (as will be shown later) but it performs poorly for Cases #1 and #2 (*e.g.* "*breast cancer*" is a correct expression but "*lymphoma cancer*" is redundant).

$$Score\_C(candidate) = \frac{hits("Hearst\_pattern("keyword","candidate")")}{hits("candidate")} \qquad (4)$$

This third score uses the pattern itself as part of the query, joining it to the keyword and the candidate with double quotes (*e.g. hits("keyword such as candidate")*). This kind of queries is the most concrete one and indicates that the relation between terms should be taxonomic. However, it can be too restrictive in some situations (especially for noun phrases like Cases #4 and #5 that involve many terms and result in longer queries) and, in consequence, the recall may be compromised. Moreover, for each possible pattern, a different score can be computed and, potentially, different results can be obtained. In §6.3.1 we include a detailed evaluation on how those different scores affect the final result for a particular case of study.

Considering the described cases and the fact that, at this stage, our main objective is to be able to select Case #1 extractions and reject Case #2 ones, we use (4) as our selection score. In order to obtain the maximum generality, a different query for each Hearst's pattern is composed and executed, and the maximum score is selected.

Once values for all candidates have been computed, those that exceed a threshold are selected. This threshold controls the selection procedure's behaviour. It should be restrictive enough to maximize performance for Cases #1 and #2, even compromising a little bit the quality of Cases #4 and #5, which will be considered more carefully later. However, the value should be tuned considering the reduced amount of hits potentially obtained by the score's numerator (which involves several words with double quotes) in comparison with the high genericity of the denominator. Considering those facts, we empirically recommend a threshold with an order of magnitude of 1E-5.

An overview of the described process with an illustrative example is presented in Table 10.

Table 10. Heart's based learning overview: query, sample URL, sample web text (matching pattern in **bold**), analysed sentences (valid candidates and candidate verbs in **bold**), statistical analysis of candidates (selected ones in **bold**).

Web Query	"cancers such as"
URL	http://www.dh.sa.gov.au/pehs/cancer-maps/cancer-maps-91-00.htm
Sample text	[...] There are several clear patterns which emerge on some of the maps. Firstly, **cancers such as breast, melanoma and prostate cancer**, which require screening or a medical check for detection, almost always have higher incidence rates in high socio-economic status areas such as eastern and inner southern Adelaide. [...]
Analysed sentences	[ADVP Firstly/RB] ,/, [NP cancers/NNS] [PP such/JJ as/IN] [NP **breast/NN** ,/, **melanoma/NN** and/CC **prostate/NN cancer/NN**] ,/, [NP which/WDT] **[VP require/VBP]** [NP screening/NN] or/CC [NP a/DT medical/JJ check/NN] [PP for/IN] [NP detection/NN] ,/, [ADVP almost/RB always/RB] **[VP have/VBP]** [NP higher/JJR incidence/NN rates/NNS] [PP in/IN] [NP high/JJ socio-economic/JJ status/NN areas/NNS] [PP such/JJ as/IN] [NP eastern/JJ and/CC inner/JJ southern/JJ Adelaide/NNP] ./.
Candidate evaluation (thres=1E-5)	Hits("cancers such as breast") = 12.774 Hits("breast") = 137.310.395 Score = **9.3E-5** <hr> Hits("cancers including melanoma") = 2.432 Hits("melanoma") = 864.002 Score = **2.4E-3** <hr> Hits("cancers including prostate cancer") = 1.827 Hits("prostate cancer") = 2.405.772 Score = **7.59E-4**

In addition to the described filtering, a minimum number of hits for the constructed queries is also required in order to avoid misspelled terms. As this is an absolute measure, we set a common value for the different search engines that have been considered (presented in §3.4.3). However, finer tuning can be performed focusing the analysis only on a particular search engine. As this value also depends on the length of the particular queries, it is relaxed proportionally to the number of query terms, from several dozens of hits for one word terms (a minimum that, even for rare concepts, a search engine such as MSNSearch, typically ensures) to a unique hit for terms with more than three words. The particular value is not as important as the order of magnitude which scales in function of the number of words queried.

The result of this first learning process is a list of terms that are marked as *preselected* or *pre-rejected*. This particular notation is used because, as stated in §5.2.1.3, some of the acquired and evaluated concepts using Hearst patterns can be potentially retrieved again using noun phrase-based patterns. Due to the especial characteristics presented by those last extractions (less affected by ellipsis and decontextualizations, as introduced in §5.2.1.2), we can re-evaluate them with more confidence. Concretely, as will be described in the next section, (pre-)selected terms of Case #3 corresponding to ellipsis, can be corrected and (pre-)rejected terms of Case #4 corresponding to multiple word hyponyms, can be recovered.

5.2.2.2 Noun phrase-based extraction

The next step is quite similar to the first one but considering patterns based on noun and adjective phrases (as our previous work presented in [Sánchez and Moreno, 2006a]).

In this case, the search engine is queried again but only with the initial keyword. The clear text obtained from the set of web resources is parsed to find matchings of the keyword. The immediate anterior word is extracted and selected as a hyponym candidate if it is a noun or an adjective but not a stop word (using a morphologic analyser and a pre-compiled list of stop-words).

Those new candidates are added to the set of candidates obtained in the previous step. In the case in which a candidate was already in the list, it is marked to be a noun phrase (*e.g. lung cancer*), regardless of being a noun phrase or a single word term or being pre-selected or pre-rejected in the previous step. With this mechanism, we try to solve problems about ellipsis (Case #3: *e.g. "cancers such as lung"*) that may appear with Hearst's based extractions in pre-selected candidates (the *"lung"* incorrect extraction will become the *"lung cancer"* correct candidate). This shows how this second pass using the noun phrase-based pattern can improve the precision of the final results.

Once all resources have been parsed, the new retrieved candidates and those re-marked as noun phrases (mentioned in the last paragraph) that were pre-rejected in the previous stage are evaluated using web scale statistics to infer the degree of relevance of the particular taxonomic relationship. With this mechanism, we give a second chance to the potentially incorrectly rejected candidates and improve the recall for the Case #4 extractions. In this case, due to the nature of the relationship (expressed by noun phrases), *Score_B* is the most adequate one. It is able to contextualize enough the search (in contrast to *Score_A*) but without being too restrictive (as *Score_C*). The numerator's score is much simpler (without the pattern's terms) than for the Heart's case and, in consequence, a higher threshold should be used. We recommend a value at least two orders of magnitude higher (*i.e.* 1E-3) and a higher number of minimum appearances, starting from several hundreds.

In this phase of the learning, a method for distinguishing between common terms - that can become subclasses for the domain's taxonomy- and named entities –that, in our case are modelled as instances- is also applied over the full set of candidates. This method is described in §5.3 and uses simple heuristics about capitalization to perform the distinction. This additional mechanism helps to improve the quality of the final set of results by distinguishing real world entities (that should populate the ontology) from domain conceptualizations (that compose the ontology itself).

An overview of the described process with an illustrative example is presented in Table 11.

At the end, we obtain a final set of selected candidates joining those pre-selected during the Hearst's extractions and those re-marked, re-evaluated or newly retrieved and finally selected during this second stage. They become subclasses of the initial concept and are stored in the ontology. In order to provide a more consistent structure, if several morphological forms for a specific concept exist, all of them are considered and stored (as the keyword-based search engines used may return different results for each one) but they are tagged as *equivalent* classes.

Table 11. Pattern-based learning overview: query, sample URL, sample web text (hyponym candidate and named entity candidate in **bold**), analysed sentences (valid hyponym candidates and candidate verbs in **bold**), statistical analysis of candidates (selected ones in **bold**). Check the next section for the named entity evaluation procedure.

Web Query	"cancer"
URL	http://www.cancerproject.org/survival/cancer_facts/index.php
Sample text	[...]Cancer is the second leading cause of death in the United States, causing one in every four deaths. In 2003, 556,000 Americans died of cancer. The most common types of cancer diagnosed in Americans include **prostate cancer**, **breast cancer**, and **colorectal cancer**.[...] Eighty percent of cancers are due to factors that have been identified and can potentially be controlled, according to the **National Cancer** Institute.[...] Dietary factors also play a significant role in cancer risk. At least one-third of **annual cancer** deaths in the U.S. are due to dietary factors.[...]
Analysed sentences	[NP The/DT most/RBS common/JJ types/NNS] [PP of/IN] [NP cancer/NN] [VP diagnosed/VBN] [PP in/IN] [NP Americans/NNPS] **[VP include/VBP]** [NP **prostate/NN cancer/NN**] ,/, [NP **breast/NN cancer/NN**] ,/, and/CC [NP **colorectal/NN cancer/NN**] ./. [NP Eighty/JJ percent/NN] [PP of/IN] [NP cancers/NNS] **[VP are/VBP]** [ADJP due/JJ] [PP to/TO] [NP factors/NNS] [NP that/WDT] [VP have/VBP been/VBN identified/VBN] and/CC [VP can/MD potentially/RB be/VB controlled/VBN] ,/, [PP according/VBG] [PP to/TO] [NP the/DT **National/NNP Cancer/NNP** Institute/NNP] ./. [ADVP At/IN least/JJS] [NP one-third/NN] [PP of/IN] [NP **annual/JJ cancer/NN** deaths/NNS] [PP in/IN] [NP the/DT U.S./NNP] **[VP are/VBP]** [ADJP due/JJ] [PP to/TO] [NP dietary/NN] factors./.
Candidate evaluation (thres=1E-3) (conf=75%)	Hits("prostate cancer") = 2.405.772 Hits("prostate") = 4.853.001 Score= **0.49** ─────────────────────── Hits("breast cancer") = 7.195.755 Hits("breast") = 137.310.395 Score=**0.052** ─────────────────────── Hits("colorectal cancer") = 840.917 Hits("colorectal") = 869.995 Score=**0.96** ─────────────────────── Hits("annual cancer") = 22.426 Hits("annual") = 65.001.936 Score=*3.4E-4* ─────────────────────── Upper_case("National Cancer") = 41 Lower_case("National Cancer") = 0 Confidence = **100%**

5.3 Discovery of named entities

One of the hardest problems of the knowledge acquisition process is to decide when a term has to be considered as a *subclass* or as an *instance*; even for a knowledge engineer this can be a challenging issue [Lamparter *et al.*, 2004]. In both situations, it shares a taxonomic relationship with its respective superclass. However, in the case of instances, they ideally represent real word entities that cannot be refined anymore (they are leaves of the taxonomic tree). In this sense, there is a wide agreement in considering *named entities* as real world individualities and, in consequence, as instances for populating an ontology.

In our case, considering our unsupervised approach for extracting and selecting terms that are taxonomically related, the probability of selecting a named entity as a subclass of a particular concept is quite high. Certainly, our noun phrase-based extraction and statistical scores deal in the same manner with the class-superclass (*e.g. breast cancer*) and the named-entity-class (*e.g. NCCN Cancer*) relationships. On the one hand, this is an interesting point as we are able to retrieve named entities with a good degree of confidence; on the other hand, they cannot be distinguished from other classes, resulting in a poorly structured hierarchy. In order to avoid this situation, we have developed an additional method integrated within the taxonomic learning process for distinguishing between concepts that become classes and named entities that are represented as instances. However, as our approach is unsupervised, the instance semantics remains unknown (*i.e.* we cannot infer if a named entity discovered for a particular ontological concept is a *person*, *organisation*, *event*, etc.). This fact may represent a limitation from the ontology population point of view but, in our case, as we only intend to improve the taxonomic structure, the presented issues are beyond the scope of our work.

Following the same principles of unsupervision and scalability, the approach that we propose is based on the fact that a named entity (in contrast with common concepts) is presented, in most situations of the English language, in capital letters. Thus, if a term extracted using the mentioned taxonomic patterns is presented in this form, it will be considered as a named entity candidate. Again, in order to check that the candidate is a truly valid one, we check it against a Web search engine in order to obtain statistics. However, as most search engines do not distinguish between lower and upper letters, we cannot obtain them directly using the scores presented in §5.2.2. In consequence, some level of analysis has to be performed.

In more detail, the methodology works in the following way:

- During the taxonomic learning process, the set of candidates that have been extracted for a specific concept are processed in order to decide if they are named entities or concepts. Following the presented heuristic, if the candidate starts with one or more capital letters, it will be marked as a named entity candidate; otherwise, it will be considered as a domain concept candidate. Note that a term can be considered as a named entity and a concept candidate at the same time if it has been found represented in both forms.

- For each named entity candidate, a query to the Web search engine is constructed by joining the candidate with its hierarchical path (*e.g. National Breast Cancer*), in order to retrieve a corpus of documents from which a final decision will be taken.

- The first N web sites returned by the search engine are evaluated in order to find the way in which the candidate is spelled: the number of times that it is represented with upper and lower letters is counted. A minimum number of web resources and hits is necessary in order to obtain reliable results and avoid misspellings (following the same guidelines introduced in previous sections for the taxonomic case).
- Once the process is completed, a confidence measure is computed (5):

$$Confidence = \frac{\#Upper}{\#Upper + \#Lower} * 100 \tag{5}$$

It represents the most common way of representing the word (upper or lower case) for each candidate. If the result is above a certain threshold (should be higher than 50%, *e.g.* 75% for very reliable results), the candidate will be considered as a named entity (included in the ontology as an instance) and not as a domain concept (modelled as subclasses). If the candidate is not considered as a named entity, it will be evaluated as a concept candidate with the taxonomic procedure explained in §5.2.2.

At the end of the process, all the terms found for a specific concept will be selected and tagged as named entities or domain concepts. As a result of this procedure, the structure and readability of the final knowledge representation can be improved, providing a certain (albeit semantically limited) degree of automatic ontology population for the desired domain.

5.4 Non-taxonomic learning

Up to this point, we are able to retrieve taxonomic relationships and organise domain concepts in a hierarchical way. However, in order to construct a semantic structure with good domain coverage, non-taxonomically related concepts should also be considered. As this aspect is certainly the less tackled one in the ontology learning process [Kavalec *et al.*, 2004], novel contributions in this area are necessary.

Following the same philosophy as in the taxonomic case, we use language regularities in the form of patterns as an effective technique to extract knowledge in an unsupervised way. However, for the non-taxonomic case, aside from a reduced set of predefined relationships (*e.g.* meronymy, antonymy, synonymy, *etc*), there do not exist finite lists of domain independent patterns, as non taxonomic relationships are typically expressed by a verb that relates a pair of concepts [Schutz and Buitelaar, 2005]. If we want to use a pattern-based approach to extract non-taxonomic knowledge, a previous step for learning *domain-dependent* patterns (based on verb phrases) is required. The learned patterns composed by domain concepts and associated verb phrases (*e.g. "breast cancer is caused by"*) allow constructing web search queries and obtain non-taxonomic relation candidates. Final selected relations can be labelled directly using the corresponding verb phrase. As stated in §4.2, previous research in non-taxonomic learning typically tackles the detection of correlated concepts first, leaving the labelling problem to a posterior (or even unresolved) stage. On the contrary, we use automatically learned verbs as the base for retrieving and labelling non-taxonomic relation candidates.

Again, despite the unsupervised nature of the proposed method, the knowledge already acquired in the previous step is used as a bootstrap to contextualize the search process and create queries. In this case, as shown in Figure 11, apart from the initial domain keyword, we receive a set of candidates for domain verbs compiled during the taxonomic analysis. All these data represent a knowledge base from which to start the non-taxonomic learning process.

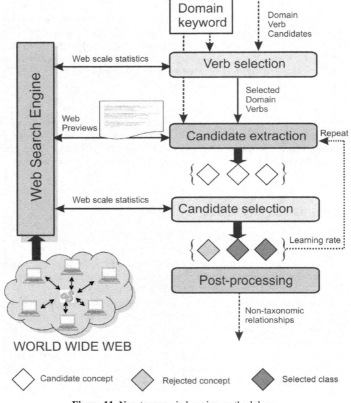

Figure 11. Non-taxonomic learning methodology.

So, in this section, we present an *automatic methodology for discovering non-taxonomic relationships from the Web*. From a general point of view, this task involves *i)* the discovery and selection of verbs –non-taxonomic labels- used for expressing non-taxonomic relationships in a specific domain and *ii)* the discovery and selection of concepts non-taxonomically –verb labelled- related.

So, the *main contributions* of the developed methodology are:

1. A method for selecting relevant domain-related verb phrases extracted during the taxonomic analysis and using them to construct domain dependent patterns.

2. A method for using those learned domain patterns to extract and select non-taxonomic relationships via lightweight linguistic and statistical analyses. An integrated, domain independent, automatic and unsupervised learning process using an incremental learning approach is presented.

3. An automatic evaluation procedure (shown in §6.5) for checking the quality of the obtained results against WordNet for domains in which that electronic repository offers good coverage.

5.4.1 Verb extraction and selection

As above, the first step in our non-taxonomic learning methodology is the discovery of patterns that express non-taxonomic relationships. In this case, those relationships are typically expressed by a verb relating a pair of concepts. Due to the potential amount of verbs available in the English language, we should find which of them are truly relevant for the particular domain.

In order to obtain a reliable verb corpus, during the taxonomic learning process described in §5.2, we compile a set of verbs that are apparently related to the domain's keyword. Concretely, using the same morphologic and syntactic analysis performed over the taxonomic pattern's neighbourhood (the sentence in which the matching for the search query has been found), we also extract the verb phrase of the sentence. In many situations a conjugated verb with, optionally, a preposition is retrieved. However, due to the unsupervised nature of our approach, we cannot have a semantic understanding of the particular verb phrase sense. In consequence, due to the enormous variability of verbal forms (according to subject number, verbal tense, passive and conditional constructions, use of adverbs, *etc*...), problems regarding the lack of understanding may arise.

In order to avoid those natural language related problems we have opted for a simple approach: as we only intend to extract labelled relationships, only those verbal forms that express a relation in an assertive way are extracted. Concretely, verb phrases are extracted taking into consideration the following:

- Only present tenses are allowed.
- No ambiguous constructions are allowed: future, conditionals or modal verbs.
- Verb phrases including modifiers in the form of adverbs of any kind are rejected.
- Verb phrases including a composition of verbs (*e.g. tends to develop in*) are not considered as it is difficult to realize in which manner the main verb's meaning is being modified. The only exception is the verb "to be", used to construct the passive form (very common in the English language).
- Prepositions are allowed and attached to the particular verb.
- Verbs expressing taxonomic relations are rejected (is/are, include, *etc.*) as we prefer to treat the taxonomic case independently as described in §5.2.

Those verbs fulfilling the restrictions are finally extracted and classified in function of their position within the sentence and the apparent role of the domain's keyword:

predecessors (*e.g.* "*causes* hypertension") or *successors* (*e.g.* "hypertension *is treated with*") of the domain's keyword.

The next step consists on realizing which verbs are really closely related to the searched domain. The objective is to select those verbs that express a domain specific relationship, which can be later used to learn concrete non-taxonomic relationships.

Again, as described during the taxonomic learning, we use a statistical analysis to measure the degree of relationship between the domain and the verbs in an unsupervised way. As has been previously introduced, in order to obtain a robust measure (that considers an amount of resources as large as possible), we use web-scale statistics that represent the distribution of a queried concept in the whole Web. Concretely, for each verb phrase candidate that has been extracted as a *predecessor* of the initial keyword, we compute the following web search based relatedness score (6). We have used similar queries as in the taxonomic noun phrase-based extraction. Concretely, the double colon ("") contextualizes enough the query to conclude that the verb phrase is really used to express a relationship in which the domain's keyword is the object:

$$Score(verbPhrase, domainKey) = \frac{hits("verbPhrase\ domainKey")}{hits("verbPhrase")} \qquad (6)$$

Alternatively, if the candidate has been extracted as a *successor* of the domain's keyword, we compute the relatedness score (7) in the following way:

$$Score(domainKey, verbPhrase) = \frac{hits("domainKey\ verbPhrase")}{hits("verbPhrase")} \qquad (7)$$

This last score states that the verb phrase is really used to express a relationship in which the domain's keyword is the subject. There can be situations in which the same verb has been retrieved both as a successor and a predecessor (*e.g.* "hypertension *is associated with*" and "*is associated with* hypertension"). In that case, both scores are computed and stored separately as two different domain dependant patterns.

The obtained values are used to rank the list of verb phrase candidates. This allows us to select those that are more closely related to the analysed domain (see examples in Table 12, for the *hypertension* domain) in order to use them as the base for learning non-taxonomic relationships. Due to the similarity of the presented non-taxonomic scores with those used during the noun phrase-based taxonomic learning, the same threshold range may be established. However, in this case, the concrete value of the threshold is not as critical as in previous cases. This is because, in general, any of the discovered verb phrases can be correctly used in the domain keyword's context; the limit is set to distinguish those verbs that express domain dependant relationships from the general ones. This filter will potentially improve the throughput of posterior non-taxonomic learning steps, limiting the result's scope. However, due to the fuzzy nature of the selection/rejection boundary it will depend more on the user's expected amount of results and the available time for performing analyses than on the particular domain. Consequently a wide range of thresholds can be established (*e.g.* from 1E-3 to 1E-5).

Table 12. Firsts (selected) and lasts (rejected) elements of the ranked list of verb phrases for the *Hypertension* domain, classified according to their position (PREdecessors or SUCcessors of the keyword).

Verb phrase	Position	Relatedness
suffer from	PRE	0.00122
is associated with	SUC	6.89E-4
is treated with	SUC	6.52E-4
is caused by	SUC	3.58E-4
accelerates	SUC	3.45E-4
is associated with	PRE	3.43E-4
is inherited	SUC	3.30E-4
affects	SUC	3.16E-4
causes	PRE	2.46E-4
reduces	PRE	2.26E-4
causes	SUC	2.24E-4
increases	SUC	2.20E-4
are treatable	SUC	2.01E-4
develops	SUC	1.55E-4
reduces	SUC	1.10E-4
...	...	...
publishes	*PRE*	*3.25E-6*
see	*PRE*	*2.77E-6*
are listed below	*SUC*	*2.45E-6*
welcome	*SUC*	*1.48E-6*
point to	*SUC*	*3.24E-7*
check out	*PRE*	*9.54E-8*
believe in	*SUC*	*5.18E-8*

5.4.2 Retrieval and selection of related concepts

Once related verb phrases have been selected, they are used to construct the domain related patterns. Those express non-taxonomic relationships and can be employed to discover related concepts. In order to do this, and following the same philosophy as with the taxonomic patterns, we query a web search engine with the patterns "verb-phrase domain-keyword" or "domain-keyword verb-phrase" depending on the role of the domain's keyword. In this manner, we retrieve a corpus of resources containing the specified query. Our objective at this stage is to evaluate their content in order to obtain concepts that immediately precede (*e.g.* "*high sodium diet* is associated with hypertension") or succeed (*e.g.* "hypertension is caused by *hormonal problem*") the queried pattern. Those new concepts become candidates for being non-taxonomically related with the initial keyword, labelling this relation with the verb phrase.

However, due to the same reasons as during the verb-phrase extraction, the quality of the candidate extraction may be affected by the lack of semantic understanding of our approach. Extracting a piece of text -the particular pattern instance- from its con-text -the whole sentence- may result in weird relationships due to decontextualization problems. In addition, due to the nature of the searched relationships (based on verbs), this problem is more important than in the taxonomic case. So, in order to avoid as many natural language derived problems as possible, only those sentences containing the pattern's instance that match with a set of simplicity rules (typically called "text nuggets" [Pasca, 2005]) are evaluated. Concretely sentences must be of the form:

<Sentence> [NP Subject] [VP Verb] ([PP Preposition]) [NP Object] </Sentence>

The domain's keyword must appear in the subject or the object in function of its role within the particular verb phrase. Other noun phrases before the subject and after the object, or modifiers such as adverbs or subordinate constructions, are not allowed. In this manner we avoid ambiguity problems and consider only knowledge expressed in an assertive way. In addition, in the noun phrase where the domain's keyword appears, no other modifiers (adjectives) are allowed as they probably specify a more specific concept that will be treated in future iterations (*e.g.* a relationship defined for *pulmonary hypertension* and not for the general concept). Only meaningless words such as determinants are allowed in the extracted noun phrases. In any case, the new discovered concept (subject or object) can be composed by several words (*e.g. diuretics* but also *diuretic therapy*).

One may wonder if this approach may be too restrictive, as this simplistic form is not the usual way of expressing knowledge in natural language. If we were dealing with a limited repository this would be an issue, as many complex but valid assertions might be omitted. In this case, the data sparseness problem (introduced in §4.1) may be more important than for the taxonomic (Hearst) case, due to the non-taxonomic pattern complexity and the heavy filtering of sentences. However, when dealing with an enormous repository with a high redundancy such as the Web, the sparseness problem is reduced [Buitelaar *et al.*, 2003; Velardi *et al.*, 2003], as it is much more probable to find the same knowledge expressed in many different forms (with different degrees of formal complexity). This simplistic approach has proved to be effective when dealing with big, heterogeneous, noisy, ambiguous environments like the Web [Pasca, 2005].

However, it is important to note that the fact of applying restrictive constraints over the text analysis in order to avoid natural language problems does not imply that the relationship expressed in the extracted nugget is valid. In consequence, once a set of new concepts has been extracted through the analysis of sentences, the next step is to decide which of them (*e.g.* "*high sodium diet*") are related to the searched domain (*e.g.* "*hypertension*"). In order to perform this selection process we use again web scale statistics about the co-occurrence of those two terms. In this case, the relatedness score is computed in the following manner (8):

$$Score(Concept \; domainKey) = \frac{hits("domainKey" \; AND \; "Concept")}{hits("Concept")} \quad \textbf{(8)}$$

In this case, the AND operator ensures that those two terms co-occur within the text but not necessarily in the same sentence. This is a more relaxed score in comparison to the taxonomic ones because the non-taxonomic relationships can be expressed in many different ways (involving different verbal forms or additional sentence components). If we used double quotes or added the verb phrase (that needs to be properly conjugated) to the query the amount of obtained results would be very reduced in many situations, becoming too restrictive to obtain robust measures.

Those concepts (see some examples in Table 13, for the *hypertension* example) whose relatedness to the initial keyword is higher than a specific threshold are selected and incorporated into the ontology. The score's numerator is the most general until this moment as the AND operator (and not double colons) is used. In consequence, the threshold range should be higher than in previous cases to maintain a similar selection behaviour. We recommend a value among 1E-1 and 1E-2. Again, the particular value is not as important as in the taxonomic case due to the fuzziness that characterizes non-taxonomic relationships. The relation is labelled according to the verb phrase used to discover it (*e.g. "high sodium diet" "is associated with" "hypertension"*). Note that the direction of the relation corresponds to the role that each concept plays in the sentences (subject or object).

Table 13. Examples of verb-labelled non-taxonomic relations for the *Hypertension* domain.

Subject (NP)	Verb (VP)	Object (NP)	Relat.
hypertension	is treated with	antihypertensives	0.55
hypertension	is treated with	diuretics	0.54
high sodium diet	is associated with	hypertension	0.512
hypertension	accelerates	renal disease	0.49
hypertension	is treated with	vasodilators	0.47
adrenergic receptor gene	is associated with	hypertension	0.469
hypertension	is associated with	atherosclerosis	0.436
hypertension	is caused by	excessive salt intake	0.399
hypertension	is associated with	cerebrovascular disease	0.339
hydroxylase deficiency	is associated with	hypertension	0.327
hypertension	is associated with	cardiovascular disease	0.257
sleep apnea	is associated with	hypertension	0.216
excess alcohol consumption	is associated with	hypertension	0.215
obesity	is associated with	hypertension	0.182
hypertension	is caused by	hormonal problem	0.159
...	...	...	...
sufficiency	*is associated with*	*hypertension*	*0.006*
unit	*is associated with*	*hypertension*	*0.004*
hypertension	*accelerates*	*the development*	*0.003*

An overview of the described process with and illustrative example is presented in Table 14.

Table 14. Non-taxonomic learning overview: query, sample URL, sample web text (matching sentence in **bold**), analysed sentences (valid concept in **bold**), statistical analysis of candidates (selected ones in **bold**).

Web Query	"is associated with hypertension"
URL	http://google.com/answers/threadview?id=266407
Sample text	[...] **Heavy drinking is associated with hypertension**. A study has shown that alcohol stimulates the activity of the sympathetic nervous system, which as already mentioned above results in increased blood pressure:[...]
Analysed sentences	[NP **Heavy/NNP drinking/NN**] [VP is/VBZ associated/VBN] [PP with/IN] [NP hypertension/NN] ./.
Candidate evaluation (thres=0.01)	Hits("heavy drinking") = 185.836 Hits("hypertension" AND "heavy drinking") = 14.873 Score = **0.08**

During the specification of the verb-labelled non-taxonomic relationships, if we detect that the verb form is expressed in passive voice (*e.g. "hypertension"* -> *"is caused by"* -> *"excessive salt intake"*), we also include the *inverse relation* establishing the appropriate relation direction and verb label in active voice (*e.g. "excessive salt intake"* -> *"cause"* -> *"hypertension"*).

5.4.3 Processing relation labels

The last important aspect of the non-taxonomic learning process is referred to the relations themselves. Even though we are able to detect that two concepts are related in some way and label those relations according to a verb (expressed by a particularly conjugated verb phrase), this last information means nothing to a computer-based knowledge driven tool that could use the acquired data for reasoning. In order to tackle this problem, and thanks to the fact that verbs are a much more reduced set of linguistic elements than nouns and adjectives, we can take profit of available semantic classifications of verbs.

In this sense, Levin's [Levin, 1993] is the most complete and widely used classification of English verbs. She observed that verbs that exhibit similar syntactic behaviour are also semantically related. Her approach reflects the assumption that the syntactic behaviour of a verb is determined in large part by its meaning. Verbs in a class may share many different semantic features, without designating one as primary. As a result, she provided a classification of over 3000 verbs according to their participation in alternations involving NP and PP constituents. Levin defines approximately 200 verb classes, which she argues reflect important semantic regularities.

Levin's classes, although a valuable starting point, do not currently provide information that is complete enough or precise enough to inform lexical entries or to serve as a clustering Gold Standard. Both Levin's classes and repositories such as WordNet have limitations that hamper their use as general classification schemes. Some authors [Palmer *et al.*, 1998] have developed a refinement of Levin's classes, intersective Levin's classes, which are more fine-grained and which exhibit more coherent sets of syntactic frames and associated semantic components. As a result, the VerbNet [Kipper *et al.*, 2000] electronic repository has been developed. It is a tool that provides structured semantic information about verbs. Concretely, for each verb class, it provides thematic roles, syntactic frames, selectional restrictions for the arguments in each frame and semantic predicates with a time function. The current status of Verbnet includes:

- 237 top-level classes, 194 additional subclasses.
- 5000 verb senses (3800 lemmas).
- 23 thematic role types.
- 36 semantic restrictions on thematic roles.
- 131 syntactic frames (357 thematic role variants).
- 55 syntactic restrictions.
- 94 semantic predicates.

Considering the usefulness of this kind of information about verbs and sentence constituents, we intend to add it to the extracted verb labelled relationships. This may bring a certain degree of semantic content necessary for reasoning and inference. However, before applying directly those tools, as VerbNet's classification does not cover the complete set of verbs (especially when dealing with prepositional verb forms), we perform an analytic process to extract the main verb from a retrieved verb phrase, considering the verbal form, auxiliary verbs and prepositions.

As shown in Table 15, the most interesting verb related information is:

- *Verb class*: identifying the particular class to which the verb semantically belongs allows us to deduce its main semantic features. Moreover, we can detect different verbs belonging to the same class and, in consequence, expressing similar semantic relationships.
- *Thematic roles*: they indicate the role that each element -subject and object- plays (*e.g.* agent, patient, cause, *etc.*) for the sentence in which the particular verb is used. This provides a base from which to perform further analyses allowing a higher level of understanding of the discovered non-taxonomic relationships.

Table 15. Examples of VerbNet semantic content associated to some of the discovered verb phrases for the hypertension domain: verb class, list of verbs in the same class and thematic roles are presented.

Verb phrase	suffer from
Root infinitive	suffer
Verb class	marvel-31.3-4
Verbs in class	[ache, hurt, suffer]
Thematic roles	[Cause[], Experiencer[+animate], Cause[], Experiencer[+animate]]
Verb phrase	is caused by; causes
Root infinitive	case
Verb class	engender-27
Verbs in class	[beget, cause, create, engender, generate, shape, spawn]
Thematic roles	[Predicate[], Theme1[+abstract], Theme2[+abstract]]
Verb phrase	is associated with
Root infinitive	associate
Verb class	amalgamate-22.2-2
Verbs in class	[associate, conjoin, entangle, muddle, pair, team, affiliate, associate, compare, confederate, confuse, entangle, incorporate, integrate, muddle, pair, total, identity]
Thematic roles	[Agent[+animate OR +abstract], Agent[+animate OR +machine], Patient1[+concrete], Patient1[], Patient2[+animate OR +abstract], Patient2[]]
Verb phrase	is inherited
Root infinitive	inherit
Verb class	obtain-13.5.2
Verbs in class	[accept, accumulate, appropriate, borrow, cadge, collect, exact, grab, inherit, receive, recover, regain, retrieve, seize, select, snatch]
Thematic roles	[Agent[+animate OR +organization], Source[+concrete], Theme[]]
Verb phrase	develops
Root infinitive	develop
Verb class	grow-26.2
Verbs in class	[develop, evolve, grow, hatch, mature]
Thematic roles	[Location[], Theme[], Agent[+animate OR +machine], Asset[+currency], Beneficiary[+animate OR +organization], Material[+concrete], Product[+concrete], Agent[+animate], Material[+concrete], Product[+concrete]]

At the moment, all this information is no further processed. Semantically grounded inference or natural language understanding is beyond the scope of this work and will be presented as a line of future work.

5.5 Ontology post processing

As shown in Figure 8, before incorporating the results of the iterative taxonomic and non-taxonomic learning into the domain ontology, a final step is performed. The distributed and incremental learning approach may raise some problems when constructing the final structure concerning how each individual result should be added to the ontology. For that reason, we have included a post processing stage that merges the partial results in the final structure in an intelligent way. We perform some analyses that try to detect redundancies, induce implicit semantic relationships (like multiple inheritance) and extract new knowledge (like class features). In this manner, we intend to take the maximum profit of the acquired knowledge, obtaining a more compact, coherent and tied structure without requiring further web analyses.

However, it should be taken into consideration that discovered redundancies and implicit relationships of ontological facts are limited to the scope of the constructed domain ontology, as the range of the analysis is the set of discovered ontological terms. Moreover, as this is a completely unsupervised process and no further web-based analyses are performed, we limit the post processing to those cases in which we can be quite sure that extracted conclusions are correct.

In this section we offer an overview of several aspects that can be taken into consideration in order to improve the quality of the final structure. As one can see in Table 16, the new knowledge automatically discovered and added to the ontology thanks to the post-processing stage is referred to the taxonomic aspect. It covers the extraction of new equivalences (detecting equivalent morphological forms as described in §5.5.1) new *is-a* relationships (due to multiple inheritance as presented in §5.5.2), and domain features (attributes associated to classes as introduced in §5.5.3).

Table 16. Comparison of the number of ontological entities obtained for the taxonomic aspect of the ontology for the *Cancer* domain before and after the final step of post-processing.

Ontological components	Pre-processing	Post-processing	Increment
Subclasses	1593	1593	N/A
is-a relationships	1593	1785	+192
Equivalences	210	848	+638
Instances	632	632	N/A
Features	0	82	+82

5.5.1 Detection of redundant and equivalent concepts

The fact of performing individual and partial analyses in an incremental way may result in discovering terms or relationships already acquired. In order to avoid redundant classes and the repetition of previously performed analyses, a control mechanism has been included.

Concretely, each class discovered from each analytical step is evaluated before including it into the final ontology. We compare it using a stemming algorithm with the already present ones:

- In the case that the exact (morphological form) is already present, the new concept is omitted, adding, to the already present one, all the new discovered relationships.
- In the case in which the concept is the same but it is presented in a different derivative form (*e.g.* plural, gerund), the class is added but specifying a relation of equivalence between them. Ontologically, a relation of equivalence means that both classes are virtually equivalent, sharing the same (past, present and future) relationships. However, we store and analyse each morphological form for convenience, as many keyword-based search engines do not consider the different derivative forms of the specified query. In this manner, we are potentially able to retrieve, in the future, a more complete corpus for the same concept.
- If the new concept is different to the previous ones, it will be included and further analysed taxonomically and non-taxonomically until the algorithm decides to finish the analysis. It is important to note that each new concept is placed in the correct taxonomic level (*i.e.* if we are adding the concept "*cranial radiotherapy*", it will be included as a subclass of the "*radiotherapy*" class, creating that last one in the case in which it was not present). In this manner the final ontology maintains the level of abstraction at each taxonomic level, regardless of the way in which the particular concept has been obtained. In any case, we only perform further analyses for the concrete discovered concept ("*cranial radiotherapy*") and not for its taxonomic structure ("*radiotherapy*").

For the noun phrase-based taxonomic classes, an additional analysis is performed to detect implicit equivalence relationships. More concretely, in some domains, a particular subclass may be stated in different forms, altering the order of the corresponding modifiers (*e.g. amperometric glucose biosensor* and *glucose amperometric biosensor*). However, both classes refer to the same semantic concepts and, in consequence, share the same characteristics. In that case, we compare the full taxonomic path of each pair of noun phrase-based classes and mark equivalent classes.

5.5.2 Processing multiple inheritance

As introduced in §4.1, noun phrase-based hyperonyms can be quite frequent in many domains. In the English language, it is quite common to define a specialisation by adding nouns or adjectives that constrain the semantic range of the main term [Grefenstette, 1997]. In our learning approach, the order in which modifiers are added in the text may result in different subclasses. However, in many situations, the particular order does not influence the final meaning.

For example, imagine that we are able to discover several noun phrase-based hyponyms for the *Cancer* domain such as *breast cancer, lung cancer, colon cancer*, but also *metastatic cancer*. Then, in a further iteration, we are able to find that *breast cancer* has a new subclass that is *metastatic breast cancer*; however, when analysing *metastatic cancer*, we are not able to retrieve any subclass of the form *breast metastatic cancer* as this is not a common way of expressing that concept. However, semantically, due to the nature of the syntactic construction, both classes have the same meaning and should be defined as equivalent. In other words, the discovered *metas-*

tatic breast cancer should be defined as a subclass of both the *breast cancer* and the *metastatic cancer* subclasses. With this multiple relationship, the subclass will inherit the characteristics of both superclasses.

The fact that a particular noun phrase-based subclass shares modifiers with other superclasses is a very typical situation (as one can see from the results presented in Table 16). Considering the described procedure for all the discovered classes, we are able to detect and specify new taxonomic relationships without any further analyses. Those relationships (*e.g.* the fact that several types of *metastatic cancers* exist) are, in many situations, hidden by the way in which specialisations are expressed in natural language. However, they add more semantic content to the domain ontology, resulting in a more complete structure.

Some examples of new taxonomic relationships discovered for different domains are present in Table 17 and Table 18.

Table 17. Examples of new taxonomic relationships discovered for the *Cancer* domain.

Class	Direct superclass	New superclass
colon_rectal_cancer	rectal_cancer	colon_cancer
invasive_bladder_cancer	bladder_cancer	invasive_cancer
invasive_breast_cancer	breast_cancer	invasive_cancer
invasive_cervical_cancer	cervical_cancer	invasive_cancer
metastatic_bladder_cancer	bladder_cancer	metastatic_cancer
metastatic_brain_cancer	brain_cancer	metastatic_cancer
metastatic_breast_cancer	breast_cancer	metastatic_cancer
metastatic_cervical_cancer	cervical_cancer	metastatic_cancer
metastatic_colon_cancer	colon_cancer	metastatic_cancer
metastatic_colorectal_cancer	Colorectal_cancer	metastatic_cancer
metastatic_esophageal_cancer	esophageal_cancer	metastatic_cancer
metastatic_gastric_cancer	gastric_cancer	metastatic_cancer
metastatic_kidney_cancer	kidney_cancer	metastatic_cancer
metastatic_liver_cancer	liver_cancer	metastatic_cancer
metastatic_lung_cancer	lung_cancer	metastatic_cancer
metastatic_prostate_cancer	prostate_cancer	metastatic_cancer
metastatic_rectal_cancer	rectal_cancer	metastatic_cancer
metastatic_testicular_cancer	testicular_cancer	metastatic_cancer
metastatic_thyroid_cancer	thyroid_cancer	metastatic_cancer

Table 18. Examples of implicit taxonomic relationships discovered for the *Sensor* domain.

Class	Direct superclass	New superclass
acceleration_position_sensor	position_sensor	acceleration_sensor
analog_temperature_sensor	temperature_sensor	analog_sensor
electrochemical_oxygen_sensor	oxygen_sensor	electrochemical_sensor
photoelectric_proximity_sensor	proximity_sensor	photoelectic_sensor
pyroelectric_motion_sensor	motion_sensor	pyroelectic_sensor
ultrasonic_flow_sensor	flow_sensor	ultrasonic_sensor
ultrasonic_motion_sensor	motion_sensor	ultrasonic_sensor
ultrasonic_proximity_sensor	proximity_sensor	ultrasonic_sensor

Another issue regarding multiple inheritance is the presence of redundant relationships. In some cases (*e.g.* for the *mammal* domain), we can retrieve the same concept (*e.g. whale*) at different taxonomic levels (*e.g. whale is-a mammal* and *whale is-a aquatic_mammal*) with superclasses that, at the same time, are taxonomically related (*e.g. aquatic_mammal is-a mammal*). This will result in an explicit multiple inheritance that is redundant with the proper definition of *subclass*. In order to treat those cases, they are processed in the post-processing stage, maintaining the most specific(s) relation(s) (*e.g. whale is-a aquatic_mammal*) and suppressing the redundant general one(s) (*e.g. whale is-a mammal*). This can bring a more compact and coherent structure. Some examples of redundant taxonomic relationships and the result of this processing stage for the *mammal* domain are presented in Table 19.

Table 19. Examples of redundant taxonomic relationships: for a concept, its *superclasses*, the *superclasses of its superclasses* and *the final set of filtered superclasses* are presented.

Class	Superclasses	Super-Superclasses	Final Superclasses
Whale	*Mammal*	-	-
	Aquatic_mammal	Mammal	Aquatic_mammal
	Marine_mammal	Mammal	-
	Cetaceans	Marine_mammal	Cetaceans
Bat	*Mammal*	-	-
	Small_mammal	Mammal	Small_mammal
Human	*Mammal*	-	-
	Large_mammal	Mammal	Large_mammal
	Primates	Mammal	-
	Apes	Primates	Apes
Lion	*Mammal*	-	-
	Large_mammal	Mammal	Large_mammal
	Carnivores	Mammal	Carnivores
Rat	*Mammal*	-	-
	Small_mammal	Mammal	-
	Rodent	Small_mammal	Rodent
Mammoth	*Mammal*	-	-
	Large_mammal	Mammal	Large_mammal
	Extinct_mammal	Mammal	Extinct_mammal

5.5.3 Automatic extraction of class features

Going a step further in the analysis of implicit relationships among taxonomic terms, we may consider the following case: imagine that we have found that a particular modifier (and its corresponding subclasses) has been retrieved for different branches of the taxonomic tree. For example, following with the same examples presented in the previous sections, we have found, from the taxonomic analysis, that several types of cancers (*e.g. bladder cancer, breast cancer* and *cervical cancer*) share a common modifier and their corresponding subclasses (*e.g. invasive bladder cancer, invasive breast cancer* and *invasive cervical cancer*).

On the one hand, in the case in which an *invasive cancer* subclass has been found, the situation will share the same principles enounced for making explicit new taxonomic relationships (*i.e.* defining all three cancers also as subtypes of *invasive cancer* as stated in the previous section).

On the other hand, the fact that the modifier has been found in *different* taxonomic branches may state that this is a *common* characteristic of several subclasses. Certainly, in many domains, there may exist many ways of classifying the same concepts according to different features shared by a community of individuals [Sabou, 2006]. For example for the *sensor* domain, we may classify them according the physical magnitude measured (*e.g. temperature sensor*) but also according to their running principle (*e.g. ultrasonic sensor*). In other cases, like the one stated for the *cancer* domain, we can consider that several classes may present a particular *attribute* or *feature* (*e.g.* several *cancers* can or cannot be *invasive*). In both cases, there exist several ways of structuring or classifying the domain's entities.

Applying these principles over our results, we have designed a procedure for automatically discovering common *features* or *attributes* for several classes. Concretely, in a similar manner as in the case of multiple inheritance, we evaluate all the modifiers present in all taxonomic branches. In the case in which a particular one is found in two or more subclasses belonging to different taxonomic branches (*e.g. invasive bladder cancer* and *invasive breast cancer*), the particular modifier will be specified as a *feature* (the fact of being or not *invasive*). It is defined at the taxonomic level of the more specific common taxonomic node (in the example, at the *cancer* level).

In this manner, we have automatically discovered a set of features specified at the corresponding taxonomic level that can be considered as attributes that may (or not) be present in the possible subclasses or individuals (*e.g.* a *cancer* may be *metastatic* or *invasive,* and a *breast cancer* may be, in addition to *metastatic* and *invasive*, also *recurrent* and *operable*). This adds more semantic content to the domain ontology without requiring any further analyses.

As an example of the kind of features that we are able to extract, some of them are summarized in Table 20 and Table 21. It is important to note the corresponding taxonomic level in which each feature is defined. For example, we have found that *Cancers* can be *invasive* and *metastatic* (as several immediate subclasses with those modifiers have been found); however, other attributes such as the property of being *operable*, *inoperable* or *recurrent* have been discovered in deeper levels of the taxonomy (cancer subclasses). Of course, due to the nature of taxonomies, each attribute defined at a certain level is inherited by all of their subclasses.

Analyzing the results in more detail, one may observe that the same feature appears in a considerable amount of different subclasses (*e.g. recurrent* appears in *bladder, breast, colon, ovarian, prostate* and *rectal* cancers), but not in the main root. It is possible that in this case, the particular feature can be defined at a higher level of the taxonomy. However, we have preferred to adopt a more rigid approach in order to ensure the correctness of the results. Of course, the fact that this analysis is based only on particular results establishes a direct dependence between the discovered features and their degree of generality and the results' size and coverage (recall).

Table 20. Examples of features discovered for several classes of the *Cancer* domain.

Class	Features
cancer	invasive, metastatic
bladder_cancer	recurrent
breast_cancer	hereditary, operable, recurrent
colon_cancer	hereditary, invasive, nonpolyposis, polyposis, recurrent
gallbladder_cancer	unresectable
gastric_cancer	distal, operable, unresectable
lung_cancer	inoperable
mesothelioma	inoperable
ovarian_cancer	recurrent
pancreatic_cancer	unresectable
prostate_cancer	hereditary, recurrent
rectal_cancer	distal, recurrent, unresectable

Table 21. Examples of features discovered for several classes of the *Sensor* domain.

Class	Features
sensor	capacitive, optic, ultrasonic
camera_sensor	megapixel
flow_sensor	thermal
humidity_sensor	resistive
image_sensor	linear, megapixel, thermal
motion_sensor	solar
oxygen_sensor	wideband
position_sensor	linear, rotary
pressure_sensor	piezoresistive, resistive

As far as we know, very little research has been performed in the field of discovering class attributes for ontology learning. In consequence, our proposal, even being a simplistic and preliminary approach, can be considered as a novel contribution.

5.5.4 Ontology annotation

Finally, as an additional step, apart from to the ontological information (classes, relationships and instances) that defines the semantics of a domain and allows performing inference, we include additional meta-information in our domain ontology.

Concretely, we add as "annotations", information about how the learning process has been performed. This includes statistical scores for the different relatedness measures, corpus size, *etc*. This may give the user additional information about the confidence that the system gives to a particular class or relationship (according to the results of the statistical analyses). Moreover, we store the web resources that have been iteratively retrieved, associated to the corresponding concept. Those resources are structured and categorized as will be described in chapter 7. This represents an added value for the final domain ontology as, in addition to the domain's knowledge, the ontology has been automatically populated with related web resources. This can be interesting for the user as it provides a direct access to the Web in a highly structured fashion (in comparison to web site lists presented by a Web search engine).

As will be described in chapter 7, this information is used by an especially designed application to provide a rich and customisable visualization of knowledge.

5.6   Relevant aspects of the learning process

Up to this point, we have offered a detailed explanation on how each step of the learning process is performed. However, some questions regarding the specific access to the web resources, the information used at each step as a bootstrap and issues about finalisation (*i.e.* how to decide when the algorithm should continue the analysis or stop the exploration) should be considered.

5.6.1   Efficient access to the web content

Even though our main objective is to offer the best results and not the shortest response time, there are some ways to speed-up the process while maintaining the quality of the final ontology. Due to the particular nature of our approach much of the runtime is employed in accessing the Word Wide Web whenever we are querying a web search engine or accessing a particular web site. As the Web's response time is, in many situations, orders of magnitude higher than the runtime required to process the web content, any improvement in this aspect can represent a great difference from the runtime performance perspective.

The first improvement is related to the web search engine used to perform queries for obtaining web sites or web scale statistics. In order to avoid the saturation of one particular search engine, denegation of service or the degradation of performance due to introduced courtesy waits, we have implemented several interfaces with different search engines such as Google, Yahoo, Altavista, AlltheWeb and MSNSearch. In this way, we can alternate from one to another in several searches or even combine two of them taking into consideration their characteristics introduced in §3.4.3. Concretely, the only search engine that is able to perform without any limitations and offers a great response time is MSNSearch. However, for very concrete domains with very few available resources, other search engines with better coverage (Google) may be needed to have a corpus wide enough. In that case, the combined use of other search engines becomes almost mandatory (*e.g.* Google for retrieving web resources from which to extract candidates and MSNSearch or Yahoo for obtaining statistics from which to compute relative scores).

The second point that influences the performance is the way in which the content of web resources is accessed. For a particular query that returns a set of web sites that are potentially interesting, we typically access each particular web URL, download its content and start working on it. This can represent an important overhead depending on the Internet connection bandwidth, the size of the web site and the server's response times. However, there are alternative ways of accessing web content partially, such as the previews offered by web search engines (called snippets, as introduced in §3.4.2). In our case this can be particularly useful because our pattern-based extraction of candidates only considers a short context for the constructed query. However, those previews only cover *one* matching for the particular query and, if several instances can be found on the same web site, they will be omitted.

So, in order to decide the convenience of using one approach or the other to access web content, we conducted a simple experiment: for a particular domain (*cancer*), we queried a web search engine using different queries that are typically required for different steps of the learning process (Hearst's, Noun Phrase-based and non-taxonomically learned patterns). Then, we evaluated the first N returned web sites and counted the number of extractions of candidates that our system was able to obtain in each case. The results were the following:

- When using Hearst's patterns (*e.g. "cancer such as"*), we were able to extract 7 candidates from the first 10 web sites, obtaining an extraction ratio of 0.7 with no more than 2 extractions of candidates per web site. This low number was expected, due to the concrete nature of the pattern.
- When using the noun phrase-based pattern (*i.e. "cancer"*) we were able to extract 112 candidates from the first 10 web sites, obtaining a ratio of 11.2 with a maximum of 31 extractions of candidates per web site. This situation is expected as these patterns are typically found as indexes, labels or partial classifications.
- When using several non-taxonomic learned patterns (*e.g. "cancer is caused by"*, *"is associated with cancer"*), we were able to extract between 8 and 13 candidates from the first 10 web sites, obtaining an extraction ratio between 0.8 and 1.3 with no more than 3 extractions of candidates per web site. Again, those low numbers were expected, due to the concrete nature of the pattern.

In consequence, for the first and the third cases, it is quite convenient to use web search previews that typically cover the maximum of 1 or 2 matchings (with a narrow context) per site. This can also be applied to the evaluation of named entities which only needs to evaluate a reduced amount of candidate matchings. This speed up things greatly as parsing one page of results is equivalent in terms of learning performance to access and parse up to 50 individual web sites. On the other hand, only for the noun phrase-based patterns, we decided to access and parse the full web sites due to the high amount of useful information that we are potentially able to obtain.

5.6.2 Adaptive corpus size

In several steps of the learning process we have mentioned the fact that a set of web resources is retrieved from a specific query and analyzed to extract candidates. On the one hand, the most domain related and updated web resources are presented first by the search engines ranking algorithms [Ridings and Shishigin, 2002] and, in consequence, the quality of the web sources tends to decrease once the most relevant sites have been evaluated. On the other hand, due to the amount of redundancy, once we have evaluated a certain percentage of the full set, obtaining new valid knowledge will be more difficult [Jans, 2000]. Thus, just evaluating a reduced amount of the full set can give us quite good quality results. In consequence, this parameter can be set auto-matically in function of the potential size of the domain.

In previous experiments [Sánchez and Moreno, 2006a] we observed in many do-mains that the growth of the number of discovered concepts (and in consequence the *recall*) follows a logarithmic distribution in relation to the size of the search. This is caused in part by the redundancy of information and the relevance-based sorting of web sites made by the search engine. Moreover, arrived at a certain point in which a considerable amount of concepts has been discovered, precision tends to decrease due to the growth of false candidates. As a consequence, analysing a large amount of web sites does not imply obtaining better results than with a more reduced but accurate corpus. Illustrative results that support those conclusions are presented in Figure 12 and Figure 13 for the *Cancer* and *Biosensor* domains.

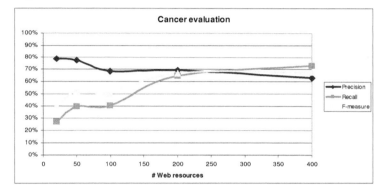

Figure 12. Evaluation results for the *Cancer* taxonomy in function of the number of analysed web resources against the MESH standard classification.

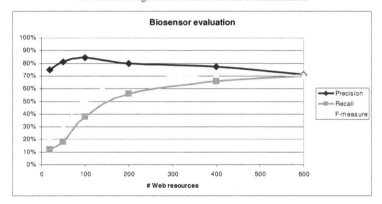

Figure 13. Evaluation results for the *Biosensor* taxonomy in function of the number of ana-lysed web resources against a domain expert's opinion.

In those cases, different executions of the taxonomy learning methodology with several fixed corpus sizes were performed. Then, the one iteration of the taxonomic learning is executed and results are manually evaluated following the procedure, measures and criteria that will be described in §6.3.

However, how big should this set be in order to obtain results with good recall without compromising the precision? It will depend on several factors, like the domain's generality, the quality of the web sources, the ranking policy of the search engine or the concreteness of the constructed query. For example, when recursively evaluating deeper levels of taxonomic relationships, the amount of resources needed to obtain the potentially available domain subclasses becomes smaller. This is because in the first levels (*e.g. cancer*), the spectrum of the candidate concepts is wider than in the last ones (*e.g. metastatic breast cancer*) where the searched concept is much more restrictive and fewer valid results can be found.

Due to the automatic, domain independent and dynamic nature of our proposal this parameter cannot be set *a priori*. Thus, we need a mechanism that sets the web resource corpus size dynamically at runtime, providing feedback about how the learning is evolving in order to decide whether to continue evaluating more resources or not.

In order to tackle this problem, we propose an incremental analytic methodology: the amount of web resources analyzed during each learning step is increased until the system decides that most of the knowledge for the particular query has been already acquired.

More concretely, for a particular query (*i.e.* each taxonomic pattern for each discovered concept), we retrieve and analyse a reduced set of web resources (*e.g.* 50), extracting candidates and selecting related ones through the described statistical analyses. At the end of the process, if the percentage of selected terms from the list of extracted candidates is high, this indicates that the queried concept is particularly productive and a deeper analysis will potentially return more results. In this case, we query again the search engine with an offset to obtain an additional set of web sites (*e.g.* the next 50 web sites) and repeat the learning stage. The process is iteratively executed until the global percentage of selected terms (computed from the accumulation of results of each iteration) is equal or falls below a certain threshold or no more knowledge has been acquired in that iteration. This indicates that most of the knowledge related to the queried concept has been already acquired because most of the last retrieved terms have been rejected.

The particular learning thresholds can be configured in relation to the particular learning step (*i.e.* taxonomic or non-taxonomic learning) and the user's personal preferences in order to tune up the system's behaviour. In this manner, one may specify to perform a very exhaustive taxonomic analysis and a subtle (and fast) non-taxonomic one. Typical thresholds used during our tests vary from 70% of selections (very constrained, small potential corpus) to 20% (very loose, wide potential corpus).

In order to illustrate this process, in Figure 14 we analyse the learning trace obtained for an execution of the taxonomy learning process for the *Cancer* domain considering a learning threshold of 60%:

-   From the list of taxonomic patterns, the first is "*cancer(s) including*". The system queries the search engine and analyses the first 50 web sites. The result of the selection process applied over the retrieved candidates is: 15 new candidates, 9 new selections, learning rate=60%.

- As the result is equal to the established 60%, the system stores the partial results and picks up the next pattern (*"cancer(s) such as"*) and starts the process again by querying the 50 first web resources to the search engine. In this case, the results are: 11 new candidates, 9 new selections, learning rate=81%. As this value is above the minimum, it queries again the search engine retrieving the next 50 web resources. In this case, the results considering the 100 resources already analysed for this pattern are: 20 candidates, 15 selections, learning rate=75%. The process continues iteratively until 250 web resources are analysed, obtaining the following results: 34 candidates, 21 selections, learning rate=61.76%. In the next iteration no new candidates are found so the process finishes.

- The next pattern (*"such cancer(s) as"*) offers, after analysing 100 web resources, 13 new candidates, 6 selections, learning=46,15%.

- In consequence, the next pattern is queried and the process is repeated. When all the patterns have been used 1100 web sites have been analysed (more precisely, as stated in §5.6.1, their previews), obtaining a total of 173 candidates and 43 selections, with a global learning rate of 24%. As expected the more patterns are evaluated the less productive they become. Due to the high size and redundancy of the Web, it is very common to retrieve the same knowledge (in this case, hyponymy candidates) is different forms (patterns). In consequence, most of the domain candidates are retrieved using a reduced set of patterns.

- At this point, as described in §5.2.2.2, the noun phrase-based taxonomy learning process starts by fully retrieving and analysing 50 web resources. However, as most of the valid candidates have been already acquired, only one iteration is performed and the process is finished.

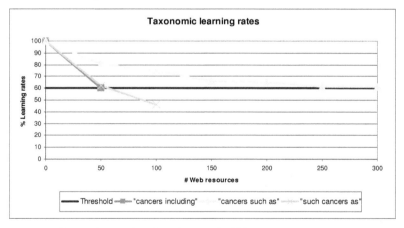

Figure 14. Evolution of learning rates for different taxonomic patterns.

Applying this algorithm to all of the discovered concepts, highly productive ones with many subclasses receive more learning effort -higher amount of analysed web resources in several iterations- (*e.g. childhood_cancer, prostate_cancer* or *leukaemia* with 3 or more additional iterations) than less productive ones (*e.g. malignant_cancer, oral_cancer, gallbladder_cancer* with only one iteration per pattern).

A similar procedure is followed during the non-taxonomic analysis using the learned verb phrase-based patterns as seed for retrieving web resources. As an example, for the *hypertension* domain presented in §5.4, we have obtained the following learning trace (see Figure 15 to follow the explanation):

- The first verb phrase-based query is "*suffer from hypertension*". Analysing the first 50 results, we obtain 2 candidates but none of them is selected, giving us a learning rate of 0%. In consequence, the next verb phrase is selected.
- Querying "*hypertension is associated with*" results after evaluating the first 50 results in 7 candidates and 5 selections, providing a learning rate of 71,4%. So, the process continues by retrieving the next 50 results. Due to the high productiveness of this verb phrase for the domain it iterates until 200 web resources, point in which the number of candidates is 38 with 22 selections, resulting in a learning rate of 57,8% that is below the specified 60% threshold.
- The query "*hypertension is caused by*" provides more than an 80% of selected candidates. However, at the third iteration, no more new candidates are retrieved and, in consequence, the process is stopped.
- When all the verb phrases have been queried, the most productive ones have been "*hypertension is associated with*", "*hypertension is caused by*" and "*is associated with hypertension*" with 3 or more additional iterations.

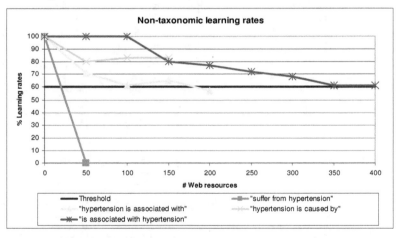

Figure 15. Evolution of learning rates for different non-taxonomic patterns.

One can see from the presented examples that the behaviour observed in Figure 12 and Figure 13 for the precision and recall measures corresponds to the tendency presented by the learning rates corresponding to the most productive patterns (typically defined by the evaluation order). A certain equilibrium between precision, recall and learning throughput can be achieved at the point in which the learning rate falls below a threshold. In consequence, the particular threshold value in conjunction with the candidate selection policies presented in previous sections has an important influence on how the learning evolves. As will be shown in some practical applications in §7.2, they will allow to adapt the learning process to the particular user's requirements (*i.e.* high precision, high coverage or high throughput).

Using the presented feedback mechanism through the full process we ensure, in addition, the correct finalization of each learning step, with a dynamic adaptation of the effort dedicated to analyse each concept. Moreover, we are able to obtain results with a good coverage regardless of the generality or concreteness of the specific domain. From the runtime performance point of view, this approach provides a good learning/effort ratio as the algorithm decides to continue with the analysis only of the apparently productive concepts, discarding the unproductive ones.

Further evaluations of the results obtained using this adaptive mechanism will be offered in chapter 6.

5.6.3 Bootstrapping

Even though we start the ontology construction process from scratch, thanks to the incremental learning methodology, after each learning step, a partial set of results is available. Concretely, once the first one-level taxonomy has been obtained, which knowledge can be used in further steps as bootstrap. In this manner we are able to improve future searches (*i.e.* deeper taxonomic analysis or non-taxonomic relationships) by creating more contextualized searches and retrieving more concrete resources.

In more detail, each acquired subclass for the initial domain's concept can be used as a seed for further taxonomic and non-taxonomic learning steps. In this case, we can use the immediate superclass as a bootstrap. Concretely, we attach that superclass to each web query performed (*e.g.* "*leukaemia*" AND "*cancer*") in further analyses for retrieving web resources or computing statistics. In this way, queries derived from the taxonomic analysis can result in: "*leukaemia such as*" AND "*cancer*"; queries derived from the non-taxonomic analysis may be: "*leukaemia is related with*" AND "*cancer*". One may see that we force the co-occurrence of the particular query and the immediate superclass. Using this approach, we try to specify the context in which the particular concept should be analyzed. This is especially useful when the analyzed subclass is polysemic or it is used in several domains, because the additional knowledge used in the learning process can constrain and guide it to the corresponding "sense". As a consequence, the more knowledge is acquired, the more informed the learning process is.

Another knowledge that can be used as a bootstrap is the compiled and selected list of domain verbs related to a particular concept. As described in §5.4.1.1, those verbs are extracted during the taxonomic analysis of a particular concept *(e.g. cancer)* and filtered and used during the non-taxonomic stage. This process is repeated for each recursive execution so, for each new subclass *(e.g. breast cancer)* of the initial one *(e.g. cancer)* an additional list of domain verbs is compiled. However for all the concepts contained in the same taxonomy, the list of verbs retrieved for a particular superclass are, in general, adequate for any of its subclasses. In consequence, and in order to improve the throughput of the analysis, the list of domain verbs retrieved for a particular class is inherited and used during the non-taxonomic analysis by all of its subclasses. Using this mechanism, two advantages arise:

1) Considering the list of selected and rejected verbs for all of the superclasses of a particular class can save us from performing a considerable amount of Web search queries. Many of the verbs that we are able to retrieve during the taxonomic analysis of a particular subclass have been potentially acquired for its superclasses and, in consequence, we do not need to perform again the web-based filtering process described in §5.4.1.1.

2) Due to the higher degree of concreteness of a subclass in relation to its superclass and considering the adaptive behaviour of our learning algorithm described in §5.6.2, the size of the taxonomic analysis is potentially reduced in function of the taxonomic level. In consequence, the amount of verbs (and their associated non-taxonomic relationships) that we are able to retrieve for a particular subclass may be considerably reduced in comparison to its superclass. This negative aspect can be neutralized thanks to the inheritance of the verb lists already acquired for the corresponding superclasses.

In addition to all those aspects, once a multilevel taxonomy for the domain's keyword and a set of non-taxonomically related concepts for each taxonomic class have been recursively obtained, new domains of knowledge can be explored. Concretely, each new non-taxonomically related concept can be used as the seed of a new learning process, obtaining a multidimensional structure. In that case, in order to avoid excessive semantic distance from the initial domain, previously obtained concepts can be also attached to search queries to contextualize the search.

As an example, if we explore the *Cancer* domain, in addition to the multi-level taxonomy that represents the different types of cancer, we can find that a particular one -*liver cancer*- is non-taxonomically linked with the relation *is caused by hepatitis*. Then, the new concept *hepatitis* can be the object of new recursive taxonomic and non-taxonomic analyses. However, we attach the concept *"liver cancer"* to each formulated query in order to maintain the context in which our analysis is focused. The process is recursively repeated adding the immediate anterior concept to the queries corresponding to the new one. The recursion finishes when no more new subclasses are selected. Thanks to the constrained queries, the potential corpus will be narrower and the algorithm may decide to stop the analysis earlier. Our objective is to control the correct finalisation of the process (as introduced in previous sections) unsupervisedly and automatically, avoiding an excessive semantic distance between related concepts. In any case, a hard limit of 2 non-taxonomic levels from the initial domain is established. The depth of the taxonomic structure is not constrained.

An example of the multi-level structure that we are able to obtain using this mechanism is presented in Figure 16.

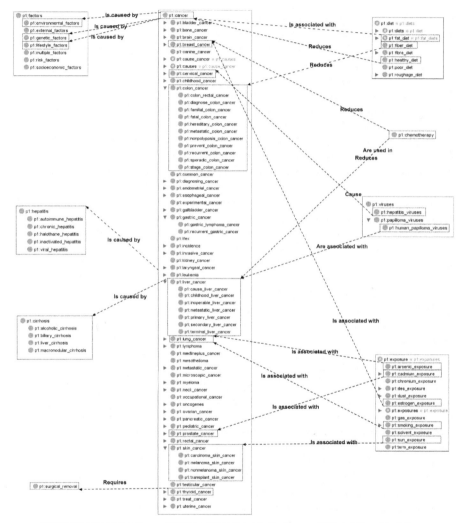

Figure 16. Part of the *Cancer* ontology obtained using the incremental learning methodology.

5.7 Semantic ambiguity

Up to this point, we have covered the full methodological process for creating a domain ontology from scratch. We have considered the main ontological elements such as domain concepts, taxonomic and non-taxonomic relationships and even some degree of automatic ontology population. However, we have omitted the issues regarding the inherent ambiguity that arises when dealing with natural language resources. As mentioned in chapter 4, dealing with semantic ambiguity is a very complex aspect and it is beyond our primary goals.

However, two additional approaches adapted to our learning process and disambiguation needs have been developed to tackle polysemy and synonymy. They should be interpreted as procedures that may improve the structure or coverage of the final results. They are not integrated with the rest of the learning methodology and their real influence in the results is left for future developments.

In more detail, for dealing with polysemy, an algorithm for clustering sense-related terms for a given keyword is presented in §5.7.1; for dealing with synonymy, a method for discovering synonyms of a given keyword is introduced in §5.7.2.

5.7.1 Word sense disambiguation

One of the main problems when analyzing natural language resources is *semantic polysemy*. In our case, for example, if the primary keyword has more than one sense (*e.g. virus* can be applied over "malicious computer programs" or "infectious biological agents"), the resulting ontology may contain concepts from different domains (*e.g.* "*iloveyou virus*", "*immunodeficiency virus*"). Although these concepts have been selected correctly, it could be interesting that the branches of the resulting taxonomic tree were somehow grouped if they belong to the same sense of the immediate "father" concept.

Attempting a general, unsupervised solution is a very complex task that is nowadays researched by many authors obtaining limited performances [Senseval, 2004]. In our case, we do not intend to present a primary contribution in this area, but only to introduce the first approaches of a methodology adapted to our learning process that can be useful for well distinguished word senses. As introduced in §4.4.1, it is based on the context where each concept has been extracted, concretely, the web resources that contain it. We can assume that each website is using a word in a concrete sense, so all candidate concepts that typically co-occur should belong to the same keyword's sense. The observation that words tend to exhibit only one sense in a given discourse or document was tested by Yarowsky [Yarowsky, 1995] on a large corpus (37.232 examples). The accuracy of the claim was very high (around 99% for each tested word), which shows that it can be exploited. Applying this idea over a representative set of documents (as the whole Web) we can find some consistent relations and construct clusters of terms associated to the main meanings of the initial keyword. Concretely, we use the same principles of statistical analyses and web-scale statistics to obtain robust measures about co-occurrence.

At the end of the process, if a word has N well distinguished meanings, the resulting taxonomy for this concept will be grouped in a similar number of sets, each one containing the classes that belong to a particular meaning.

The algorithm begins from the taxonomy generated in previous steps. For a given concept of the taxonomy (for example the domain keyword: *virus*) and a concrete level of depth (for example the first one), a classification process is performed by joining the concepts which belong to each keyword sense. Taking into consideration the premises stated above, this process is performed by a *clustering algorithm* that joins the more similar concepts, using as a similarity measure the degree of co-occurrence between set of concepts:

- In order to compute the similarity between concepts, for each possible pair of concepts of the same taxonomic level (see Figure 17), a query to the search engine involving each pair is constructed. In a similar manner as for the relatedness scores for the taxonomic and non-taxonomic analysis, the following score is computed (9).

$$Similarity(Concept\_A, Concept\_B) = \frac{hits("Concept\_A" \; AND \; "Concept\_B")}{Max(hits("Concept\_A"), hits("Concept\_B"))} \quad (9)$$

We are computing the relative degree of co-occurrence between a pair of terms in relation to the most general one (that covers a wider spectrum of web resources). So, the higher it is, the more similar the concepts are (because they are frequently used in the same context). Note that in this case we use the AND operator as we measure the degree of co-occurrence between terms and not a specific relation as in the taxonomic case.

- With these computed measures, a similarity matrix between all concepts is constructed. The most similar concepts (in the example, *hiv* and *herpes* have the highest co-occurrence) are selected and joined indicating that they belong to the same keyword's sense. The joining process is performed by creating a new class with those concepts and removing them individually from the initial taxonomy.

- For this new class, the similarity measure to the remaining concepts is computed, considering the most distant one (10) (furthest neighbour: *complete linkage*). In consequence, no more Web search engine queries are required. Other measures like taking into consideration the nearest neighbour (*single linkage*) or the arithmetic average have also been tested, obtaining worse results: as they are higher and less restrictive measures, they tend to join all the classes, making it difficult to distinguish the final set of senses.

$$Similarity(Class(A, B), C) = Min(Similarity(A, C), Similarity(B, C)) \quad (\mathbf{10})$$

- The similarity matrix is updated with these values and the new most similar concepts/classes are joined (building a dendrogram as shown in Figure 17 and Figure 18). The process is repeated until no more elements remain disjoint or the similarity is below a minimum threshold. However, for domains with well distinguished senses, no threshold is needed in order to detect final clusters: they are automatically defined when the similarity equals zero (no co-occurrence between some of

their subclasses). This is caused by the use of the restrictive *complete linkage* as
the joining criteria.

The result is a partition (with 2 elements for the *virus* and *organ* examples) of
classes that groups the concepts that belong to a specific meaning. The number of final
classes is, for well differentiated senses, automatically discovered by the clustering
algorithm. Note that this methodology can be applied to a set of terms at any level of
the taxonomy.

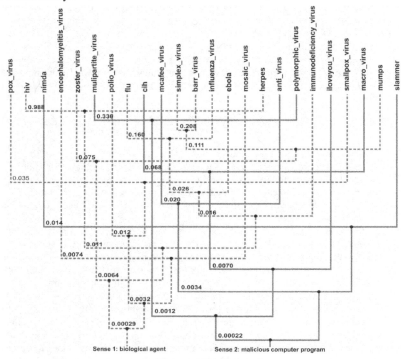

Figure 17. Dendrogram representing semantic associations between classes found for the *virus*
domain. Two final clusters are automatically discovered when similarity equals zero. Note that
nimda, *cih*, *iloveyou* and *slammer* are computer virus names.

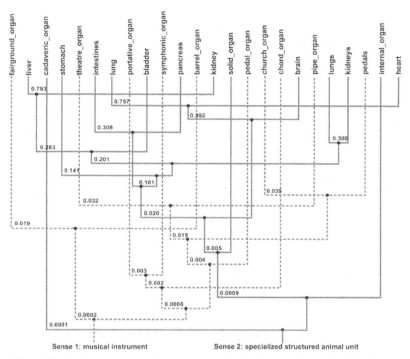

Figure 18. Dendrogram representing semantic associations between classes found for the *organ* domain. Two final clusters are automatically discovered when similarity equals zero.

Through several executions of the presented methodology for different domains, we have observed that, even though it is able to group and detect the main well distinguished senses related to a polysemic word, it performs worse for similar ones (whose classes tend to be joined) or very specific concepts (whose classes may remain disjoint). In consequence, it should be considered as an additional help for improving the readability of the results in well distinguished polysemic domains.

5.7.2 Discovery of synonyms

The detection of synonyms is an important task when using keyword-based web search approaches in order to explore more exhaustively the corpus of web resources that really covers a knowledge domain.

Even though we do not intend to provide an exhaustive or general contribution to this complex area, we have developed a methodology adapted to our learning procedure and our learning corpus for discovering synonyms.

It uses the noun phrase-based taxonomical branches obtained by the algorithm presented in §5.2.1.2 and, again, a web search engine. Our approach is based on considering the longest branches of noun phrase-based subclasses (*e.g. hormone ablation resistant metastatic prostate cancer*) of our hierarchy and using them as the constraint (search query) for obtaining new documents covering the same topic but, maybe, using alternative forms of the same concept.

The assumption of the algorithm is that the longest noun phrases of our taxonomy contextualize enough the search to obtain, in most cases, synonyms of the same semantic concept. The procedure, in this case, is inverse to the construction step: in that case we used an initial keyword to obtain a taxonomy; now we use that taxonomy to obtain equivalent forms for that keyword.

Concretely, the methodology works as follows:

- Select the longest branches (at least 3 words) of the obtained taxonomy, without considering the initial keyword (*e.g. hormone ablation resistant metastatic prostate*). Due to their high degree of concreteness, they define specifically the domain of knowledge to explore, without problems of polysemy or semantic ambiguity. The longer the branches are, the more contextualized the search will be but the fewer documents will be retrieved.
- For each branch, we make a query in the search engine and retrieve a set of web resources. This can be performed in two ways:
  - Setting only the multiword term as the query (*e.g. "hormone ablation resistant metastatic prostate"*). That will return the webs containing this sentence without caring about the next word. Most of them will contain the original keyword, but a little amount will use synonyms, ensuring that all pages will belong to the desired domain but slowing the search. This is the procedure followed to obtain the results included at the end of this section.
  - Specifying the query not to contain the original keyword (*e.g. "hormone ablation resistant metastatic prostate" –cancer*). The set of pages (if there is any) will only contain alternative words. This will speedup the search considerably but perhaps valid resources will be omitted (those in which both the keyword and the alternative word(s) co-occur).
  In any case, a reduced set of web sites (among 50-100) is enough to discover a good set of valid candidates. This is because the most query-related ones are typically found sooner than invalid ones as, following the initial premise, similar synonyms are the ones that co-occur more frequently with their respective contexts, in this case, noun phrase's suffixes.
- Search among the text of the obtained web resources for the specified query and evaluate the following word: the position that originally was occupied by the initial keyword (*e.g. cancer*). Due to the high contextualization defined by the queried noun phrase, the word found in that position is considered to be a candidate for synonym (*e.g. carcinoma*). As we are looking into a very narrow context, in the same way as for the taxonomic and non-taxonomic learning steps, this analytic step can be accelerated by working only over the snippets presented by the web search engine.

- Repeat the process for each website and each multiword term and count the number of appearances of each candidate. A stemming morphological analysis is also performed to group different forms of the same word.

- Once the process is finished, a list of candidates has been obtained. Again, in order to select reliable ones, a procedure to check the suitability of each candidate using web-based statistics is performed. For each candidate, a series of new queries to the web search engine using again noun phrase concepts is performed. In this manner, we check if this candidate is commonly used as an alternative form to express the same concept in the domain. For each multiword, a set of queries is constructed joining a suffix from that noun phrase and the new candidate. For example, for the *Cancer* domain, the *Carcinoma* candidate and the *hormone ablation resistant metastatic prostate* concept, the domain constrained queries that can be performed are: *"prostate carcinoma"*, *"metastatic prostate carcinoma"*, *"resistant metastatic prostate carcinoma"*, *"ablation resistant metastatic prostate carcinoma"* and *"hormone ablation resistant metastatic prostate carcinoma"*. The longer the queries are, the more constrained and domain dependent they will be but, at the same time, the more difficult the retrieval of matching web sites will be. So, for example, queries of 2, 3 and 4 terms from each concept can be considered in this step. Each one is queried and the number of returned hits is considered. However, instead of evaluating the number itself (which will depend more on the generality of the multiword than on the candidate itself), we only consider the fact that the query has returned a minimum number (*e.g.* 10 hits). Thus, the number of queries that have returned some results is counted and weighted depending on the number of involved terms (11). If several derivative forms are available for the same candidate, their maximum relevance is considered.

$$relevance = \sum_{i=min\_terms}^{i=max\_terms} (i - min\_terms + 1) * \#queries\_with\_i\_terms\_returning\_min\_results \quad (11)$$

- This final value represents the relevance of the candidate to become a final synonym for the domain, and allows selecting the most similar ones. As a refinement, it can be normalised in function of the number of total possible queries (12), obtaining a final percentage that eases the selection process (establishing a minimum threshold). In addition, with this measure, it is easy to detect and directly discard misspelled candidates as they typically return zero values.

$$relative\_relevance = \frac{relevance}{\sum_{i=min\_terms}^{i=max\_terms} (i - min\_terms + 1) * \#total\_queries\_with\_i\_terms} * 100 \quad (12)$$

The described methodology has been tested with several domains obtaining promising results. For illustrative purposes, in Table 22, Table 23 and Table 24, results for the *Cancer*, *Sensor* and *Disease* domains are presented, respectively.

Table 22. Firsts and lasts elements of the sorted list of synonym candidates for the *Cancer* domain. From the obtained taxonomy, 31 classes of 3 terms and 16 classes of 4 terms have been considered, evaluating 100 web sites including the original keyword.

Concept (root)	Derivatives	Relevance	Relative_relev
cancer	cancer, cancers	61	96.82%
carcinoma	carcinoma, carcinomas	30	47.62%
tumor	tumor, tumors	25	39.68%
tumour	tumours, tumour	24	38.09%
neoplasm	neoplasms	7	11.11%
testi	testis	6	9.52%
bladder	bladder	5	7.93%
malign	malignancies, malignant	3	4.76%
epithelioma	epitheliomas	2	3.17%
carcino	carcino	2	3.17%
skin	skin	2	3.17%
mitosi	mitosis	1	1.58%
....	....	....	....
carcinomabiomed	carcinomabiomedical	0	0%
tumortreat	tumortreatment	0	0%
forelimb	forelimb	0	0%
tumorsovarian	tumorovarian	0	0%

Table 23. Firsts and lasts elements of the sorted list of synonym candidates for the *Sensor* domain. From the obtained taxonomy, 17 classes of 3 terms and 1 class of 4 terms have been considered, evaluating 100 web sites including the original keyword.

Concept (root)	Derivatives	Relevance	Relative_relev
sensor	sensor, sensors, sensores	17	89.47%
transduc	tranducer, transducers	4	21.05%
measure	measurement	2	10.5%
circuit	circuit	2	10.5%
signal	signal	2	10.5%
transmit	transmitter, transmitters	2	10.5%
exce	exceeds	1	5.26%
differ	differences	1	5.26%
....	....	.....	.....
element	element	0	0%
rel	relative	0	0%
code	codes	0	0%

Table 24. Firsts and lasts elements of the sorted list of synonym candidates for the *Disease* domain. From the obtained taxonomy, 84 classes of 3 terms and 24 classes of 4 terms have been considered, evaluating 100 web sites including the original keyword.

Concept (root)	Derivatives	Relevance	Relative_relev
diseas	disease, diseases	122	92.24%
disord	disorder, disorders	17	12.87%
syndrom	syndrome, syndromes	13	9.84%
lesion	lesions	7	5.3%
condit	condition, conditions	7	5.3%
stenosi	stenosis	7	5.3%
atherosclerosis	atherosclerosis	6	4.54%
infect	infections, infection, infectivity, infects	6	4.54%
stenos	stenoses	6	4.54%
obstruct	obstruction, obstructions	5	3.78%
health	health	5	3.78%
occlus	occlusion	5	3.78%
involve	involvement	5	3.78%
caus	causes	4	3.03%
problem	problems	4	3.03%
viru	virus	4	3.03%
resist	resistant, resistence	4	3.03%
.....	.....	.....	.....
antibodycrhon	antibodychronic	0	0%
diseasefelin	diseasefeline	0	0%
infectiwalt	infectiwalter	0	0%
diseasekaren	diseasekaren	0	0%
diseasedisord	diseasedisorder	0	0%
diseaseinform	diseaseinformation	0	0%

These results can be used to enrich the learning procedure as a wider and more complete corpus of resources can be retrieved from a keyword-based search engine, potentially improving the final recall. However, one should evaluate if the potential improvement of the final results obtained with this additional step affects negatively to the final precision, as more noise can be added to the learning corpus when querying through those alternative forms (sometimes not truly equivalent). This question is left for future development.

5.8 Summary

In this chapter, a detailed explanation of the novel methodologies proposed for each of the main ontology learning steps has been presented.

First, the taxonomic aspect has been addressed by using a combination of linguistic patterns for extracting hyponym candidates. An empirical study has been performed in order to design a method in which the best characteristics of each pattern-based approach are exploited to potentially improve the final results. This assumption will be justified in §6.3.1, in which an evaluation of results obtained for different domains and for each pattern are compared using standard IR measures.

In addition to the taxonomic relations, a method to distinguish between concepts that become subclasses and named entities that become instances has been designed. Based on capitalization rules, as will be shown in §6.4, it can improve the quality of the final taxonomic results by providing a more coherent ontological structure.

The next important issue considered has been the retrieval of non-taxonomic verb labelled relationships. Even using the same principles as for the taxonomic pattern-based approach, in this case we have introduced a previous step for learning domain related linguistic patterns using verb labels. The results obtained from the application of those learned patterns for the extraction of non-taxonomic relationships will be evaluated against an electronic repository (WordNet) in §6.5.

All those processes are iteratively repeated for each new discovered concept until the algorithm decides to stop the analysis based on the feedback measures provided by the learning process. In this manner, we can adapt automatically the size of the analysed corpus and the finalisation of the learning process in function of the domain nature and the amount and quality of the information sources available in the Web.

The semantic structure obtained after this incremental learning process is post processed and stored in an ontological way.

Finally, a pair of methods for dealing with semantic ambiguity especially adapted to our working environment has also been developed. They can be used as the base for further improvements: a final integration into the learning methodology may result in a potential improvement of the result quality. They are evaluated against WordNet in §6.6 (for the word sense disambiguation) and §6.7 (for the synonym discovery).

All these novel methods have been especially designed to operate in a fully automatic and unsupervised way. This brings benefits when using them for performing knowledge related tasks over highly changing technological domains in which other learning methods cannot be applied (as introduced in chapter 2).

In addition to these interesting characteristics, the developed methods have been designed in a way that distinguishes them from other classical ontology learning approaches. On the one hand, they are especially adapted to the Web, using lightweight analytical procedures in order to obtain a good scalability in such an enormous repository. On the other hand, they are fully integrated with available Web search engines in order to obtain, in an efficient way, the corpus to analyse and the web scale statistics from which to compute especially designed relevance measures.

At the end, we have presented a system that is able to learn a domain ontology from scratch. As will be shown in §7.1, thanks to the definition of different learning tasks in an incremental way, we have implemented them in a distributed way that can take profit from the resources and computational power of several computers of a network to improve the learning throughput.

Chapter 6

Evaluation

As introduced in chapter 4, evaluation is the final and mandatory step that should be performed in any ontology learning approach. This is especially important in unsupervised approaches like the present work due to the lack of expert's intervention.

Regarding our proposal, specific evaluation methods for each ontology learning step have been designed. Our objective is, on the one hand, to demonstrate the viability of the proposed learning methodologies in constructing domain ontologies from scratch and, on the other hand, to justify some of the decisions or hypothesis formulated in the previous chapter.

Due to the fully automatic nature of our approach, the amount of evaluated candidates and finally selected concepts can be considerably high. In consequence, the evaluation process may be a long and tedious process if it is tackled in a manual way (like many other approaches as presented in chapter 2). This is aggravated in the cases in which no gold standards to which compare the results are available or in which the results are no easy to classify (such as for the non-taxonomic case).

Due to all those reasons, except for the taxonomic case for which the manual evaluation is more feasible (thanks to the available standard classifications for well studied domains), we have opted for an automatic or at least semi-automatic approach. However, due to the lack of general purpose automatic evaluation procedures [Buitelaar *et al.*, 2004], this requires to design and implement especially adapted solutions. In consequence, we present several approaches to evaluate ontological results in an automatic way by comparing them to other approaches or against electronic general purpose repositories (WordNet). This can be also considered as a contribution to the ontology learning field.

Thus, in this chapter we offer an overview of the evaluation issues that have been addressed and the evaluation procedures that have been designed:

- In §6.1, an introduction to the ontology learning evaluation criteria and a formalisation of the different evaluation measures used to quantify the quality of the obtained results are presented. Classical IR measures of *precision*, *recall* and *F-measure* have been used.
- Next, in §6.2, we introduce the WordNet general purpose electronic repository and describe some characteristics that can be exploited in order to design automatic evaluation procedures.

- In §6.3 we detail the evaluation process of the taxonomic learning, discussing the influence of the use of different web-scale statistical scores and linguistic patterns over several well distinguished domains.
- In §6.4 we present the automatic evaluation procedure designed to test the named entities extracted during the taxonomic learning.
- In §6.5 we discuss the issues that arise when evaluating non-taxonomic relationships, presenting an approach to test our results against WordNet.
- In §6.6 and §6.7 we introduce evaluation procedures designed to test our methods for dealing with semantic ambiguity against WordNet.

6.1   General evaluation criteria and quality measures

Automatically created domain ontologies consist on *i)* sets of concepts (which can or cannot be related to the domain) and *ii)* sets of relationships linking pairs of concepts (which can or cannot be related with the specified relationship). So, in order to check the correctness of the learned ontology, we have evaluated, at the same time, the retrieved and selected concepts belong to the domain's scope and they are correctly related (by means of *is-a, instance-of, verb-labelled non-taxonomic* relationships).

Considering that the presented ontology learning methodology is divided in several stages according to the nature of the learned relationships, a different evaluation criterion has been used at each stage. Specific details will be provided in the corresponding section but, in general, the quality of the results is measured in the same way. Concretely, concept-per-concept evaluations are performed at each stage, checking the correctness of the specified relationships by comparing them against a gold standard, a domain expert's opinion or by means of a general purpose semantic repository. As a result, and in order to provide comparable measures of result's quality, we compute typical quality scores widely used in Information Retrieval: *Recall, Precision* and *F-Measure*.

Recall (13) shows how much of the existing knowledge is extracted. To calculate the recall, the number of correctly selected items is divided by the overall number of domain items.

$$Recall = \frac{\#correctly\ selected\ entities}{\#domain\ entities} \tag{13}$$

For the taxonomic case, recall is obtained counting the number of truly taxonomically related concepts selected by the algorithm in relation to the full set of taxonomic entities belonging to a domain. This implies that we have to be aware about a limited and complete set of domain specialisations. In other words, a complete gold standard is necessary (not available for many domains, especially technological ones).

In addition to concrete taxonomic domains, for the non-taxonomic case, measuring recall is much more difficult as non-taxonomic relationships do not represent a finite set that can be classified or stored. In those cases, the *Local Recall* (14) can be computed. This measure considers that the domain's scope is limited to the corpus of documents analysed by the learning algorithm (*i.e.* the set of web resources). It is computed as the rate between the number of correctly selected entities against the full set of correct entities extracted from the analysed corpus.

$$Local\_Recall = \frac{\#\,correctly\ selected\ entities}{\#\,correctly\ retrieved\ entities} \qquad (14)$$

In our case, the domain's scope is determined by the full set of candidates (taxonomic or non-taxonomically related depending on the situation) retrieved from the analysed corpus of web resources. As this composes a finite set whose correctness can be evaluated, as stated above, local recall can be computed by dividing the number of correctly selected (taxonomically or non-taxonomically related) concepts against the full set of correctly retrieved entities.

Despite its locality, this score can give a measure of how good the learning procedure is in accepting or rejecting candidates based on statistical measures. This measure is consistent with the recall metric used in TREC conferences [Alfonseca and Manandhar, 2002] and has been used by several authors such as [Etzioni *et al.*, 2005], to evaluate automatically obtained knowledge.

Precision (15) specifies to which extent the knowledge is extracted correctly. It is computed as the ratio between the correctly extracted items and the whole number of extracted ones.

$$Precision = \frac{\#\,correctly\ selected\ entities}{\#\,total\ selected\ entities} \qquad (15)$$

Precision can be computed for all the results sets (taxonomically and non-taxonomically related terms) by evaluating the correctness of the selected entities against a gold standard, the expert's criteria or other learning approaches.

In addition to those individual measures, the *F-Measure* (16) provides the weighted harmonic mean of precision and recall, summarizing the global performance of the selection process. This eases the comparison of different approaches.

$$F - Measure = \frac{2 * Precision * Recall}{Precision + Recall} \qquad (16)$$

In the same way as for the *Recall*, a *Local F-Measure* (17) can be computed considering the *Local Recall* instead of the global one.

$$Local\_F - Measure = \frac{2 * Precision * Local\_Recall}{Precision + Local\_Recall} \qquad (17)$$

Additionally to those *quantitative scores* (certainly useful in order to give an objective measure), we have also examined the results from a *qualitative point of view*. In this case, domain experts can examine the result's structure and the nature of the typical semantic mistakes in order to derive interesting conclusions. This qualitative evaluation, albeit subjective, can be useful for understanding to which degree the obtained results can be useful for certain applications.

6.2   WordNet overview

WordNet is a general purpose semantic electronic repository for the English language. As shown in chapter 2, it has been extensively used as a base of knowledge for ontology learning. In our case, we have used it for performing automatic evaluations for domains with good semantic coverage. In this section, an overview of its characteristics, structure and potential usefulness for our purposes is described.

Although we plan to use knowledge repositories to help on the evaluation process, this fact does not affect the "domain-independent/unsupervised" premise. The idea is to be able to demonstrate the quality and suitability of the learning procedure in obtaining results for well known domains and to establish the base of trustworthiness on the obtained results for any other possible domain (like specific technological domains not included in WordNet such as *Biosensors* for which we have been able to obtain quality results [Sánchez and Moreno, 2006a]).

WordNet[13] is the most commonly used online lexical and semantic repository for the English language. Many authors have contributed to it [Daudé *et al.*, 2003; Farreres *et al.*, 2004; Meaning, 2005] or used it to perform many knowledge acquisition tasks (see §2.2). In more detail, it offers a lexicon, a thesaurus and semantic linkage between the major part of English terms. It seeks to classify words into many categories and to interrelate the meanings of those words. It is organised in synonym sets (synsets): a set of words that are interchangeable in some context, because they share a commonly-agreed upon meaning with little or no variation. Each word in English may have many different senses in which it may be interpreted: each of these distinct senses points to a different synset. Every word in WordNet has a pointer to at least one synset. Each synset, in turn, must point to at least one word. Thus, we have a many-to-many mapping between English words and synsets at the lowest level of WordNet. It is useful to think of synsets as nodes in a graph. At the next level we have lexical and semantic pointers. A semantic pointer is simply a directed edge in the graph whose nodes are synsets. The pointer has one end we call a *source* and the other end we call a *destination*.

Some interesting semantic pointers are:

o   *hyponym*: X is a hyponym of Y if X is a (kind of) Y.

o   *part meronym*: X is a part meronym of Y if X is a part of Y.

o   *member meronym:* X is a member meronym of Y if X is a member of Y.

o   *attribute*: A noun synset for which adjectives express values. The noun *weight* is an attribute, for which the adjectives *light* and *heavy* express values.

o   *similar to*: A synset is similar to another one if the two synsets have meanings that are substantially similar to each other.

Finally, each synset contains a description of its meaning, expressed in natural language as a gloss. Example sentences of typical usage of that synset are also given.

All this information summarizes the meaning of a specific concept and models the knowledge available for a particular domain. Using this information it is possible to compute the similarity and relatedness between concepts. There have been some ini-

---

[13] http://wordnet.princeton.edu/

tiatives for computing these measures, such as the software *WordNet::Similarity* [Pedersen *et al.*, 2004]. It offers an implementation of some standard measures that have been widely used by several authors to perform different WordNet-based disambiguation tasks [Budanitsky and Hirst, 2001; William, 2002].

More concretely, *similarity measures* use information found in an *is-a* hierarchy of concepts and quantify how much a concept A is like another concept B. WordNet is particularly well suited for similarity measures, since it organizes nouns into *is-a* hierarchies and, therefore, it can be adequate to evaluate taxonomic relationships. However, as described, concepts can be related in many ways beyond being similar to each other (*i.e.* through the mentioned semantic pointers). This information, in conjunction to gloss descriptions, can be brought to bear when creating *measures of relatedness*. As a result, those last measures are more general than similarity ones.

Table 25. Classification of measures of semantic similarity and relatedness and their relative advantages and disadvantages as stated in [Pedersen *et al.*, 2006].

Type	Name	Principle	Pros	Cons
Path Finding	Path Length	Count of edges between concepts	- Simplicity	- Requires a consistent hierarchy - No multiple inheritance - WordNet nouns only - *IS-A* relations only
	[Wu and Palmer, 1994]	Path length to subsumer, scaled by subsumers path to root	- Simplicity	- WordNet nouns only - *IS-A* relations only
	[Leacock-Chodorow, 1998]	Finds the shortest path between concepts	- Simplicity	- WordNet nouns only - *IS-A* relations only
	[Hirst and St-Onge, 1998]	Based in WordNet synsets	- Measures relatedness of all parts of speech - More than *IS-A*	- WordNet specific
Info. Content	[Resnik, 1998]	Information Content (IC) of the least common subsumer (LCS)	- Uses empirical information from corpora	- Does not use the IC of individual concepts, only that of the LCS - WordNet nouns only - *IS-A* relations only
	[Jiang and Conrath, 1997]	Extensions of Resnik; scale LCS by IC of concepts	- Takes into account the IC of individual concepts	- WordNet nouns only - *IS-A* relations only
Context Vector Measures	[Patwardhan and Pedersen, 2006]	Creates context vectors that represent meaning of concepts from co-occurrence statistics	- Relatedness POS - No structure required - Uses Knowledge implicit in a corpus	- Definitions can be short, inconsistent - Computationally intensive

The available measures (compared in Table 25) can be grouped in three types:

- *Path finding*: as a similarity measure, it finds the path length between two concepts in the *is-a* hierarchy of WordNet. The path length is then scaled by the depth of the hierarchy in which they reside to obtain the relatedness of the two concepts.
- *Information content*: it indicates the specificity of a concept. Information content is derived from corpora, and it is used to augment the concepts in the WordNet *is-a* hierarchy. The measure of relatedness between two concepts is the information

content of the most specific concept that both concepts have in common (*i.e.* their lowest common subsumer in the *is-a* hierarchy).

- *Context vector*: it does not depend on the interlinkage between words that, in some situations, has a poor coverage in the WordNet. In more detail, this measure incorporates information from WordNet glosses as a unique representation for the underlying concept, creating a co-occurrence matrix from a corpus made up of the WordNet glosses. Each content word used in a WordNet gloss has an associated context vector. Each gloss is represented by a gloss vector that is the average of all the context vectors of the words found in the gloss. Relatedness between concepts is measured by finding the cosine between a pair of gloss vectors.

From all of these measures, context vector ones offer the best performance in general situations [Patwardhan and Pedersen, 2006]. Moreover, they do not depend on the degree of semantic interlinkage between the considered concepts (that is mainly limited to taxonomic relationships). In consequence, they are adequate for evaluating general relationships. For that reason, we use them during the non-taxonomic evaluation as a measure of comparison with our web-based statistical scores.

Additionally, we have used a path length based similarity measure to design an automatic evaluation procedure for the semantic disambiguation algorithms. They are limited to the taxonomic aspect and, consequently, a similarity measure based on *is-a* WordNet hierarchies is more suitable than a more general relatedness score.

However, all measures have limitations because they assume that all the semantic content of a particular term is modelled by semantic links and/or glosses in WordNet and, in consequence, in many situations, truly related terms obtain a low score due to the relative WordNet's poor coverage for specific domains [Turney, 2001]. However, these measures are some of the very few fully automatic general purpose ways of evaluating knowledge acquisition results.

6.3 Taxonomy learning evaluation

This section has two main purposes. On the one hand, we will show the potential learning improvement in the results that the designed approach (concretely, the specific combination of patterns and the designed statistical scores) may offer in comparison with other alternatives that we have also considered. On the other hand, we will show and evaluate the results that our learning methodology is able to return for several well distinguished domains of knowledge.

A possible first step for automatic evaluation can be the comparison of the obtained taxonomies against hypernym/hyponym hierarchies of general domain semantic repositories as WordNet. However, this solution cannot be applied in many cases in which, due to the concreteness of the domain, many correct terms are missing in a general domain repository as WordNet. Moreover, concepts composed by several words (*e.g. colorectal cancer*) that are very frequent in our taxonomies have a particularly reduced coverage in WordNet.

From another point of view, thanks to the importance of the taxonomic aspect in structuring knowledge, many -manual- efforts have been put in defining appropriate hierarchies of concepts for many domains of knowledge (Gold Standards). In consequence, there exist standard classifications for well known and well structured domains of knowledge. The *Gold Standard evaluation* approach assumes that it contains all the extractable concepts from a certain corpus and it contains only those. In reality though, Gold Standards omit many potential concepts in the corpus and introduce concepts from other sources (such as the domain knowledge of the expert) [Sabou, 2006]. In order to compensate those imperfections and, in cases in which no standards are available, *concept-per-concept evaluation* by a domain expert can be performed [Navigli *et al.*, 2004]. So, the evaluation of taxonomic results is carried by means of Gold Standards and expert's opinion.

Considering the evaluation criteria presented in §6.1, the concept-per-concept evaluation is carried by analysing the raw list of taxonomic candidates retrieved during the corpus analysis. The domain relatedness of each concept and the validity of the taxonomic relationships are evaluated by a domain expert or using a Gold Standard. This is then compared against the list of selected and rejected concepts defined by means of web-based statistics, computing the mentioned standard measures of *recall*, *precision* and *F-measure*.

Note that in all of the following examples, the procedure to distinguish between candidates for subclass (domain concepts) or instances (named entities) described in §5.3, is applied by default. As will be shown in §6.4, this additional step contributes to increase the precision of the final results without compromising the recall.

Note also that for all of the presented evaluations and results of this section, a learning threshold of 60% and the default selection threshold guidelines introduced in §5.2.2 have been applied. All queries were performed to MSNSearch as it does not impose any limitation in relation to the allowed number of queries.

6.3.1 Evaluating the taxonomy learning hypotheses

Once the general evaluation procedure has been explained, we are ready to perform some tests. First, we start by checking some of the hypotheses mentioned in §5.2.1 and §5.2.2 about how linguistic patterns combinations and web scale statistical scores perform. We have used one taxonomic iteration of the *Cancer* domain as a case of study because, as presented in §5.2.1, it covers all of the different extraction cases that we have identified and it is widely considered in many standard repositories. Different executions with the same conditions are performed with different implementations of the learning procedure (considering different linguistic patterns and web scale statistics). Results are then evaluated against a Gold Standard and conclusions about the learning performance are extracted.

As Gold Standard we have used the MESH[14] classification of *neoplasms* (scientific term for referring to cancers). Concretely, MESH (*Medical Subject Headings*) considers different overlapping ways of classifying neoplasms. We have used the classification "*Neoplasms by Site – Tree C04.588*" as our Gold Standard because this hierarchy offers the widest coverage for the domain. The concrete evaluation procedure is

---

[14] http://www.nlm.nih.gov/mesh/

performed in the following way: every concept of the list of retrieved ones is queried on the MESH Browser[15]. If the query results in one matching corresponding to the C04.588 (which indicates that it belongs, taxonomically, to the *cancer* domain) it is considered as correct. When a concept is not found, considering the limitations presented by Gold Standard evaluations as stated above, an expert is requested to check if the particular concept is taxonomically correct or not. For example, *metastatic cancer* is not a considered as a cancer subclass in MESH as it classifies cancers as parts of the body, but it can be considered as a correct subclass of cancer according to the stage of development. Those concepts (*e.g. chemotherapy*) which may belong to the cancer domain but are not taxonomically related are considered as incorrect. When the full set of concepts has been analysed, the result is compared against the selection and rejection decision performed by the developed learning algorithm in order to detect correctly or incorrectly selected or rejected concepts. As a result, we can compute *precision* and *local recall* (considering the list of retrieved concepts as the domain scope) measures as defined in §6.1. In order to compute the global *recall* (that considers the full domain scope), we consider the number of subclasses of the C04.588 tree (102) plus those identified as correct by the expert.

The first test regards the selection of Hearst-based candidates through statistical analyses. In §5.2.2, 3 scores where defined, being *Score_A* the most widely used [Turney, 2001] and *Score_C* the one selected in our approach as the best to contextualize queries and select the most related candidates. In order to prove this hypothesis, we have run 3 one-shot taxonomic executions with the same conditions and compared the behaviour of the selection procedure using each score. Figure 19 shows the result of the evaluation of the selection procedures.

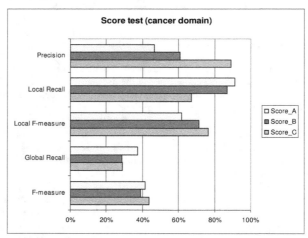

Figure 19. Evaluation of the performance of each score used for the selection of candidates extracted through Hearst's patterns.

[15] http://www.nlm.nih.gov/mesh/MBrowser.html

We can see how there is a direct relation between the degree of contextualization that each score brings and its precision in the selection procedure. However, the inverse relation can be observed for the local recall. Considering that the Hearst's extraction is the first step of the learning process and that the pre-rejected terms can be re-evaluated during the noun phrase-based extraction stage (as presented in §5.2.2.2), we prefer to maximize the precision of this phase. In consequence, as *Score_C* improves the other ones globally in terms of F-measure (by margins of 5-15% locally) and maximizes the precision greatly (over 30-45%), is the most adequate for complementing Hearst-based extractions with the rest of the learning process.

The next step is addressed to show the convenience of combining the different linguistic patterns in the way proposed in §5.2.2. Several tests have been performed, considering each pattern independently (Hearst's with *Score_C* and noun phrase-based with *Score_B* as described in §5.2.2) and both.

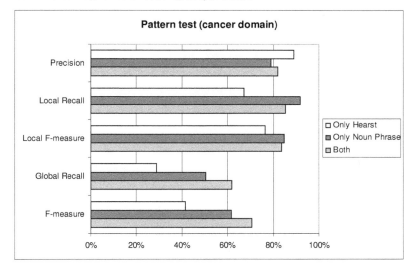

Figure 20. Evaluation of the performance of extraction and selection of candidates according to the specific pattern(s) employed.

Analysing the result shown in Figure 20, we can see that both kinds of patterns behave in a quite complementary way: Hearst's patterns in conjunction with *Score_C* tend to show high precision (89%) but low local recall (67%), whereas the noun phrase-based pattern with *Score_B* presents the inverse behaviour (79% and 92% respectively). This is very convenient as both can compensate each one and, finally, as shown by the F-measure, provide a result that is considerably better (by margins up to 28%) than the one obtained by a single pattern.

Considering the extraction cases presented in §5.2.1, we can observe that Hearst-based extraction is able to retrieve and distinguish between Cases #1 (*cancer such as leukaemia*) and #2 (*cancer such as radiotherapy*), which can only be retrieved through Hearst's patterns, providing a good selection precision. However, recall, mainly referred to the incorrect rejection of Case #4 (*cancer such as breast cancer*), is low due to the restrictive selection procedure that affects negatively to the queries with many terms. Case #3 (*cancer such as lung*) is also present, affecting slightly the precision as ellipsis is a problem when using these patterns.

Then, adding the noun phrase-based extractions and the final selection procedure over the partial results, we can improve the global recall. This is due to the selection of Case #3 extractions, thanks to the less restrictive queries based on *Score_B* (maintaining a good precision), and the correction of the selection of Case #4 extractions, as these patterns do not suffer from ellipsis.

At the end of the process, we have been able to obtain an acceptable global recall for the domain (61.8%), maintaining a good level of precision (82%). Those facts can be summarized in the improved F-measure (70.5% in contrast to 61.5% and 41.5%).

Considering that additional sets of Hearst-based patterns exist (see [Agichtein and Gravano, 2000; Iwanska et al., 2000; Pasca, 2004; Snow et al., 2004]), one may wonder if introducing additional sets to the taxonomic analysis may improve considerably the result's recall. Considering the behaviour observed in §5.6.2 for the learning rates of successive pattern iterations, we believe that the size and high redundancy of the Web makes it possible to obtain representative results using a reduced set of general patterns. Regarding the present work, our opinion is that recall can be more affected by tuning learning and selection thresholds than from overheading the taxonomic analysis with new patterns. However, this question is left for future development (see chapter 8).

6.3.2   Evaluating several domains of knowledge

After discussing the potential improvement that our approach can bring for taxonomy learning, we present complete taxonomic evaluations performed over well distinguished domains. The evaluation criteria is the same as in the previous cases but, due to the enormous and overwhelming amount of candidates to evaluate (more than ten thousands in total), the evaluation has been applied to those classes which have at least 100 candidates (the most representative ones).

First, the *cancer* domain used up to this moment is evaluated analysing the multi-level taxonomy (a part is presented in Figure 21). It can be considered as a good test bed for both types of patterns as it is composed by single word terms like *leukaemia* and noun phrases like *breast cancer* in a similar percentage. The evaluation procedure is the same already described in the previous section. In this case, however, the expert's intervention is higher as concrete multiple word terms are barely covered by MESH.

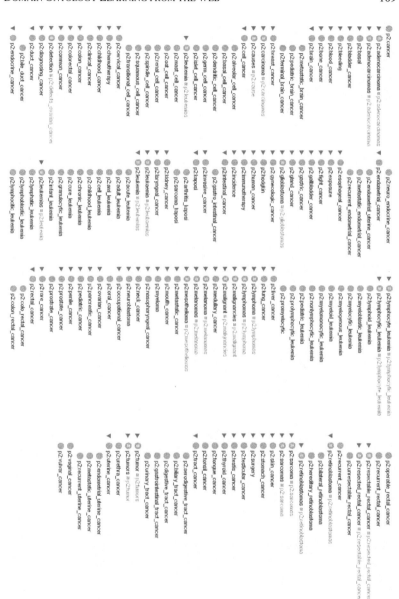

Figure 21. Part of the multi level *Cancer* taxonomy with a total of 1458 classes.

Considering only those classes with more than 100 subclass candidates, we have evaluated the 1st level taxonomy (with 260 candidates for cancer specialisations) and 16 subclasses of the 2nd taxonomic level (which represent a total set of 2249 candidates). The candidates belonging to subclasses wrongly selected in the 1st taxonomic level (*e.g. surgery*) have been evaluated independently (*e.g. surgery* is an *incorrect* subclass of *cancer* but *maxillofacial surgery* is a *correct* type of *surgery*). The results of the evaluation are summarized in Table 26 and Figure 22.

Table 26. Taxonomic evaluation for the *Cancer* domain. Number of correctly and incorrectly selected and rejected classes. A total of 16 subclasses evaluated for the 2nd level.

1st taxonomic level

	Right	Wrong	Total
Selected	73	16	89
Rejected	159	12	171
Total	**232**	**28**	**260**

2nd taxonomic level (16 classes)

	Right	Wrong	Total
Selected	417	143	560
Rejected	1641	48	1689
Total	**2058**	**191**	**2249**

1st and 2nd taxonomic level

	Right	Wrong	Total
Selected	490	159	649
Rejected	1800	60	1860
Total	**2290**	**219**	**2509**

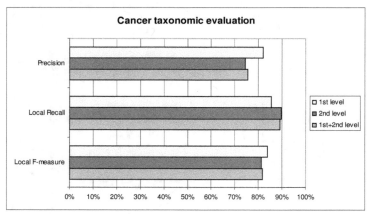

Figure 22. Taxonomic evaluation for the *Cancer* domain.

Next, we have selected two extreme cases. The first is the *mammal* domain, shown in Figure 23, in which single word terms prevail (*e.g. cat, cow, dog* but also *aquatic mammal*) and the *sensor* domain, shown in Figure 24, in which specialisations expressed by adding nouns and adjectives to the initial terms are the most common case (*e.g. temperature sensor, biological sensor, pressure sensor*, but also *sonar*).

The *mammal* domain is, in fact, especially interesting due to the large amount of equivalent terms and redundant taxonomic cycles (*e.g. whales is-a mammal, aquatic_mammal, marine_mammal* and *cetaceans*, being *aquatic_mammal is-a mammal* and *cetaceans is-a marine_mammal*). This shows the effectiveness of the taxonomy post-processing stage introduced in §5.5.

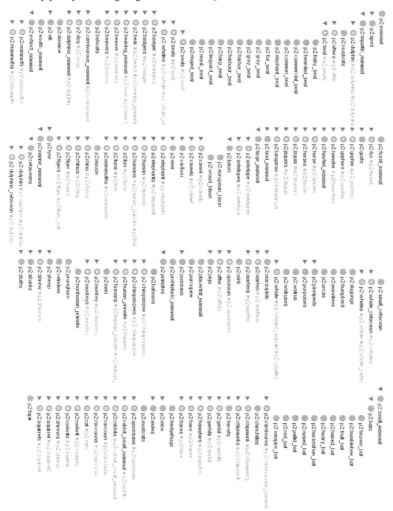

Figure 23. Part of the multi level *Mammal* taxonomy with a total of 957 classes. A total of 122 redundant taxonomic relationships were detected and removed.

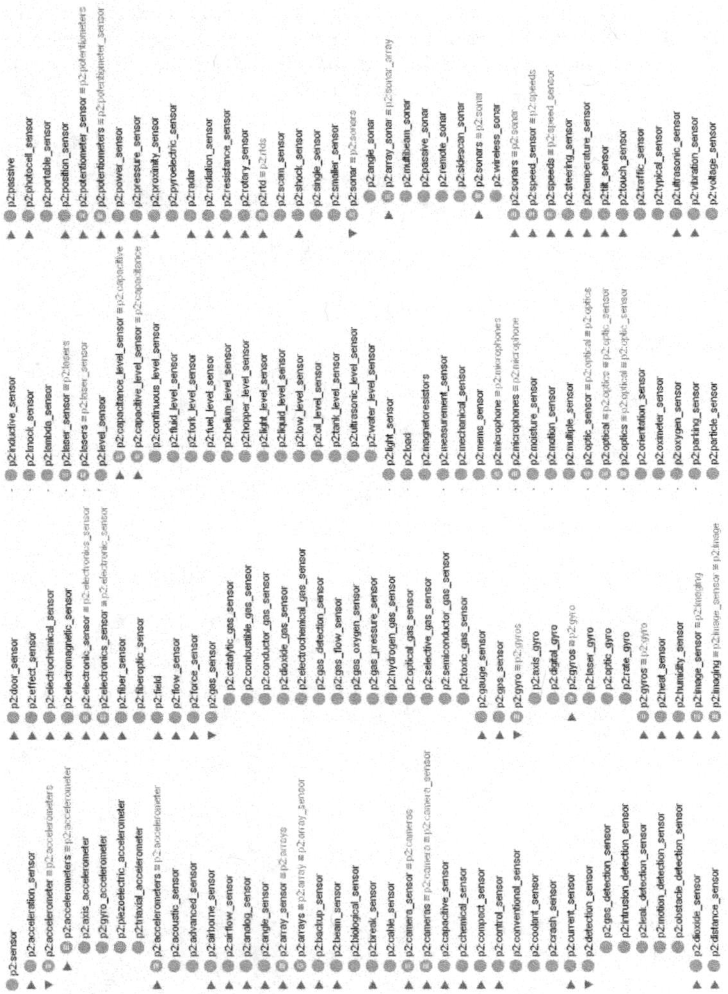

Figure 24. Part of the multi level *Sensor* taxonomy with a total of 868 classes.

In both cases, an expert based concept-per-concept multi-level evaluation has been performed. Precision, local recall and local F-measure have been computed in the same way as in the cancer domain but, as no Gold Standard has been used, no global recall is provided. We have evaluated those classes with 100 or more candidates.

For the *mammal* domain, evaluation is quite easy as one has only to check if a particular concept is a mammal (*e.g. dolphin, dog, cat, etc.*) or a mammal category (*e.g. aquatic mammal, marine mammal, etc.*). We have evaluated the 1st taxonomic level (with 245 candidates) and 19 subclasses of the 2nd level representing a total of 2493 candidates. Results are summarized in Table 27 and Figure 25.

Table 27. Taxonomic evaluation for the *Mammal* domain. Number of correctly and incorrectly selected and rejected classes. A total of 19 subclasses evaluated for the 2nd level (those with more than 100 candidates).

1st taxonomic level

	Right	Wrong	**Total**
Selected	79	5	**84**
Rejected	141	20	**161**
Total	**220**	**25**	**245**

2nd taxonomic level (19 classes)

	Right	Wrong	**Total**
Selected	173	54	**227**
Rejected	2207	59	**2266**
Total	**2380**	**113**	**2493**

1st and 2nd taxonomic level

	Right	Wrong	**Total**
Selected	252	59	**311**
Rejected	2348	79	**2427**
Total	**2600**	**138**	**2738**

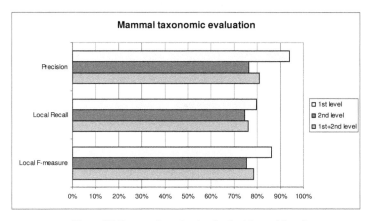

Figure 25. Taxonomic evaluation for the *Mammal* domain.

For the *sensor* domain, subclasses have been considered as correct if they indicate the measured magnitude (*e.g. force, speed, temperature, etc.*) and/or the type of measuring transducer (*e.g. optic, electrochemical, etc.*). We have evaluated the 1st taxonomic level (with 262 candidates) and 12 subclasses of the 2nd level representing a total of 1986 candidates. Results are summarized in Table 28 and Figure 26.

Table 28. Taxonomic evaluation for the *Sensor* domain. Number of correctly and incorrectly selected and rejected classes. A total of 12 subclasses were evaluated for the 2nd level (those with more than 100 candidates).

1st taxonomic level

	Right	Wrong	Total
Selected	75	18	**93**
Rejected	159	10	**169**
Total	**234**	**28**	**262**

2nd taxonomic level (12 classes)

	Right	Wrong	Total
Selected	211	73	**284**
Rejected	1380	60	**1440**
Total	**1591**	**133**	**1724**

1st and 2nd taxonomic level

	Right	Wrong	Total
Selected	286	91	**377**
Rejected	1539	70	**1609**
Total	**1825**	**161**	**1986**

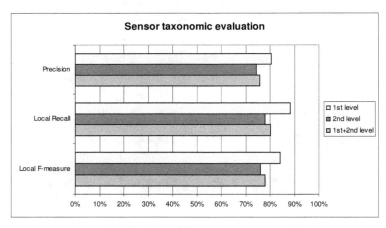

Figure 26. Taxonomic evaluation for the *Sensor* domain.

The presented results show a consistent global performance, with a very similar F-Measure through the different domains, with values above 80% for the first level and above 75% for the considered subclasses. This shows that our approach performs well and robustly with independence of the taxonomic nature of the particular domain of knowledge (in which a particular type of pattern can be more or less suitable). One can also realize from the tables that the percentage of rejected candidates is much bigger for the subclasses than for the root concept. This is expected, as concrete concepts present a much narrower scope (*i.e.* valid subclasses). This fact influences a bit negatively the quality of the deeper taxonomic levels, as the system has to deal with a higher amount of false candidates. However, proportionally, extraction quality is maintained at a reliable level. Considering each domain individually, *cancer* offers the most consistent results, followed by *sensor*. *Mammal*, on the contrary, offers the major divergence between the 1st taxonomic level and the rest. This domain's quality is hampered by its generality and some problems regarding polysemy (*e.g. baseball bat, hot dog, etc.*). Bootstrapped information contributes to minimize the problem by contextualizing queries, but the unsupervised learning may be affected due to the lack of semantic understanding.

Besides the presented quantitative evaluation, results have been examined from the domain expert's point of view. This qualitative evaluation [Sabou, 2006], can bring some interesting conclusions about the kind of results one can expect:

- Some of the mistakes (about a 10%) presented in the taxonomic structure are caused by the particular morphologic and syntactic analyser used during the parsing of text (more details in chapter 7). Some subclasses such as *"diagnosing cancer"* (which are hardly distinguished from truly noun phrase-based hyponyms using the designed scores) could be filtered if a better analyser or a wider text context were considered.
- The obtained taxonomies tend to be quite big containing, in many situations, concepts that are not modelled in gold standards and from related domains. However, it seems that the cleanness of the ontology is not of major importance for the ontology engineer [Sabou, 2006]. Related concepts offer additional information about the domain and facilitate comprehension about its structure. In this sense, recall is more interesting than precision.
- In many domains, and especially for noun phrase-based hyponyms, deep level subclasses are defined as a concatenation of different classification criteria (*e.g. metastatic breast cancer, electrochemical oxygen sensor*). Those, evaluated as correct, are useful to automatically discover domain features (*i.e.* simpler, generally binary, classification characteristics), as introduced in §5.5.3.

6.4 Evaluation of named entities

The manual evaluation of named-entities is a harder task than in the taxonomic case. The fact of the Web being an open and highly dynamic environment with a virtually unlimited amount of potential entities makes unviable the availability of any standard repository. In consequence, gold standard-based evaluations are not possible.

An alternative way for evaluating results can be the comparison with other well-known named entity detection techniques applied over the same corpus and domain. As mentioned in §4.3, there exist supervised approaches that are able to retrieve with high confidence a reduced set of broad categories of named entities. Those approaches rely on a considerable amount of pre-tagged training data from which to infer classification criteria.

In the present work, we have used a *named-entity detection package trained for several types of named entities for the English language* (OpenNLP, more details will be offered in §7.1.4) that is able to detect some named entities in categories like *organizations, persons,* and *locations*. It is based on *maximum entropy models* [Borthwick, 1999] and uses an enormous corpus of millions of pre-selected named entities grouped in the mentioned categories as the knowledge base.

The evaluation is performed by testing if the named-entities extracted and selected by our methodology are also selected by the mentioned detection tool. Both approaches are applied over the same context: the snippets returned by the web search engine when querying a named entity candidate. The named entities discovered by the detection package are compared with the final list of selected and rejected named entities provided by our selection procedure (described in §5.3). In the same manner as in the taxonomic case, this evaluation will give us sets of correctly and incorrectly selected and rejected candidates. From those sets, we are able to compute the *precision* and *local recall* of the obtained results in an automatic way, comparing our algorithm against a well known supervised approach.

However, due to the automatic nature, its results are relative and conclusions should be extracted with care. This is because, as any other automatic approach, the named-entity detection package used as the model does not present a 100% precision and its recall is limited to predefined sets (*persons, organizations* and *locations*). In addition, in our case, the particular named entity semantics is not considered (*i.e.* the fact that ontology instances should be *persons* or *organisations*).

The evaluation measures obtained for the same domains used during the taxonomic evaluation are shown in Table 29, Table 30 and Table 31 (a minimum of confidence of 60% was specified and 50 web documents were considered per candidate). Thanks to the automatic nature of the evaluation, we have easily evaluated the named entities discovered for the first *two* taxonomic levels for each domain.

Table 29. Evaluation results for named-entity sets discovered in the first *two* taxonomic levels for the *Cancer* domain against an automatic named-entity detection package. Number of correctly and incorrectly selected and rejected classes.

	Right	Wrong	Total
Selected	125	2	**127**
Rejected	320	83	**403**
Total	**445**	**85**	**530**

Table 30. Evaluation results for named-entity sets discovered in the first *two* taxonomic levels for the *Sensor* domain against an automatic named-entity detection package. Number of correctly and incorrectly selected and rejected classes.

	Right	Wrong	Total
Selected	206	16	**222**
Rejected	435	91	**526**
Total	**641**	**107**	**748**

Table 31. Evaluation results for named-entity sets discovered in the first *two* taxonomic levels for the *Mammal* domain against an automatic named-entity detection package. Number of correctly and incorrectly selected and rejected classes.

	Right	Wrong	Total
Selected	517	17	**534**
Rejected	707	248	**955**
Total	**1224**	**265**	**1489**

As summarized in Figure 27, results are quite consistent through the different domains, presenting a high precision and a moderate recall. This behaviour is expected as both approaches are based on explicit (for our case) or implicit (for the detection package) rules for representing individuals in natural text. However, the detection package has a tendency of tagging any set of capitalized consecutive words. In contrast, our approach evaluates several candidate appearances in order to discover the most common way of representing a particular entity. The greedier behaviour of the detection package explains the differences reflected in the recall measure.

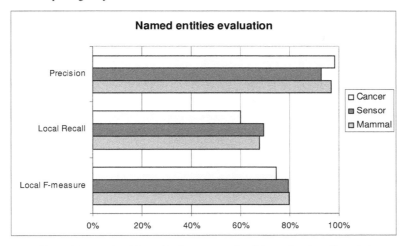

Figure 27. Named entities evaluation measures for different domains of knowledge.

As this evaluation process is integrated in our learning methodology and performed at execution time, the evaluation can be presented to the user at the end of the learning process. As a result, we can retrieve, in many situations, the full name associated to an individual extracted by the named-entity detection tool: in cases in which the name of an individual is composed by several words (*e.g. Global MEMS Sensor Developments*), for which we are only able to detect a word subset (*e.g. MEMS Sensor*) the detection package identifies the full set of words. This complete name can be incorporated as additional information in the final structure, as shown in Table 32, Table 32 and Table 34. Note that named entities are associated to the corresponding class as an instance, but without considering the individual's semantics (*i.e.* the fact that a particular ontology should be populated by *persons*, *events*, *organisations*, *etc.*).

Table 32. Examples of *named-entity* sets found for several classes of the obtained taxonomy for the *Sensor* domain (50 web documents evaluated for each candidate and minimum confidence of 60%).

Class	Named entity	Full named-entity name	Conf.
Sensor	Bayer	*RGBE Bayer Sensor*	93.54
	Nokia	*Nokia Sensor*	83.70
	ITP	*ITP Sensor Workshop*	68.62
	MEMS	*Global MEMS Sensor Developments*	84.44
	QuickBird	*QuickBird Sensor Model*	87.5
Airflow sensor	AKCP	*ACKP Airflow Sensor SNMP Environmental Monitoring*	82.60
	Ford	*Windstar Ford Airflow Sensor*	73.33
Humidity sensor	Vaisala	*Vaisala humidity sensor*	100.0
	Smartec	*SMARTEC Humidity Sensor*	82.60
	SMD	*SMD Humidity Sensor Element*	76.47
Oxygen sensor	Audi	*Audi Oxygen Sensor*	77.57
	Benz	*Mercedes Benz Oxygen Sensor*	64.93
	BMW	*BMW Oxygen Sensor*	74.12
	Cadillac	*Cadillac Oxygen Sensor*	72.88
	Chrysler	*Chrysler Oxygen Sensor*	79.88
	Delorean	*DELOREAN Oxygen Sensor*	69.23
	Ferrari	*Ferrari Oxygen Sensor*	83.87
	Hyundai	*Hyundai Oxygen Sensor*	69.31
	Suzuki	*Suzuki Oxygen Sensor*	74.83
	Volvo	*Volvo Oxygen Sensor*	81.90
Pressure sensor	Sensotec	*Tri-Clover Sensotec Pressure Sensor*	85.71
	Sunx	*Sunx Pressure Sensor*	61.29
Image sensor	KODAK	*KODAK Image Sensor Solutions*	94.78
Motion sensor	Apple	*Apple Motion Sensor*	83.78
	ActiveEye	*ActiveEye Motion Sensor*	73.77
Occupancy	DECORA	*Leviton Decora Occupancy Sensor Switch*	78.57
	HVAC	*HVAC Occupancy Sensor*	81.39
	Novitas	*Energy NOVITAS OCCUPANCY SENSOR*	78.94

Table 33. Examples of *named-entity* sets found for several classes of the obtained taxonomy for the *Cancer* domain (50 web documents evaluated for each candidate and a minimum confidence of 60%).

Class	Named entity	Full named-entity name	Conf.
Cancer	American	*American Cancer Society*	92.07
	Canadian	*Canadian Cancer Society*	92.85
	Georgia	*Georgia Cancer Coalition*	92.79
	National	*National Cancer Institute*	86.67
	Macmillan	*Macmillan Cancer Relief*	82.85
	NCI	*NCI Cancer Bulletin*	97.05
	Regional	*Gibbs Regional Cancer Center*	85.45
Breast cancer	Israeli	*National Israeli Breast Cancer Screening Program*	96.49
	Massachusetts	*Massachusetts Breast Cancer Coalition*	87.87
	University	*Bastyr University Breast Cancer Research*	95.56
Cervical cancer	Multicenter	*Multicenter Cervical Cancer Study Group*	96.07
Childhood cancer	British	*British Childhood Cancer Survivor Study*	86.20
	Canadian	*Canadian Childhood Cancer Surveillance and Control Program*	83.33
	Kingdom	*United Kingdom Childhood Cancer Study*	100.0
Colorectal cancer	Anderson	*Anderson Colorectal Cancer*	65.21
	National	*National Colorectal Cancer Awareness Month*	83.56
	Norwegian	*Norwegian Colorectal Cancer Prevention*	96.15
Gastric cancer	Dutch	*Randomized Dutch Gastric Cancer Group*	76.92
	International	*International Gastric Cancer Congress*	97.14
Lymphoma	Coventry	*Coventry Lymphoma Association Support Group*	71.42
	University	*Louisiana State University Lymphoma Rescue Protocol*	68.18
	World	*2nd World Lymphoma Awareness Day*	79.66
Melanoma	Biggane	*Mollie Biggane Melanoma Fund*	100.0
	Institute	*Joseph Hospital Cancer Institute Melanoma Program*	85.71
	Sydney	*Sydney Melanoma Diagnostic Centre*	100.0

Table 34. Examples of *named-entity* sets found for several classes of the obtained taxonomy for the *Mammal* domain (50 web documents evaluated for each candidate and a minimum confidence of 60%).

Class	Named entity	Full named-entity name	Conf.
Mammal	Florida	*Florida Mammal Species Distributions*	75.67
	Kansas	*Kansas Mammal Meetings*	86.66
Bat	American	*First American Bat Mitvah*	100.0
	California	*California Bat Conservation Fund*	80.0
	Mexico	*New Mexico Bat Survey*	100.0
Cetacean	American	*American Cetacean Society*	83.09
	British	*British Cetacean Site*	91.66
	Conservation	*Science and Conservation Cetacean Society*	87.5
	Spanish	*Spanish Cetacean Society*	89.09
Dolphin	Discovery	*Swim Discovery Dolphin*	63.93
	International	*International Dolphin Conservation Program*	80.28
	Island	*Island Dolphin Care*	85.54
	Project	*Project Dolphin Safe Association*	78.57
Whale	Allied	*Allied Whale*	96.55
	Harbor	*Harbor Whale Watching*	82.05
	Institute	*Mammal Research Institute Whale Unit*	92.0
	University	*Southern Cross University Whale Research Centre*	82.14
	Vermont	*Vermont Whale Watching Directory*	86.66
Primate	Laboratory	*Laboratory Primate Newsletter*	63.88
	National	*National Primate Research Centers*	93.10
	University	*Duke University Primate Center*	91.30
	Wisconsin	*Wisconsin Primate Research Center*	92.98
Mammoth	Columbian	*Columbian Mammoth*	94.36
	International	*First International Mammoth Conference*	92.30
	Jose	*The San Jose Mammoth*	74.28
Cat	German	*German Cat Federation*	91.17
	International	*International Cat Association*	95.12
	Massachusetts	*Massachusetts Cat*	84.0

As a final test, and in order to illustrate the benefits of including the detection of named entities as an additional step of the taxonomy learning process, we have conducted some taxonomy learning processes omitting this phase. Evaluating the same described domains and comparing the results with those presented in §6.3 (which include by default the named entity detection stage) we have observed an average precision decrease of 6% with negligible local recall differences. This difference is caused by the additional noise introduced by the lack of a proper distinction between individuals and concepts in the unsupervised learning. Certainly, without considering named entities, some candidates fulfilling the required scores will be selected erroneously as subclasses (whereas they should be considered as instances). Introducing the detection of named entities, those candidates will be correctly classified (as named entity candidates have preference over subclass ones), improving the quality of the final structure. So, considering the limitations of our approach for ontology population, the taxonomic quality improvement is the main reason why we have introduced this complementary stage in the ontology learning process.

6.5   Evaluation of non-taxonomic relationships

The problem of evaluating non-taxonomically related terms is even more complex than the issues presented in previous sections [Schutz and Buitelaar, 2005]. Various proposals have been made for comparing ontologies on the lexical as well as on the taxonomic level, which can be used to evaluate against a *gold standard*. However, non-taxonomic relationships are rarely contained in a gold standard. In fact, an investigation of the structure of existing ontologies via the Swoogle[16] ontology search engine [Ding *et al.*, 2004] has shown that domain ontologies very occasionally model this kind of relationships.

   Due to the problems of finding gold standards, and the difficulty of evaluating those kinds of relations by means of a domain expert due to their fuzziness, we have focused our efforts on the automatic side. However, as already commented in §6.4, automatic evaluations, despite their objectiveness, offer more inaccurate results than manual ones due to the imperfect nature of the sources and methodologies compared.

   Regarding the evaluation methodology, it shares the same principles with the taxonomic case. Non-taxonomic relations involve a pair of concepts belonging to a specific domain and labelled using a verb. Consequently, the evaluation should test if concepts are appropriately related. As our base to select a relation between a pair of concepts are the statistical scores computed from the Web, we can centre the evaluation in the comparison of those scores with other relatedness measures between concepts. As mentioned in §6.2, for the English language there exists the WordNet repository, and using its stored information (lexicon, thesaurus, and semantic linkage) it is possible to compute the similarity and relatedness between concepts. *Similarity measures* tend to be well suited to evaluate taxonomically related terms as they are based in WordNet's *is-a* hierarchies. However, other general relations and natural language glosses included for each concept can be considered when computing *measures of relatedness*. As a result, these measures tend to be more general and, in our case, more adequate for evaluating non-taxonomically related terms.

   As discussed in §6.2, among the different existing relatedness measures we have chosen a context vector measure (concretely *gloss-vector* [Patwardhan and Pedersen, 2006]) because it does not depend on WordNet's interlinkage between words and seems to offer the best performance [Patwardhan and Pedersen, 2006].

   During the evaluation, we check the selection quality of our Web-based relatedness measure between two non-taxonomically related candidate concepts by comparing it against *gloss-vector*. Concretely, we query the *WordNet::Similarity* software package for each pair of candidates for being non-taxonomically related, whenever both are

---

[16] http://swoogle.umbc.edu/

contained in WordNet. Unfortunately, this last requirement forces the omission in the evaluation process of a considerable amount of concrete technological terms and those composed by several words. One may also realize that the evaluation does not consider the verb used to label the relations. This is because WordNet-based relatedness measures are intended for nouns (concrete things with specific meaning). However, as in our case final concepts are obtained through verb phrases, their quality (evaluated here) also depends on the adequacy of extracted verbs.

Once both scores have been obtained (*web-based* and *gloss-vector*), establishing the same selection thresholds (following the guidelines stated in §5.4), we can evaluate the correctness of our candidate selection procedure computing correctly classified concepts (selected or discarded) and incorrectly classified ones (selected or discarded). As a result, precision and local recall measure can be obtained. Global recall is not considered as no gold standard is employed.

The concrete evaluation tests have been carried out for some of the already presented domains, by running an iteration of the non-taxonomic learning process for the initial domain's keyword. Some examples of the obtained results have been already shown in Figure 9, Figure 16 and in Table 13, included in chapter 5. In Table 35, Table 36, Table 37 and Figure 28, the evaluation results are presented. A selection threshold of 0.1 for both measures has been established.

Table 35. Evaluation of non-taxonomic candidate concepts for the *Cancer* domain. Number of *Selected* and *Rejected* concepts using the Web-based selection procedure compared to the gloss-vector criteria (*right* or *wrong*) for the same selection threshold. Only 70% (124 concepts) were evaluated as the rest were not contained in WordNet.

	Right	Wrong	Total
Selected	99	23	**122**
Rejected	1	1	**2**
Total	**100**	**24**	**124**

Table 36. Evaluation of non-taxonomic candidate concepts for the *Sensor* domain. Number of *Selected* and *Rejected* concepts using the Web-based selection procedure compared to the gloss-vector criteria (*right* or *wrong*) for the same selection threshold. Only 40% (103 concepts) were evaluated as the rest were not contained in WordNet.

	Right	Wrong	Total
Selected	52	16	**68**
Rejected	11	24	**35**
Total	**63**	**40**	**103**

Table 37. Evaluation of non-taxonomic candidate concepts for the *Hypertension* domain. Number of *Selected* and *Rejected* concepts using Web-based selection procedure compared to the gloss-vector criteria (*right* or *wrong*) for the same selection threshold. Only 74% (311 concepts) were evaluated as the rest were not contained in WordNet.

	Right	Wrong	Total
Selected	76	68	**144**
Rejected	106	61	**167**
Total	**182**	**129**	**311**

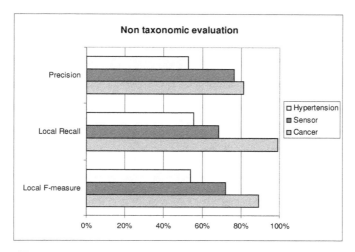

Figure 28. Summary of non-taxonomic evaluation measures for three domains of knowledge.

Analysing these results, we can extract the following conclusions:

- Only a percentage of the full set of non-taxonomic relationships (40%-75%) has been evaluated using WordNet. This is caused by the presence of concrete domain terms that are not contained in WordNet and, in consequence, cannot be evaluated using WordNet-based relatedness measures.

- For the *cancer* domain, we have obtained high quality results, as most of the extracted candidates represent correct relationships. WordNet has a high coverage for this domain, containing even a representative amount of cancer types.

- For the *hypertension* domain, quality is much lower. Analysing this last case in more detail, we have observed that the poor performance is caused in many situations by the way in which *gloss-vector* (and in general all WordNet-based relatedness measures) works. As has been introduced previously, relatedness measures completely depend on WordNet's coverage for each specific concept (semantically expressed by pointers or glosses); in consequence, when concepts are poorly considered in WordNet, those measures return a value that does not fully represent reality. In contrast, our measure depends on the Web's coverage for a particular term. For example, on the one hand, *gloss-vector* returns a low value of 0.04 for the relationship between *atherosclerosis* and *hypertension,* even though the first is a problem commonly derived from the second. This is because, in WordNet, this fact is not mentioned in the *atherosclerosis'* gloss. On the other hand, for other general concepts such as *family,* the returned value is 0.169. In contrast, our measure depends on the Web's coverage for a particular term and, taking into consideration its size compared to WordNet, it can be seen why we are able to provide more consistent results over a wider set of concepts (returning a value of 0.47 for *artherosclerosis* and 0.0069 for *family*).

- The *sensor* domain represents an intermediate case but, due to the low percentage of evaluated relationships (40%) caused by the low coverage of WordNet for technological domains, measures are not as reliable as in the other two cases.

The final conclusion is that the evaluation results based on relatedness measures highly depend on WordNet's coverage for the particular domain. In contrast, our Web-based relatedness score hardly presents this handicap thanks to the high coverage offered by the Web for almost every possible domain of knowledge.

Additionally, analysing the kind of results obtained from the qualitative point of view, some conclusions can be extracted:

- The retrieved concepts tend to be, in many situations, quite specific. This is caused by the score-based selection that ranks higher those concepts that only co-occur with the specific domain. Considering that our goal is to compose a domain ontology this is quite convenient as the discovery of very concrete concepts is necessary to present a complete structure.
- From the list of verbs compiled and selected for a certain domain, only a reduced set is really productive. Most of the valid discovered relationships are associated to a reduced amount of verb phrases. So, at the end, the verb selection process is not very critical and mainly influences on the execution performance (less invalid verbs to evaluate).
- Most of the invalid extracted relations are referred to incomplete phrase objects (*e.g.* *"sensor provides linear..."*) which are caused by the narrow context (snippets) considered during the analysis. A higher precision is expected by performing the analysis over complete sentences, at the cost of a much higher runtime.

6.6 Word sense disambiguation evaluation

As our polysemy disambiguation algorithm has been designed as a complement for our taxonomy learning methodology, and not as a general purpose approach, the evaluation procedure has been designed accordingly.

Considering the cluster-based disambiguation of taxonomic hierarchies presented in §5.7.1, the purpose of the evaluation procedure is to check two main aspects: *i)* each cluster of concepts is properly associated to one of the senses of the corresponding superclass, and *ii)* each concept is contained in the adequate cluster.

Considering those goals and the way in which WordNet, as described in §6.2, organises each concept in function of its corresponding senses (*synsets*), we have designed an especially adapted WordNet-based evaluation of our results. Even though this repository does not contain all of the possible concepts, polysemy is typically presented on commonly used terms that are normally included in WordNet, rather than on missing concrete and domain specific concepts.

For dealing with the first objective of the evaluation, we try to find which of the synsets (and their associated glosses) of the superclass (*e.g. organ*) is the most appropriate for the set of concepts contained in each cluster (*e.g.* cluster1: *brain, lung, liver*; cluster2: *pipe, church, symphonic*). In other words, we have to measure which superclass synset is the most *similar* to the highest amount of cluster components. As we are working with subclass terms that are taxonomically related with the superclass, we can take profit of the hierarchical structure of WordNet. Concretely, as described in §6.2, semantic linkage with *is-a* relationships can be used to compute similarity measures [Pedersen *et al.*, 2004]. For that reason, contrarily to the non-taxonomic evaluation in which we have used a *relatedness* measure (*gloss vector*) we have opted for a *similarity* measure based on *path length*. It computes the number of semantic pointers that link taxonomically a pair of concepts' synsets.

Once the path length measure between each concept and superclass synset has been computed, we can obtain which of the superclass senses is the most similar to the particular concept (*e.g.* the *liver* concept is most similar to the *organ*'s synset defined as *"animal unit specialized in a particular function"*).

As a result, we select as the sense (synset+gloss) associated to each cluster, the one that appears most frequently as the most similar sense to all concepts. Evaluating this assignment, we can have an idea of the quality of the clusterization performed in relation to the number and adequacy of obtained clusters. For example, we can check if the number of clusters with different associated senses corresponds to the total number of senses of the superclass. In a similar manner, we can check if several clusters should be joined as they share the same particular sense.

On the other hand, for dealing with the second objective we can evaluate each individual concept by checking if its associated cluster is the most suitable one. Concretely, once a sense is assigned to each cluster, for each term of that cluster, we check if its corresponding selected gloss is really the most similar one (computed in the previous step). In this manner we can verify if the most similar synset for each concept is really the same that the one corresponding to its cluster. This can give us an idea on how correctly was each term classified in the concrete cluster (sense).

As an example, we offer the evaluation for the polysemic domain presented in §5.7.1: *organ*. For that noun, the following synsets are available in WordNet:
1) *A fully differentiated structural and functional unit in an animal that is specialized for some particular function.*
2) *A government agency or instrument devoted to the performance of some specific function.*
3) *An electronic simulation of a pipe organ.*
4) *A periodical that is published by a special interest group.*
5) *Wind instrument whose sound is produced by means of pipes arranged in sets supplied with air from a bellows and controlled from a large complex musical keyboard.*
6) *A free-reed instrument in which air is forced through the reeds by bellows.*

Considering the concepts found for that domain and the clusters defined after the disambiguation process, we have measured the similarity for each one versus each superclass sense. As a result, the apparently most suitable superclass sense for each concept of each cluster is obtained. Note that in the case that a particular concept has several WordNet synsets, all of them are evaluated and the most similar is taken. Note also that, due to the taxonomic nature of the similarity measure, for some items we may not be able to obtain any measure if they are not linked in WordNet with the superclass through *is-a* relationships.

Table 38. Evaluation of the concept clusters discovered for the *organ* domain.

Cluster	Concept	Superclass most similar sense
Cluster1	Cadaveric_organ	Not found
	Internal_organ	Not found
	Brain	1
	Lung(s)	1
	Heart	1
	Liver	1
	Kidney(s)	1
	Bladder	1
	Stomach	1
	Pancreas	1
	Intestines	1
	Solid_organ	1
Cluster2	Barrel_organ	3
	Fairground_organ	1
	Chord_organ	Not found
	Portative_organ	Not found
	Symphonic_organ	Not found
	Church_organ	2
	Pedals	3
	Theatre_organ	1
	Pipe_organ	5
	Pedal_organ	3

Observing the results presented in Table 38, for the first cluster it is clear that the most suitable superclass sense is number 1 (*organ: a fully differentiated structural and functional unit in an animal that is specialized for some particular function*). One may see that this is the most adequate sense for the defined cluster and it indicates that is has been correctly defined. In addition, almost all of the concepts that belong to the cluster have the highest similarity against that cluster. This indicates that the concepts of the cluster are correctly classified. Only for the first two we have not been able to obtain any measure as they are not taxonomically linked with the corresponding superclass. This may indicate that they have been incorrectly classified or that they do not have an adequate coverage in the WordNet's semantic network.

For the second cluster, the most common superclass sense is number 3 (*An electronic simulation of a pipe organ*). Even though this can be a suitable sense for the cluster, one may also consider sense number 5 and even number 6 as correct. Analysing each concept independently, we can see that there is much more variability, including incorrectly obtained senses such as number 1 and 2. This may indicate that the concepts should be included in the other cluster and even in a new one. However, one can easily see that the most adequate senses are among 3, 5 and 6. This indicates the poor semantic coverage for many domains in WordNet (especially in general non medical cases).

We have applied the same procedure over the other polysemic domain presented in §5.7.2: *virus*. For that noun, the following synsets are available in WordNet:

1) *Infectious agent that replicates itself only within cells of living hosts; many are pathogenic; a piece of nucleic acid (DNA or RNA) wrapped in a thin coat of protein.*
2) *A harmful or corrupting agency.*
3) *A software program capable of reproducing itself and usually capable of causing great harm to files or other programs on the same computer.*

The evaluation results performing the evaluation process over this domain are presented in Table 39.

Table 39. Evaluation of the concept clusters discovered for the *virus* domain.

Cluster	Concept	Superclass most similar sense
Cluster1	Herpes	1
	Hiv	1
	Immunodeficiency_virus	2
	Ebola	2
	Flu	2
	Influenza_virus	2
	Zoster_virus	2
	Mumps	2
	Simplex_virus	Not found
	Barr_virus	Not found
	Smallpox_virus	2
	Pox_virus	2
	Polio_virus	2
	Encephalomyelitis_virus	Not found
	Mosaic_virus	3
Cluster2	Multipartite_virus	Not found
	Polymorphic_virus	Not found
	Iloveyou_virus	Not found
	Cih	Not found
	Macro_virus	3
	Mcafee_virus	Not found
	Anti_virus	Not found
	Slammer	1
	Nimda	Not found

In this case, the classification seems much worse even though one can easily observe that our results are, in general, quite correct. On the one hand, the most common sense for the first cluster appears to be number 2 (*A harmful or corrupting agency*), and not the correct one (*Infectious agent that replicates itself only within cells of living hosts*). In this case, due to the particular semantic organisation of WordNet's *is-a* hierarchies, the WordNet-based similarity measure behaves in an incorrect way. On the other hand, for the second cluster, much of the cluster terms are referred to computer names of virus, a very dynamic domain that can be hardly covered in a general domain repository.

Summarizing, as any other automatic approach for evaluating results, extracted conclusions should be taken with care. Our disambiguation method is designed to distinguish well distinguished senses that can really influence on the quality and structure of the final results. This characteristic does not fit very well with the proliferation of word sense distinctions in WordNet, which is difficult to justify and use in practical terms, since many of the distinctions are unclear [Agirre *et al.*, 2000]. In addition, the employed WordNet-based similarity measures heavily depend on how WordNet taxonomies are organised according to concept synsets. As has been observed, in some situations, they behave worse and are more limited than our more general Web-based similarity measures used for clustering.

6.7 Synonyms discovery evaluation

Synonym sets are information that can be extracted easily from WordNet. However these synsets are far from complete or exhaustive compared to a specific synonym thesaurus [Navigli and Velardi, 2004].

In our case, we intend to perform an automatic evaluation by comparing our list of sorted synonym candidates against the synsets presented in WordNet for a specific keyword. In WordNet, each synset groups a set of concepts that are considered to be truly equivalent, and assigns them a gloss. However, due to the proliferation of a high number of unclear word sense distinctions [Agirre *et al.*, 2000] and the fine grained semantic organization of terms, in many situations synsets are quite incomplete (*e.g. Disease* has not got any synonym). As our purpose for synonym discovery is to widen the search process using other typically equivalent forms for expressing the same concept, other semantically related terms can also be considered. Concretely, first levels of hyponym or hypernym terms for a specific concept are typically used as equivalent terms (*e.g. Cancer* is a hypernym of *Carcinoma*).

Taking these facts into consideration, the automatic evaluation procedure can be performed by employing WordNet-based similarity measures. Concretely, for each candidate that is included in WordNet, the number of semantic links between it and the original concept following hyponym and/or hypernym pointers is computed. As we are working on the taxonomic side, we use the *path length*-based similarity measures mentioned in §6.2. Those that present a semantic distance close enough (4 pointers maximum in our case) are considered to be correctly selected as final synonyms (see the last column in Table 40, Table 41 and Table 42).

Although this process is automatic, the procedure can only be considered as a first approximation of evaluation because the semantic linkage of WordNet is far from complete or exhaustive enough especially in scientific and technological domains [Turney, 2001]; as a consequence, in some cases, correct candidates are not considered (*e.g. disease* and *syndrome*).

Table 40. Firsts and lasts elements of the sorted list of synonym candidates for the *Cancer* domain. From the obtained taxonomy, 31 classes of 3 terms and 16 classes of 4 terms have been considered evaluating 100 web sites including the original keyword. Elements in **bold** represent correctly selected results.

Concept (root)	Derivatives	Relevance	Relative_relev	Correct?
cancer	**cancer, cancers**	**61**	**96.82%**	**yes**
carcinoma	**carcinoma, carcinomas**	**30**	**47.62%**	**yes**
tumor	**tumor, tumors**	**25**	**39.68%**	**yes**
tumour	**tumours, tumour**	**24**	**38.09%**	**yes**
neoplasm	**neoplasms**	**7**	**11.11%**	**yes**
testi	testis	6	9.52%	no
bladder	bladder	5	7.93%	no
malign	malignancies, malignant	3	4.76%	no
epithelioma	**epitheliomas**	**2**	**3.17%**	**yes**
carcino	carcino	2	3.17%	-
skin	skin	2	3.17%	no
mitosi	mitosis	1	1.58%	no
....	....	....	....	....
carcinomabiomed	carcinomabiomedical	0	0%	-
tumortreat	tumortreatment	0	0%	-
forelimb	forelimb	0	0%	-
tumorsovarian	tumorovarian	0	0%	-

Table 41. Firsts and lasts elements of the sorted list of synonym candidates for the *Sensor* domain. From the obtained taxonomy, 17 classes of 3 terms and 1 class of 4 terms have been considered evaluating 100 web sites including the original keyword. Elements in **bold** represent correctly selected results.

Concept (root)	Derivatives	Relevance	Relative_relev	Correct?
sensor	**sensor, sensors, sensores**	**17**	**89.47%**	**yes**
transduc	**tranducer(s)**	**4**	**21.05%**	**yes**
circuit	**circuit**	**2**	**10.5%**	**yes**
measure	measurement	2	10.5%	no
signal	signal	2	10.5%	no
transmit	transmitter(s)	2	10.5%	no
exce	exceeds	1	5.26%	no
differ	differences	1	5.26%	no
....	....	.....	.....	......
element	element	0	0%	no
rel	relative	0	0%	no
code	codes	0	0%	no

Table 42. Firsts and lasts elements of the sorted list of synonym candidates for the *Disease* domain. From the obtained taxonomy, 84 classes of 3 terms and 24 classes of 4 terms have been considered evaluating 100 web sites including the original keyword. Elements in bold represent correctly selected results.

Concept (root)	Derivatives	Relevance	Relative_relev	Correct?
diseas	**disease, diseases**	**122**	**92.24%**	**yes**
disord	disorder, disorders	17	12.87%	no
syndrom	syndrome, syndromes	13	9.84%	no
lesion	**lesions**	**7**	**5.3%**	**yes**
condit	**condition, conditions**	**7**	**5.3%**	**yes**
stenosi	**stenosis**	**7**	**5.3%**	**yes**
atherosclerosis	atherosclerosis	6	4.54%	no
infect	**infections, infection, infectivity, infects**	**6**	**4.54%**	**yes**
stenos	**stenoses**	**6**	**4.54%**	**yes**
obstruct	obstruction, obstructions	5	3.78%	no
health	health	5	3.78%	no
occlus	occlusion	5	3.78%	no
involve	involvement	5	3.78%	no
caus	causes	4	3.03%	no
problem	problems	4	3.03%	no
viru	virus	4	3.03%	no
resist	resistant, resistence	4	3.03%	no
.....	.....	.....	.....	.....
antibodycrhon	antibodychronic	0	0%	-
diseasefelin	diseasefeline	0	0%	-
infectiwalt	infectiwalter	0	0%	-
diseasekaren	diseasekaren	0	0%	-
diseasedisord	diseasedisorder	0	0%	-
diseaseinform	diseaseinformation	0	0%	-

One can see from the presented results that, in general, there exists an agreement between our most relevant candidates and those considered as correct using the described evaluation procedure. However, for the presented examples, non truly equivalent synonyms are found according to WordNet synsets. In consequence, the discovered domain lexicalizations may be useful for widening the analysed corpus of Web resources or may add additional noise to the analytic process that can influence negatively in the final results. Those questions will be discussed in the final chapter and left for further investigation.

6.8 Summary

The evaluation of any ontology learning methodology is a hard task. On the one hand, high quality evaluations can be performed through the intervention of a human expert and/or using available gold standards. However, this is hardly scalable and, in some situations (like the evaluation of non taxonomic relationships or named entities) inapplicable. On the other hand, automatic evaluations against other measures, approaches or electronic repositories, even providing objective results, may introduce compromises regarding their imperfect nature.

In our case, we have designed evaluation procedures for every ontology step, covering a wide spectrum of evaluation approaches: from fully manual evaluation for highly studied taxonomic structures to semi-automatic or fully automatic comparisons for the other cases (such as non-taxonomic relationships or named entities).

Throughout the explanation, several cases of study for different domains have been presented, illustrating how our methodologies behave in extracting knowledge according to the designed evaluation. An overview of additional –restricted- tests performed following the same learning and evaluation criteria –manual or automatic concept per concept evaluations- over other heterogeneous domains is presented in Table 43. Results are quite consistent through the different tests, and similar conclusions to those stated in the previous section can be extracted. This shows the effectiveness of the designed domain independent approach.

Table 43. Summary of evaluation results for several domains of knowledge. All test performed against MSNSearch with default parameters, restricted to two taxonomic levels and one non-taxonomic level.

Domain	Taxonomic	Instances	Non taxonomic
Equation	215 subclasses Precision = 87.8% Recall = 80%	100 named entities Precision = 88.8% Recall = 66.6%	730 concepts Precision = 91.3% Recall = 93.1%
Virus	919 subclasses Precision = 73.95% Recall = 94.6%	317 named entities Precision = 88.9% Recall = 79.5%	1709 concepts Precision = 97% Recall = 99.44%
Cpu	134 subclasses Precision = 76.6% Recall = 85.2%	164 named entities Precision = 97.2% Recall = 71.4%	121 concepts Precision = 98.1% Recall = 88.3%
Insect	668 subclasses Precision = 76% Recall = 94.6%	227 named entities Precision = 83.3% Recall = 47.7%	236 concepts Precision = 94.11% Recall = 76.2%
Tea	236 subclasses Precision = 70.3% Recall = 95.95%	87 named entities Precision = 98.8% Recall = 52.7%	1430 concepts Precision = 92.28% Recall = 98.9%

In addition to the typical quantitative measures of precision and recall, we have also analysed the results from the qualitative point of view, analysing the kind of results that one can expect from our methodology.

In more detail, for the taxonomic case, we have discussed the influence of pattern-based approaches and statistical scores obtaining, for the selected approach, the best results according to a manually performed evaluation. In addition, we have also introduced the learning performance of the named entity detection procedure against a well known supervised technique. We have also commented the precision improvement that we can expect when applying this additional step in the taxonomy learning process.

For the non-taxonomic case, conclusions are more relative as, due to its fuzzy nature, it may be difficult to obtain consensued results even between domain experts. This fact is reflected in the lack of standard classifications covering this kind of relationships. In consequence, our evaluation procedure presents a comparison between our web-scale-based scores and general purpose relatedness measures –*gloss vector*-computed automatically from the WordNet repository. In this case, the limitations of such an unsupervised approach, in conjunction to the lack of semantic WordNet's coverage for some domains, handicapped the evaluation. However, evaluation results can be used as the base for aiding further evaluation procedures, reducing the amount of cases that a human expert should analyse.

Finally, approaches for evaluating results of the disambiguation methodologies designed against WordNet have also been presented. Considering that at this stage we are working a taxonomic level, we have used *path length* similarity measures, based on *is-a* WordNet hierarchical structure. Again, automatic evaluations have shown their limitations in relation to WordNet coverage and, in consequence, the same conclusions as in the non-taxonomic case can be extracted.

Chapter 7

Implementation and applications

Up to this point we have presented the main contributions of our work, describing several specially designed methods for learning domain ontologies from the Web. In order to test their viability in a real world environment, a prototype has been developed. It includes all the different learning steps in an integrated fashion. It also contains functions for the different automatic evaluation procedures described in the previous chapter. The system has been designed and implemented in a distributed way providing, as will be described later, an efficient solution. Note that its execution over several domains has provided the example results presented in the previous sections and in the publications referenced in the Annex.

So, in §7.1, we discuss the computation complexity of the developed algorithms. As a consequence of this study and the potential improvement that can be achieved using a distributed approach, we present a system architecture based on a Multi-Agent system. Next, the formal language used to represent the results and the programming libraries, tools and software used during the development are presented.

In addition, in order to proof the viability of the proposed learning methodologies and the usefulness of the potential results, we have applied them over several real world problems as will be presented in §7.2. Concretely, in §7.2.1 we introduce a way for bringing structure to the web resources analysed during the ontology learning process of a particular domain. Next, in §7.2.2, we describe a method based on our taxonomic learning proposal to structure automatically large digital libraries. Finally, in §7.2.3, we present a distributed knowledge-based system that, using our automatically constructed domain ontologies as input, is able to perform semantically grounded Web Information Retrieval.

7.1 Prototype implementation

In previous chapters, we have described from a methodological point of view the proposed learning procedures. Through the explanation we have commented several questions regarding the scalability and efficiency of the analytical procedure in order to obtain a feasible learning throughput in such an enormous repository as the Web and for general domains of knowledge involving thousands of entities.

Even considering aspects such as the lightweight analysis or snippet-based web parsing, the knowledge acquisition can be a very time consuming task. As Table 44 shows, one iteration of the learning process for one general concept can take about 1 hour using one computer. This is mainly caused by the online accessing to web resources and the querying of web search engines. However, the runtime is reduced when dealing with specific subclasses or concrete non-taxonomically related concepts (both retrieved from the initial domain's keyword during the incremental learning process), as a narrower spectrum of web resources and candidates is available.

Table 44. Summary of results obtained for one iteration of the full learning process for several domains using one computer. All test performed against MSNSearch with default parameters.

Domain	Sub classes	Instances	Non taxonomic	Queries (statistics)	Total webs	Run-time
Sensor	55	48	444	3105	848	57 min.
Cancer	73	25	497	2298	774	48 min.
Hypertension	29	11	336	1799	664	37 min.
Colon cancer	19	9	48	765	175	11 min.
Metastatic breast cancer	9	1	11	334	74	8 min.
Papiloma virus	3	0	0	35	65	3 min.

From the analysis of the results presented in Table 44, one can observe that the runtime depends linearly on the number of access to the Web, querying a web search engine or checking a web site. However, considering that, for medium to wide analyses, the number of queries overpass the number of web sites accessed, we can conclude that the runtime depends on the number of web search engine queries (see Figure 29). More details about this assumption will be discussed in §7.1.4.

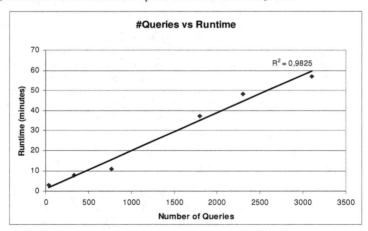

Figure 29. Runtime depends linearly on the number of Web search queries.

In any case, the incremental execution of the different instances of the learning processes (taxonomic and non-taxonomic) as new knowledge (domain concepts) is acquired may represent, for general domains, a computational cost that is hard to be assumed by one computer. For example, in the tests presented in Table 45 –considering only the taxonomic aspect- and Table 46 –restricting to 2 taxonomic levels and 1 non-taxonomic level-, one may observe the increment of runtime required to recursively analyse general domains of knowledge.

Table 45. Summary of results obtained for recursive iterations of the taxonomic learning process for several domains on one computer. All tests have been performed against MSNSearch with default parameters.

Domain	Sub classes	Instances	Queries (statistics)	Total webs	1st level runtime	Total runtime
Sensor	868	737	31455	12591	17 min.	15 hours
Cancer	1458	710	40491	11160	8 min.	21 hours
Mammal	957	1187	46308	12747	16 min.	16 hours

Table 46. Summary of results obtained the full learning process restricted to 2 taxonomic levels and 1 non-taxonomic level for several domains on one computer. All test performed against MSNSearch with default parameters.

Domain	Sub classes	Instances	Non taxonomic	Queries (statistics)	Total webs	Runtime
Equation	215	100	730	28741	12326	10 hours
Virus	919	317	1709	204450	23116	66 hours
Cpu	134	164	121	13934	4567	6 hours
Insect	668	227	236	58286	8270	20 hours
Tea	236	87	1430	57148	6471	17 hours

In order to justify this empirically observed behaviour, in the next section we analyse from a theoretical point of view, the computational complexity of the algorithms.

7.1.1 Computational complexity

As has been introduced in §7.1, the full learning process can be divided in individual tasks which correspond to the evaluation of a particular concept. The actions performed during this process are:
- The system queries a web search engine using each Hearst pattern and analyses the web snippets (grouped in sets of 50 for the case of MSNSearch). As a result of this process, a certain number of taxonomic candidates (t_l) are retrieved. They are evaluated by performing new queries into a web search engine. Considering the scores introduced in §5.2, $2ht_l$ queries are requested, where h is the number of Hearst patterns employed (all pattern-based scores are queried and the highest is used). As a result of the queries, s_l items are selected and t_l- s_l are rejected in function of the specified selection threshold. Then, depending on the learning threshold, the algorithm may decide to evaluate an additional set of resources (re-

sulting in t_2 candidates to evaluate) or continue with the next pattern. After performing all the iterations for all the Hearst patterns, a total of $2h\sum\sum t_{ij}$ queries for statistics have been performed (where t_{il} is the number of candidates retrieved for the 'i' iteration and the 'l' pattern –from a total of 'h' patterns-). As introduced in the previous section, the number of queries for statistics is the variable that mainly defines the runtime, as it is always much higher than the queries required for web IR and requires much more runtime (several orders of magnitude higher) than web parsing of fixed size results pages.

-   The taxonomic learning using Noun Phrases follows the same behaviour but, in this case, each web resource will be accessed independently, resulting in an additional number of web accesses. In addition, the parsing runtime is more nondeterministic as it depends on the size of the specific web site. In any case, queries for computing statistics typically consume most of the runtime. This results in additional $2\sum n_j$ queries, where n_j the number of noun phrase-based candidates evaluated in the iteration 'j'.

-   Additionally to the selection of taxonomic subclasses, retrieved candidates can also be evaluated as instance candidates (named entities). This process requires performing an additional number of queries (e queries are required for 'e' named entities) and parsing fixed size snippets.

-   Once the taxonomic learning is finished, the non-taxonomic phase starts by evaluating extracted verb phrases (as introduced in §5.4). Following the same philosophy, this requires new web queries for computing statistics. Concretely, $2v$ queries are needed to evaluate 'v' verb phrase candidates.

-   Each selected verb phrase is used as a pattern for learning non-taxonomic relations, similarly to the taxonomic case (search querying, snippet parsing and incremental candidate evaluation). This requires $2\sum\sum r_{kp}$ queries for statistics, where r_{kv} is the number of candidates retrieved in the 'k' iteration for the 'p' verb phrase.

-   Other tasks such as the ontology post-processing performed offline over the obtained structure do not influence in the required runtime as they have a reduced scope (typically thousands of ontological entities).

As a conclusion, the effort applied to a particular domain concept depends on its learning productiveness: the number of taxonomic relations ($t_{ij}+n_j$), non-taxonomic relations (r_{kv}), instances (e) and verb labels (v) candidates retrieved. This result in a linearly dependant amount of web queries for statistics (Q) that finally defines the runtime (18).

$$Q = Queries\_per\_concept = 2h\sum_{l}^{h}\sum_{i} t_{il} + 2\sum_{j} n_j + e + 2v + 2\sum_{p}^{v}\sum_{k} r_{kp} \quad (18)$$

Arrived at this point, we have learned the immediate relations for a particular concept (C). In function of the particular domain, the available web resources and the selection and learning thresholds, we have obtained 'x' subclasses and 'y' non-taxonomically related terms (see Figure 30). Note that for the taxonomic case the branching factor is the same as the number of subclasses, but for the non-taxonomic case we can obtain fewer classes than relationships (*i.e.* two classes can be non-taxonomically related with different verb labels).

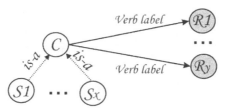

Figure 30. Learning expansion of the concept *C* with *x* taxonomic relationships and *y* non-taxonomic relationships.

The next step will consist on executing the same learning process over those $x+y$ new concepts acquired. On one computer those concepts would be sequentially analysed. Considering T the runtime for a particular concept that mainly depends on the number of web queries (Q), the final runtime would be $(x+y)T$. As this is an incremental process, multilevel relationships can be further developed and the number of concepts can grow consequently. As shown in the previous section, for general concepts, the particular 'T' has an order of magnitude of minutes, 'x' can be dozens of subclasses and 'y' may arrive to several hundreds.

The algorithm is responsible of finishing the less productive ontological branches in function of how the learning evolves as stated in §5.6.2. One should also note that due to the bootstrapped information added to the web queries (presented in §5.6.3), the more advanced the learning is, the more concrete and the less amount of new results are retrieved. In any case, non-taxonomic relationships are hard limited to a maximum of two links from the initial concept. The taxonomic subclass level is not limited but, in practice, the maximum depth achieved is about 3 or 4.

At the end, considering this kind of expansion, the final runtime on one computer where concepts are sequentially evaluated is a *polynomic* function (19).

$$Runtime = T(taxo\_concepts + notaxo\_concepts)^{\max(taxo\_depth, notaxo\_depth)} \qquad \textbf{(19)}$$

It depends on the number of taxonomic and non-taxonomically related concepts retrieved at each iteration. The exponent is the maximum depth of the relationships (typically the taxonomic depth will be higher and inferior to 4). As stated, the runtime (T) required to perform the analysis of one concept depends linearly on the web queries for statistics that, at the same time, depend linearly on the number of retrieved candidates. Considering the orders of magnitude managed (runtime in *minutes* and number of concepts in *hundreds*) one can easily realize that a sequential execution in one computer is not computationally feasible.

However, as shown in Figure 31, taking into consideration the tree like expansion of the learning process, several tasks can be performed concurrently and independently.

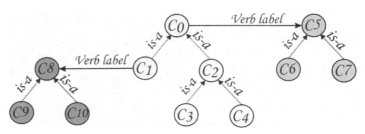

Figure 31. Basic ontological structure with tree like taxonomic a non-taxonomic relationships.

This workflow is adequate for parallel computing, as several tasks (different analyses for each new concept) can be performed at the same time without interference. In our case, the parallelisation is not only related to the computational power, but also to other resources such as the Internet bandwidth or system memory. However, the most important aspect is that the parallel execution of various learning instances through several computers can reduce the overhead of Web access, minimizing the execution waits and web search engine restrictions thanks to the distributed access from, ideally, different IP addresses. Our hypothesis is that a distributed approach of our learning methodology can represent a great improvement.

As the execution workflow is nondeterministic, as it is defined by the knowledge acquired at execution time, coordination and flexibility are fundamental. In order to tackle these execution requirements, we have used the agent paradigm. In the next section we offer an overview of this technology. Next, we provide details about the system architecture, operation and implementation, and the results representation and visualization.

7.1.2 Agents and Multi-Agent Systems

An agent [Wooldridge, 2002] is a computer system capable of flexible autonomous action in some environment. An agent has its own goals and the tools to be able to achieve them. The main properties of agents are:
- *Sociability*: an agent must be able to communicate with other agents, and cooperate with them to solve complex tasks.
- *Reactivity*: an agent is aware of the changes in the environment and responds to them in a timely fashion.
- *Autonomy*: the agent may decide whether to fulfil a given request or not, and may decide which is the best way to achieve its goals.

There are particular problems that cannot be solved by a single agent because different resources, knowledge or tools are needed. In this case, agents must cooperate, co-ordinate or negotiate with other agents to achieve their goals. This is a Multi-Agent System (MAS) [Weiss, 1999]. The main advantages of using a Multi-Agent System are:
- *Modularity*: the full problem can be divided into several tasks than can be modelled into individual agents.

- *Efficiency*: the distributed approach allows concurrent and parallel execution through several nodes of a computer network.
- *Robustness*: against failures of individual agents.
- *Flexibility*: agents can be managed (*i.e.* created, destroyed) dynamically depending on the particular execution needs of the full system.

In recent years it has been argued that MAS may be considered as the latest software engineering paradigm [Jenning, 2000; Petrie, 2001]. This is interesting for large and complex systems in several senses: (i) with geographically distributed data, (ii) with many components or entities, possibly with particular interests, (iii) with a broad scope and huge amounts of information to consider. The use of intelligent, distributed agents is an adequate approach for this type of problems.

As a conclusion, MAS provide some advantages with respect to traditional systems such as efficiency, flexibility, autonomy and highly elaborate communicative skills, and are very suitable to implement dynamic and distributed systems. Several projects applying MAS to information retrieval and knowledge acquisition such as [Gibbins *et al.*, 2003; Moreno *et al.*, 2004] are an indication that agents can provide benefits in this area.

7.1.3 Agent-based distributed ontology learning

In this section, the implementation of the presented knowledge acquisition methodologies for constructing domain ontologies over a distributed agent-based approach is presented.

In general, the main idea is to distribute the full ontology learning process into several independent tasks that can be executed on different computers. At the end of each execution, partial results obtained by each one are returned and incorporated into the domain ontology. Repeating iteratively this parallel execution model, the final ontology can be constructed transparently using the computational power of several nodes of a computer network.

The developed MAS (*Multi-Agent System*) is composed of several autonomous entities (agents) that can be deployed around a network. Each agent can be considered as an execution unit that follows a particularly modelled behaviour and interacts (communicates) with other ones, coordinating their execution to achieve a common goal. Those agents can be created, eliminated or modified dynamically in function of the execution requirements derived from the learning process, providing an efficient utilisation of the available computational resources.

There are three kinds of agents in the MAS:

a) User Agent (UA): allows the human user to interact with the system. It offers a web interface from which the user can asynchronously manage the learning process and visualize results. Even though the ontology construction process can be fully automatic and unsupervised, through this agent, he has the possibility of configuring, initializing and controlling the construction process. In addition, the web interface represents an invaluable help for debugging during the development phase.

b) Internet Agent (IA): implements the taxonomic and non-taxonomic learning methodology as described in chapter 5. For a specific concept, it performs a single execution of the developed learning methods, composing a partial ontology containing the new taxonomically and non-taxonomically related concepts. Those new concepts can be recursively analysed using new instances of IAs. The coordinated and parallel execution of several IAs with different concepts allows obtaining a set of partial results that can be joined and interrelated in order to build the final domain ontology. As this construction process is very time consuming, in order to provide an efficient solution, this kind of agents are placed in different computer nodes from a network that provides the required hardware resources (*i.e.* available RAM and/or internet bandwidth). They also implement mobility capabilities in order to be deployed transparently and dynamically in an available computer node.

c) Coordinator Agent (CA): it coordinates the domain ontology construction process by creating and configuring IAs to explore retrieved concepts. Concretely, each concept discovered by each partial analysis is used as a seed for further analyses by creating new IAs, bootstrapping with the knowledge already acquired, as described in §5.6.3. In addition, CA joins partial results composing the final domain ontology. It also implements load balancing policies that allow it to decide, at every moment, where to deploy each IA according to the free resources available. It is also able to restore learning state of unfinished tasks (due to software or hardware errors) by continuously monitoring the MAS state. This provides the degree of robustness necessary in distributed environments. Note that, although the ontology construction is centralised by this agent, its work load in relation to the IAs (even with several machines available) is quite reduced.

As shown in Figure 32, the process starts when the UA receives from the user the concept (*e.g. cancer*) that represents the domain to explore (step 1). This is sent to the CA. It creates a first IA that is deployed in an available network node and it starts acquiring domain knowledge (new taxonomically and non taxonomically related terms) using the methodology presented in chapter 5 (step 2). Up to this moment the learning process is executed sequentially. As a result, a set of related terms (*e.g. breast, lung, colon, radiotherapy*) is returned to the CA (step 3). The CA incorporates this knowledge into the domain ontology as classes and relationships and, for each class, a new IA is created and deployed to explore it. At this moment, a degree of parallel execution is achieved in function of the number of tasks to execute (associated to IAs) and the available computer nodes. Concurrently, those partial results are sent to the UA in order to offer an updated visualization of the obtained results.

As the different IAs finalize their analyses, several sets of taxonomically and non-taxonomically related classes are returned asynchronously to the CA that incorporates them into the ontology (step 4). The process is repeated until the algorithm decides to stop exploring each ontology branch (as described in §5.6.2). At the end, the CA is able to construct recursively an ontology that represents the available knowledge in the Web for the domain. As a final step, the CA refines the ontology in order to detect implicit relationships and attributes for each class (*e.g. metastatic cancer*) as described in §5.5 and outputs the result.

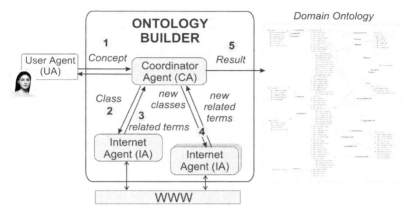

Figure 32. Multi-agent system architecture to create domain ontologies from the Web.

All the agents are deployed and executed in a computer network that provides the required computational resources and Internet bandwidth to perform the analysis (as shown in Figure 33). This network is linked to a server that manages the agent platform and provides a web interface that is managed by the UA allowing the user's access to the system from any computer with Internet connection.

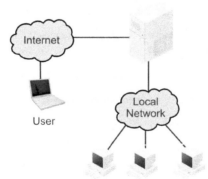

Figure 33. Agent-based knowledge acquisition physical architecture.

Note that no special requirements (computer architecture, operating system, software, computing power, *etc*) are established on the user's side as all the learning process is performed on the server's internal network and the interaction is performed via Internet. Moreover, due to the potential runtime required to finish the full learning process, the server implements a persistence mechanism to store the user's session, maintaining the state and partial results of the works currently in execution.

7.1.4 Distributed learning performance

Once the distributed agent-based system has been presented, in this section we discuss the learning performance obtained using different degrees of parallelism. In this manner we intend to show the scalability capabilities of the designed system and the performance improvement over non parallel approach (introduced in §7.1.1).

The first test consists in picking up four tasks of similar complexity (4 immediate subclasses of the *Cancer* domain) and to execute them, using the same parameters, in the following hardware configurations:

- 1 computer runs the 4 tasks: they are executed sequentially. The final runtime is computed by adding each individual runtime.
- 2 computers running 2 similar tasks: 2 tasks are modelled over an IA which are sequentially executed in one computer and in parallel with the other pair (and the other IA). The final runtime is the maximum of both sequential executions.
- 4 computers running 1 task: maximum parallelism with 4 agents. The final runtime is the maximum of the four executions.

Table 47. Performance tests for the execution of 4 similar learning tasks with different parallel conditions. Individual and total runtimes are presented.

Domain	1 node	2 nodes	4 nodes
Breast cancer	1083 s.	1093 s.	1095 s.
Colon cancer	627 s.	667 s.	705 s.
Lung cancer	980 s.	992 s.	1029 s.
Ovarian cancer	715 s.	812 s.	841 s.
Total	**3405 s.**	**2085 s.**	**1095 s.**

One can see that the improvement is very significant and proportional to the degree of parallelism (see Figure 34). It is also interesting that the execution overhead introduced by the agent and platform management is negligible in relation to the sequential approach. This is due to the complexity and heavyweight nature of tasks.

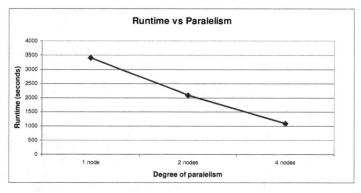

Figure 34. Increase of performance in relation to the degree of parallelism.

The following test covers the full parallel execution of a domain. In this case, we pick up one domain and execute 2 taxonomic levels sequentially (using one computer) and in parallel (using 4 computers) with automatic distribution of the work load in function of the available computational resources (following the implemented scheduling policy). From the performance obtained, we can check, in a real situation, the degree of parallelism one can except from our MAS and the behaviour of the implemented task planner.

First, we have executed the taxonomic learning (two levels) for the *Sensor* domain, which results, for the specified parameters, in 12 immediate subclasses that should be analysed. When running the full process (*sensor*+12 subclasses analyses) in one computer, it takes 6606 seconds. Next, the same test with the same search parameters is executed in a parallel environment with 4 nodes. As a result, the same amount of subclasses is obtained, but the process is finished in 2944 seconds. This represents an improvement of 224% when the hardware is increased by a 400%. Examining the execution trace and representing the task-node assignation at each moment, we can compose the Gantt diagram shown in Figure 35 (each task corresponds to each coloured interval).

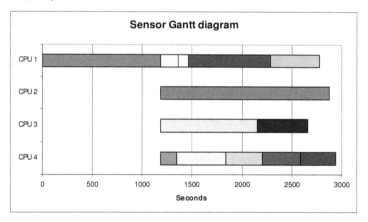

Figure 35. Distribution of taxonomic learning tasks among 4 CPUs for the *Sensor* domain.

One can see that the first task (the *Sensor* analysis) is executed alone in computer 1, as no other concepts have been discovered. Once its analysis is finished and 12 new tasks (subclasses) has been discovered, the maximum degree of parallelism is achieved, as the scheduler assigns tasks to free nodes whenever they are available. At the end, the system has to wait until all nodes have finished as no more tasks (we have limited the analysis to two taxonomic levels) remain. In consequence, the final performance is restricted by the sequential parts of the non-parallel implementation.

Regarding the runtime required for each learning task, as stated in §7.1, they depend linearly on the number of queries for statistics performed to the web search engine (see Figure 36). In this case, however, there is more variability due to the higher degree of parallelism and the finer granularity of the measured tasks.

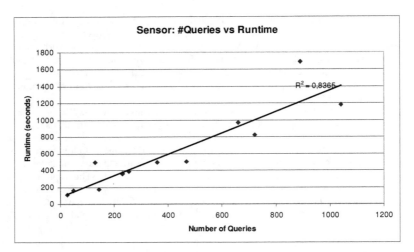

Figure 36. Number of queries *vs* runtime for each learning task (subclass) of the Sensor domain. A linear dependence can be inferred.

In the next test, we have picked a much wider domain (Cancer) and perform the same executions. This has result in 49 immediate subclasses to analyse. When executing the learning process in one computer, it lasts a total of 16505 seconds. Performing the same execution in parallel with 4 computers, the total runtime is lowered till 5634 seconds. This represents a performance improvement of 292% with and hardware increase of 400%. In this case, the task distribution among the available nodes is shown in Figure 37.

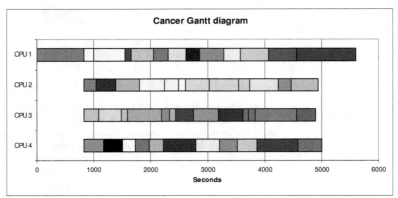

Figure 37. Distribution of taxonomic learning tasks among 4 CPUs for the *Cancer* domain.

In this case, the non fully parallel intervals are shorter than in the previous example, due to the higher amount of tasks to execute. One can see that the potential improvement of this parallel approach is higher as more tasks (concepts) to execute are available. In a complete learning process (involving hundreds of multi-level taxonomic and non-taxonomic analyses) the percentage of fully parallel execution is much higher in relation to the sequential parts and the throughput improvement will tend to be similar to the hardware resources provided. As shown in the first test of this section, the overhead introduced of the agent and parallelism management are negligible in relation to the size of the tasks to execute.

Again, the runtime of each task depends linearly on the number of queries performed (see Figure 36).

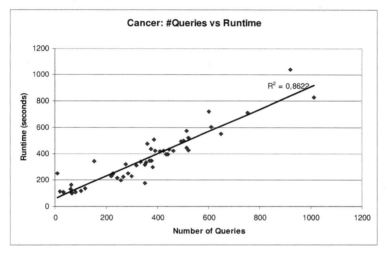

Figure 38. Number of queries *vs* runtime for each learning task (subclass) of the Sensor domain. A linear dependence can be inferred.

Considering this new execution environment, we can compare it to the sequential approach in relation to performance. As presented in §7.1.1, the computational cost in a sequential approach is a polynomic function of the number of concepts retrieved at each iteration, multiplied an amount of times defined by the maximum depth of the relationships. Without considering the limitations introduced by the available hardware or the Web search engine, in the distributed approach we can parallelise the full set of concepts retrieved, reducing the runtime of one iteration to T (the runtime required to evaluate one concept, depending linearly on the number of web queries). At the end, we are able to obtain a runtime of T^{max_depth}, where the exponent is maximum depth of the taxonomic and non-taxonomic relationships (among 2 and 4). In consequence, we can reduce the runtime from to $T(taxo\_concepts+notaxo\_concepts)^{max\_depth}$ to T^{max_depth} using a *(taxo_concepts+notaxo_concepts)* degree of parallelism.

In the real world, however, it is very unlikely to have available such an amount of hardware and, in consequence, the real runtime will depend on the maximum degree of parallelism that we are able to achieve.

In this sense, other interesting questions about the parallelisation of learning tasks that we have observed during the development are the following:

- Ideally, each learning task (modelled by the corresponding IA) will be executed exclusively in one computer. However, due to the limitation of computer nodes, in our tests, we have determined that one computer with enough hardware resources (*i.e.* 2 Gigs of Ram, Pentium4 CPU or later) is able to execute among 6 to 8 tasks (and IAs) before the performance is degraded due to the concurrence overhead.

- When executing several learning tasks in parallel, the Web search engine employed may receive a considerable amount of queries at the same time. MSNSearch scales quite well under those heavy load conditions but, for other search engines, the performance is degraded. This is motivated because, in our case, several computer nodes of the network share the same external IP and they are identified as the same machine by the search engine. In those cases, access control policies are applied, decreasing the query priority and, in consequence, increasing the response time. In order to minimize this problem, each computer executing IAs should have a different IP.

7.1.5 Formal representation of the results

There exist several standard ontology languages such as RDF[17], DAML+OIL[18] or OWL[19]. This last one, the *Web Ontology Language* is the newest one. It is a semantic mark-up language specially designed for publishing and sharing ontologies on the World Wide Web. It is developed by the WebOnt group as a vocabulary extension of RDF and is derived from DAML+OIL. It is designed to be used by applications that need to process the content of information and facilitates greater machine interpretability by providing additional vocabulary along with a formal semantics [Fensel *et al.*, 2001]. OWL is supported by many ontology visualizers and editors. There exist three different OWL specifications in which a particular ontology can be defined:

- *OWL full* is meant for users who want maximum expressiveness and the syntactic freedom of RDF with no computational guarantees. Inference is undecidable.

- *OWL DL* supports those users who want the maximum expressiveness while retaining computational completeness. It is based on Description Logic, provides a well defined semantic and allows inferences (there are available reasoners such as FACT++[20], Pellet[21] or F-OWL[22]).

- *OWL Lite* supports those users primarily needing a classification hierarchy and simple restrictions.

---

[17] Resource Description Framework: http://www.w3.org/RDF
[18] DAML+OIL WebOntology Language: http://www.w3.org/TR/daml+oilreference
[19] Web Ontology Language: http://www.w3c.org/TR/owl-features/
[20] http://owl.man.ac.uk/factplusplus/
[21] http://www.mindswap.org/2003/pellet/
[22] http://fowl.sourceforge.net/

As our main purpose is the representation of domain knowledge with full expressiveness but allowing inference, we use OWL DL. From the full set of ontological components supported by the OWL specification, we have used the following ones:

- *RDF Schemas Features*: they define basic ontological components.
  - o *Classes*: are sets of individuals with common characteristics. In our case they correspond to domain concepts.
  - o *Subclasses*: define class specializations by constraining their coverage. Class hierarchies can be specified by making one or more statements that a class is a subclass of another class. They are retrieved through several iterations of the taxonomy learning procedure.
  - o *Individuals*: Individuals are the objects in the domain. In our case they are limited to named entities found during the ontology learning.
  - o *Properties*: can be used to state relationships between individuals or from individuals to data values. Relationships in OWL are binary. There exist three types of properties:
    - • *Object Property*: it establishes relationships between pair of individuals. We have used them to define verb-labelled non-taxonomic relationships.
    - • *Datatype Property*: relates an individual to a data value (*int, string, float, etc.*). Can be considered "attributes". We have used them to define the class "features" extracted during the post-processing stage.
    - • *Annotation Property*: used to attach metadata (*e.g. version, author* or *comment*) to classes, individuals or properties. We have used them to add meta-information about the learning process and the web content.
- *Equality* and *Inequality*: allows expressing equalities and inequalities between ontological components:
  - o *Equivalent Classes*: it states that the set of individuals belonging to a particular class is the same as the set corresponding to another class. It may be used to create synonymous classes. We have used it to define the alternative class names that are referred to the same concept (during the linguistic analysis and ontology post-processing stage).
- *Property Characteristics*: they define the semantics of properties:
  - o *Inverse Property*: one property may be stated to be the inverse of another property. We have used it to define inverse semantic relationships between the passive and active voice of a non-taxonomic relationship.
- *Property Restrictions*: they define the "meaning" of classes by specifying a statement between a pair of entities (classes or datatypes) and a property with specific semantics:
  - o *SomeValuesFrom*: a particular class may have a restriction on a property that at least one value for that property is of a certain type. We have used this type of restriction to state non-taxonomic relationships between a pair of classes using a previously defined verb-labelled property.
  - o *HasValue*: for a particular class, a default value for a datatype property is stated. We have used this type of restriction to define the appropriate Boolean values of the automatically discovered domain features (previously defined as datatype properties) in the corresponding taxonomic level.

See Figure 39, Figure 40, Figure 42 and Figure 41 for examples of the concrete OWL notation used in some of the mentioned ontological components.

```
<owl:Class rdf:about="http://grusma.etse.urv.es/ontologies/cancer/#C:breast_cancer">
  <rdfs:subClassOf>
    <owl:Restriction>
      <owl:onProperty
rdf:resource="http://grusma.etse.urv.es/ontologies/cancer/#D:Is_OPERABLE" />
        <owl:someValuesFrom>
          <rdfs:Datatype rdf:about="http://www.w3.org/2001/XMLSchema#boolean"/>
        </owl:someValuesFrom>
      </owl:Restriction>
  </rdfs:subClassOf>
  <rdfs:subClassOf>
    <owl:Restriction>
      <owl:onProperty
rdf:resource="http://grusma.etse.urv.es/ontologies/cancer/#D:Is_RECURRENT" />
        <owl:allValuesFrom>
          <rdfs:Datatype rdf:about="http://www.w3.org/2001/XMLSchema#boolean"/>
        </owl:allValuesFrom>
      </owl:Restriction>
  </rdfs:subClassOf>
  <rdfs:subClassOf>
    <owl:Class rdf:about="http://grusma.etse.urv.es/ontologies/cancer/#C:cancer">
    </owl:Class>
  </rdfs:subClassOf>
</owl:Class>
```

Figure 39. *breast_cancer* is subclass of *cancer* and has two features: *Is_OPERABLE* and *Is_RECURRENT* .

```
<rdf:Description
rdf:about="http://grusma.etse.urv.es/ontologies/cancer/#I:American_breast_cancer">
  <rdf:type>
    <owl:Class rdf:about="http://grusma.etse.urv.es/ontologies/cancer/#C:breast_cancer">
    </owl:Class>
  </rdf:type>
</rdf:Description>
<rdf:Description
rdf:about="http://grusma.etse.urv.es/ontologies/cancer/#I:NCCN_breast_cancer">
  <rdf:type>
    <owl:Class rdf:about="http://grusma.etse.urv.es/ontologies/cancer/#C:breast_cancer">
    </owl:Class>
  </rdf:type>
</rdf:Description>
```

Figure 40. *American_breast_cancer* and *NCCN_breast_cancer* are instances of *breast_cancer.*

```
<owl:Class rdf:about="http://grusma.etse.urv.es/ontologies/cancer/#C:intestinal_cancer">
  <owl:equivalentClass>
    <owl:Class
rdf:about="http://grusma.etse.urv.es/ontologies/cancer/#C:intestine_cancer">
    </owl:Class>
  </owl:equivalentClass>
  <rdfs:subClassOf>
    <owl:Class rdf:about="http://grusma.etse.urv.es/ontologies/cancer/#C:cancer">
    </owl:Class>
  </rdfs:subClassOf>
</owl:Class>
```

Figure 41. *intestinal_cancer* and *intestine_cancer* are stated to be equivalent.

```
<owl:Class rdf:about="http://grusma.etse.urv.es/ontologies/cancer/#C:chemotherapy">
  <rdfs:subClassOf>
    <owl:Restriction>
    <owl:onProperty
rdf:resource="http://grusma.etse.urv.es/ontologies/cancer/#P:reduces" />
      <owl:someValuesFrom>
        <owl:Class
rdf:about="http://grusma.etse.urv.es/ontologies/cancer/#C:breast_cancer">
        </owl:Class>
      </owl:someValuesFrom>
    </owl:Restriction>
  </rdfs:subClassOf>
  <rdfs:subClassOf>
    <owl:Restriction>
    <owl:onProperty
rdf:resource="http://grusma.etse.urv.es/ontologies/cancer/#P:is_used_in" />
      <owl:someValuesFrom>
        <owl:Class
rdf:about="http://grusma.etse.urv.es/ontologies/cancer/#C:liver_cancer">
        </owl:Class>
      </owl:someValuesFrom>
    </owl:Restriction>
  </rdfs:subClassOf>
</owl:Class>
```

Figure 42. *chemotherapy* has the following non-taxonomic relationships: "*chemotherapy reduces breast_cancer*" and "*chemotherapy is_used_in liver_cancer*".

7.1.6 Prototype components

The implemented application is fully written in Java in order to achieve good interoperability with the freely available tools for Web and NL processing. Concretely, the main tools and libraries used in the development of the prototype:

- JADE 3.3[23]: the *Java Agent Development Framework* is the tool used to implement the presented Multi-Agent system. It provides a set of programming libraries for implementing agents and an execution environment in which to perform the deployment. It follows the FIPA[24] standards about how agents should be defined in order to guarantee the interoperability between applications. This version includes features about agent mobility that have been extensively used in our implementation in order to provide a fully distributed solution.
- English Stemmer 1.0[25]: it provides a stemming algorithm to find the morphological root of a word in the English language. This has been extensively used in order to detect equivalent forms of expressing the same ontological concept.
- Text processing tools from OpenNLP Tools 1.1[26]: is a mature Java package that hosts a variety of *Natural Language Processing* tools which perform sentence detection, tokenization, pos-tagging, chunking and parsing, allowing morphological and syntactical analysis of texts. It is based on maximum entropy models [Borthwick, 1999] and, in consequence it requires annotation samples. Models[27] of anno-

---

[23] http://jade.tilab.com/

[24] http://www.fipa.org/specs/fipa00001/

[25] http://sourceforge.net/projects/stemmers/

[26] http://opennlp.sourceforge.net/

[27] http://cvs.sourceforge.net/viewcvs.py/opennlp/models/

tation for each task exhaustively trained for the English Language are used (provided "officially" by the developers of the library). It has been used to analyse interesting pieces of web content (*i.e.* a pattern matching found within a particular web site). Even though the computational cost of this analysis can be high when evaluating large texts, only the particular sentence in which the keyword has been found is considered. Concretely, we have used the sentence detector and the morphological and syntactical –parts of speech- analyser.

- Named-entity tool from OpenNLP Tools 1.1[28]: it is able to detect some word patterns like *organization*, *person*, and *location* names using, again, maximum entropy models. Previously trained model files[29] with annotation examples for those categories are used in this task. We have used it for evaluation purposes, comparing its tagged terms with our extracted named entities over the same sources.
- Html Parser 1.6[30]: this is a powerful HTML parser that allows processing web content. It has been used to extract automatically clear text contained in a web resource.
- Web search engine APIs: one of the most important parts of the implemented system, as they provide access to the Web search engine services. We have extensively used them to retrieve ranked lists of web resources, statistics, snippets and html caches. In order to avoid an abusive use of a particular engine, several alternatives have been implemented.
  - o Google Web API[31]: this is the library of functions that the Google search engine provides to programmers to allow them to make queries and retrieve search results. However, the maximum amount of daily search queries per account is restricted to 1000.
  - o Yahoo Search 1.1.0[32]: in the same way as Google, Yahoo recently provided an API for accessing Yahoo Search services. Similarly, it is also limited to a maximum of 5000 queries per day, account and IP.
  - o For the other search engines that have also been considered (Altavista, AlltheWeb, MSNSearch), ad-hoc libraries for performing web queries and parsing the page of results have been implemented. They are based on analysing the query language used by each search engine and studying the format in which result pages are presented. In consequence, this is not a flexible solution as any change in both the query language and/or the result page format will require modifications of the implemented modules. In addition, many search engines impose IP limitations (MSNSearch is the only one offering an unlimited access).

- OWL API 1.4[33]: it is one of the first libraries providing functions to construct and manage OWL files. As we have selected OWL as the formal language for repre-

---

[28] http://opennlp.sourceforge.net/
[29] http://cvs.sourceforge.net/viewcvs.py/opennlp/models/
[30] http://sourceforge.net/projects/htmlparser
[31] http://www.google.com/apis/
[32] http://developer.yahoo.com/search/
[33] http://sourceforge.net/projects/owlapi

senting our learned domain ontologies, this library is used to write them in the corresponding format.

- WordNet 2.0[34] (more details in §6.2): one of the latest versions of the WordNet semantic electronic repository. As described in chapter 6, it has been extensively used for evaluation purposes.

- JWNL WordNet API 1.3[35]: offers an interface for accessing WordNet 2.0 from Java programs. It allows querying words specifying a morphological category and retrieving corresponding synsets and glosses. Moreover it also allows exploring the semantic network that links WordNet's entities.

- WordNet::Similarity 1.03[36]: offers an implementation of some WordNet-based similarity and relatedness measures between terms (more details in §6.2). Concretely, it works in conjunction with a WordNet 2.0 instance to provide the following measures: *Path length, Leacock & Chodorow, Wu & Palmer, Resnik, Hirst & St-Onge, Jiang & Conrath, Extended Gloss Overlaps, Gloss Vector, Gloss Vector (pairwise)* and *Random*. For evaluation purposes we have compared our Web-based relatedness scores with *Gloss Vector* which seems to offer the best quality measures [Patwardhan and Pedersen, 2006]. As a similarity measure used to evaluate the designed methods for dealing with semantic ambiguity, we have employed a simple *path length* derived measure as, in those cases, we are only interested in the WordNet's *is-a* hierarchies. However, as the package is implemented in Python, a wrapper module has been implemented to allow a transparent communication with our Java-based prototype.

- VerbNet 1.5 & API[37]: it is an XML-based electronic repository which contains semantic information about verbs. As introduced in §5.4.1.3, it includes refinements of Levin's classification of verbs, WordNet synsets and additional information such as thematic roles or syntactic frames. A Java-based API is provided. We have used to classify and to add semantic content to our verb labelled non-taxonomic relationships.

Moreover, we have used Protégé 3.1[38] as a visualization and edition tool. Protégé represents the latest in a series of interactive tools for knowledge-system development. It facilitates the construction of knowledge bases in a principled fashion from reusable components. It allows a variety of plug-ins to facilitate customization in various dimensions. From April 2003, an OWL extension of Protégé has been developed, featuring access to description logics reasoners and graphical editors. Concretely, we have used the OWLviz and Jambalaya plug-ins to create visual representations of an OWL file (see Figure 43 and Figure 44).

---

[34] http://wordnet.princeton.edu/

[35] http://jwordnet.sourceforge.net/

[36] http://www.d.umn.edu/~tpederse/similarity.html

[37] http://verbs.colorado.edu/~mpalmer/projects/verbnet/downloads.html

[38] http://protege.stanford.edu/download/download.html

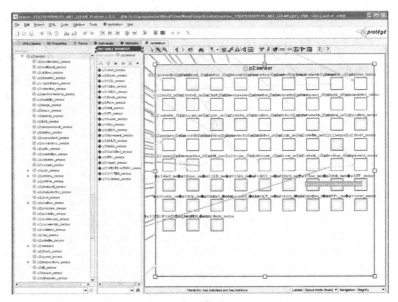

Figure 43. Taxonomic and non-taxonomic graphical visualization of the *Sensor* domain in Protégé with Jambalaya plug-in.

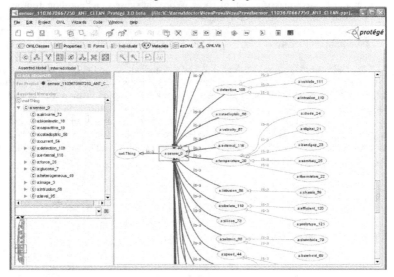

Figure 44. Taxonomic visualization for the *Sensor* domain in Protégé with OWLviz plug-in.

7.1.7 Domain ontology visualizer

Even though Protégé is certainly useful for managing ontologies, it does not scale well with big ontologies (with thousands of concepts). In consequence, due to the size of our domain ontologies, the program's performance is easily degraded and the visualization becomes confusing and overwhelming. Moreover, additional meta-information included in our domain ontologies (mainly statistics, learning traces and web resources) cannot be visualized.

For those reasons, we have developed an especially designed tool for visualizing our domain ontologies with the following features (see an example in Figure 45):

- Thanks to the efficient *ad-hoc* programming that includes a complete loading of the ontology's content on memory over especially designed data structures, it scales well with huge ontologies, maintaining a good visualization response time.
- It provides an incremental visualization centred on the domain's initial concept. In this manner, the user can recursively explore domain branches and nodes showing those parts in which he is interested. Expansion/collapse and *drag&drop* of graphical nodes are fully supported.
- It provides a two dimensional representation of taxonomic and non-taxonomic verb labelled relations.
- It used ontology meta-information to enrich the visualisation, using colours, shapes and sizes as additional visualisation dimensions to represent statistical relatedness measures for concepts and relationships.
- This quantitative meta-information also allows the implementation of visualization filters. In this manner, the user can, for example, specify a minimum relatedness value for the visualized classes and relationships, obtaining a partial visualization of the domain ontology containing only the most related entities.
- It offers direct access to the categorised list of associated Web resources (also contained in the domain ontology). In this manner the user can consult, at every moment, corresponding Web resources related to the visualized concepts.
- It has been implemented as a Web applet, offering complete integration with web-based interfaces.

The only limitations are that only an OWL subset (the part used for constructing our domain ontologies) is supported and it does not support editing ontologies.

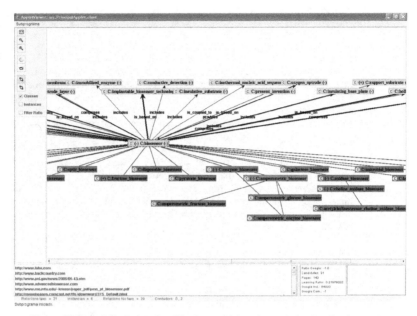

Figure 45. Especially designed and implemented domain ontology visualization applet.

7.2 Applications

Ontologies have many interesting applications. The fact of providing machine read-able semantic content to a computer program dealing with a certain domain of knowledge makes themselves an essential component to many knowledge-intensives services like:

o Information Extraction: [Buitelaar *et al.*, 2006], [Stevenson *et al.*, 05], [Maedche *et al.*, 2003].

o Information Retrieval (Semantic Search): WebKB [Martin and Eklund, 2000], SHOE [Helflin and Hendler, 2000], OntoSeek [Guarino *et al.*, 1999].

o Question Answering: [Sinha and Narayanan, 2005], [Schlobach *et al.*, 2004], Aqualog [Lopez and Motta, 2004], [Pasca and Harabagiu, 2001].

o Machine Translation: [Nirenburg *et al.*, 2004].

o Business Process Modeling: [Uschold *et al.*, 1998].

o Information Integration: [Kashyap, 1999].

o Knowledge Management (including the Semantic Web): [Fensel, 2001], [Mulholland *et al.*, 2001], [Staab and Schnurr, 2000], [Sure *et al.*, 2000].

o Software Agents: [Gluschko *et al.*, 1999], [Smith and Poulter, 1999].

In addition to the several mentioned benefits of using ontologies in knowledge related tasks, in this section we present some practical applications of our learning methodologies and obtained results for solving some real world problems. Concretely, first, we present a way to structure domain related web resources in a meaningful taxonomic way that is fully integrated with our learning methodology. Following the same principle, secondly, we introduce a way for automatically structuring web-based digital repositories using our taxonomy learning methodology. Next, we provide an example of application of our potential results to improve Web information retrieval using a knowledge-based searching platform.

7.2.1 Structuring web sites

One important application of term taxonomies in the Web environment is the meaningful organization of available web resources in order to ease the way in which the user finds and access the desired information. Hierarchical classifications are quite useful for document classification and retrieval. Users browse hierarchies of concepts and quickly access the documents associated with the different concepts.

As shown in §3.4.1, taxonomic search engines perform in that way, using a manually created (as Yahoo directory) or automatically obtained (as Clusty) structure of terms that are relevant for a domain, classifying web sites according to the available categories. That way of representing information is an improvement over classical ranked lists of webs [Magnini *et al.*, 2003], especially when the amount of returned results is overwhelming. However, as introduced in §3.4.1, the current state of both manual and automatic classification engines has serious drawbacks that impact in the quality of the results.

As our proposal performs a wide analysis over the Web in order to extract a rich repository of concepts and semantic relationships, we can take advantage of the ontology learning process. Concretely, we can classify the returned and analysed sets of web resources obtained from the search engine into that meaningful organisation. So, at the end of the process, the user will not only be able to explore relevant knowledge regarding a domain in an ontological fashion, but also to obtain the web resources that cover each concept as a topic hierarchy of web resources [Lawrie and Croft, 2003].

In our approach, each class and instance, stores the set of web sites from where it was selected (*e.g.* the *skin cancer* contains the set of web sites returned by the search engine when setting the keyword *cancer* that contain the candidate concept *skin cancer*).

Named entities are particularly interesting as, if the name is restrictive enough, it is typical than the first(s) web site(s) proposed into the hierarchical classification of web resources corresponds to the homepage for that entity.

In addition to the conceptual classification of web resources according to the discovered categories, the extra information obtained through the analysis of the web content may be useful. In some cases, we can categorize each individual web site with the context in which the covered concept is applied. Concretely, in the noun phrase-based analysis, the immediate *posterior* word for the initial keyword may bring new information about the *context of application* [Grefenstette, 1997]. In this case, those concepts are used to categorize the set of web sites associated to each class. For example, if we find that for a web site associated to the class *breast cancer* this keyword is followed by the word *research,* the web site will be categorized with this word that represents a *context of application.* This provides the user with richer information and allows him a higher level of understanding of the available resources, minimizing the selection time of the suitable ones according to his preferences.

Some examples of the proposed topic classification of web resources obtained for the *Lung Cancer* domain are shown in Figure 46.

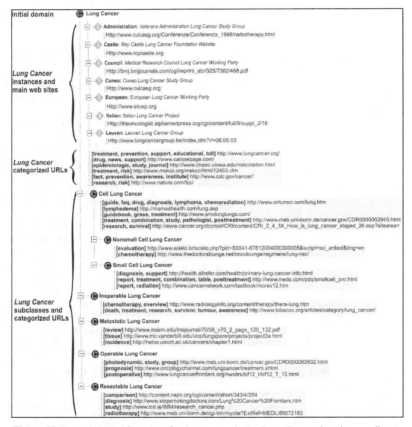

Figure 46. Example topic hierarchy of web resources in the *Lung Cancer* domain according to the discovered knowledge (instances and subclasses).

7.2.1.1 Evaluation

As a measure of comparison of the results' quality against similar available systems, we have evaluated precision and recall of our taxonomies against hand-made web directory services and taxonomic search engines (a comparison of those approaches was presented in §3.4.1). On the one hand, we have used Yahoo directory service, as it can be considered one of the most popular human-made directories. On the other hand, we have selected the taxonomic search engine Clusty that automatically presents concept hierarchies using clustering techniques. In both cases, we query the search engine and collect the returned topic categorization of web sites, considering it as a domain taxonomy. Those taxonomies are then concept-per-concept evaluated against a gold standard and/or a domain expert in the same way as described in §6.3. As a result, we can compute precision and recall for the different approaches. Local recall is only computable for our approach because rejected candidates are not available for the compared search engines.

As an example of evaluation, we present the results obtained for two well distinguished domains: a medical one (*Cancer*) and a technological one (*Biosensor*). The first one has been presented in §6.3 and evaluated against the MESH *neoplasm* classification using the same evaluation criteria. The second one is a very specific technological concept that is not found in typical semantic repositories (like WordNet). Even though the domain is highly structured, there does not exist a global consensus about the specific classification. Only the IUPAC (*International Union of Pure and Applied Chemistry*) defines some general classes and different forms of classification of biosensors according to their specific properties. Concretely, according to the specific measured entity, at least 100 different classes can be defined. This last measure has been considered when computing the global *recall*. The particular domain evaluation has been carried by a domain expert. The specific evaluation criteria is very similar to the *sensor* evaluation presented in §6.3, considering physical magnitudes and measuring principles and technologies as valid specialisations.

The evaluation of the results presented by the three approaches is presented in Figure 47 and Figure 48. Our results have been obtained with the same execution conditions presented for the taxonomic evaluation in §6.3.

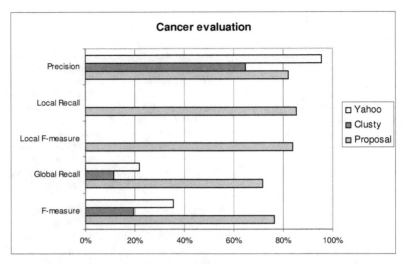

Figure 47. Evaluation results for the *Cancer* taxonomy for the proposed methodology against several taxonomic Web search engines considering the MESH standard classification.

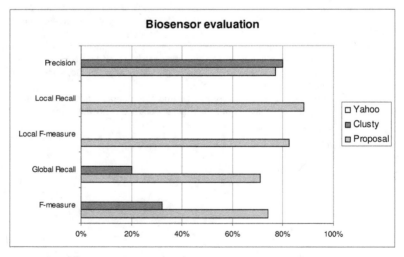

Figure 48. Evaluation results for the *Biosensor* taxonomy for the proposed methodology against a taxonomic Web search engine considering a domain expert's opinion.

Observing the figures, we can conclude that, as stated in §6.3, the correctness of our candidate selection procedure is high as the number of mistakes (incorrectly selected and rejected concepts from the candidate list), represented by the precision and local recall measures, is maintained around a 15-20% in both cases.

Compared with other web-based systems from the topic categorization point of view, our proposal surpasses easily their structuring capabilities. Comparing to the Yahoo directory, we can see that, although its *precision* is the highest, as it has been manually composed, the number of results presented (*recall*) is quite limited. Concretely, for the *cancer* domain (see Figure 47), we achieve an *F-Measure* of 76.39% that easily doubles the 35.49% presented by Yahoo. In addition, for the much more concrete technological domain, *biosensor* (see Figure 48), Yahoo is not able to provide any classification, showing the limited coverage of manual attempts of structuring information (WordNet does not contain that concept either). Compared with the automatic taxonomic search engine, Clusty, its *precision* is similar to the one presented by our proposal (both present similar mistakes due to their automatic and unsupervised nature) but its recall is very limited (it is able to return very few subclasses for the *biosensor* domain). In consequence, we achieve an *F-Measure* of 76.39% and 73.9% for the *cancer* and *biosensor* domains respectively, in comparison to the 19.45% and 32% presented by Clusty.

This comparison can give us an idea of the potential improvement that our domain structuring may bring to the topic categorization of web resources.

7.2.2 Automatic structuring of digital libraries

Digital libraries are an invaluable repository of information. Web-based digital libraries (*e.g.* Citeseer, PubMed, *etc.*) provide an environment in which the scientific production for a particular domain is stored, offering a trusted, updated and immediate repository of information. However, due to the success of these initiatives, the amount of available resources is beginning to be, so huge that the difficulty of searching and obtaining the desired information has become a serious problem in a similar way as with the whole Web but in a lower scale [Kobayashi and Takeda, 2000]. That is why the need of tools for information retrieval that ease the way in which those resources are accessed and analyzed has been growing in pair with the information itself.

Similarly to the Web, the most common way for accessing the resources is by means of the keyword-based search engines that many of these libraries incorporate. This type of search usually suffers from two problems derived from the nature of textual queries and the lack of structure in the documents: a) the difficulty to set the most appropriate and restrictive search query, and b) the tedious evaluation of the huge amount of potential resources obtained.

Taking all those points into consideration, we have designed a solution for automatic construction of structured representations (in a taxonomic fashion) of a library's content, according to the main topics discovered for a particular domain. These results are used as concrete queries for retrieving resources from the library's search engine, providing an access similar to a directory service but composed in a completely automatic and unsupervised way. The premises about the working environment and the learning bases are the same that those presented in chapters 3, 4 and 5 for learning taxonomies.

However, the difference in this case is that we consider the response time as a goal. Certainly, instead of building a domain ontology (with independence of the required time and computational resources), our purpose is to provide a usable and immediate tool for structuring digital libraries with a reasonable response time. In consequence, an especially optimised and adapted learning procedure –omitting some aspects considered in the full ontology learning- has been designed.

7.2.2.1 Constructing topic hierarchies

The base of our proposal is the analysis of the resources available for a specific domain in an electronic repository to detect the main topics covered in it. In order to perform this process automatically and unsupervisedly, two main tasks are performed: *i)* extraction of candidates that represent different topics for the domain and *ii)* evaluation of their relevance in order to select the most representative ones for constructing a taxonomy. In the same way as for the ontological case, our bases are the pattern-based linguistic analysis for extracting candidates and the statistical analyses for computing relevance measures.

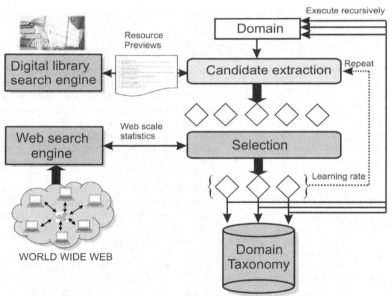

Figure 49. General schema for constructing topic taxonomies from large digital libraries.

As shown in Figure 49, the process is very similar to the taxonomic learning explained in §5.2.2. The differences introduced to improve the response time are:
- The local digital library search engine is used to retrieve resources. However, statistics are extracted by querying a general Web search engine (such as Google) in order to obtain more robust measures (based on a much wider corpus).
- Only noun phrase-based linguistic patterns are considered. The throughput of those patterns in terms of runtime *vs.* extracted knowledge is better than Hearst's ones. This is caused by the higher degree of complexity and the reduced amount of pattern instances retrieved by the later. The way of extracting candidates and computing relatedness measures is the same as described in §5.2.2.1.
- Due to the nature of the resources contained in those digital repositories (typically scientific publications), in many cases it is possible to obtain previews, abstracts or summaries of the particular resources. As we only want to extract the main subtopics for the specified domain, those pieces of text (in conjunction to the title) are typically enough for detecting them. It is usually possible to specify to the repository's search engine to show that information for each item in the results page. Only considering that page (containing dozens of resources) we can extract valuable knowledge without having to analyze large amounts of redundant information and to perform additional access to the web to download each resource.
- Even though considering the mentioned optimization, there can be thousands of potential result pages that should be accessed and processed. However, for many domains, the main interesting topics are a reduced set that can be mostly detected at the beginning of the analysis. For that reason only a reduced set of resource summaries are analyzed. As described in §5.6.2, the system automatically and dynamically decides the number of analyzed resources according to the domain's generality and the potential amount of available subtopics using learning rates as feedback measures.

At the end, we obtain a one level taxonomy that includes the main subtopics available for the particular electronic repository for the specific domain (*i.e.* a topic hierarchy of web resources [Lawrie and Croft, 2003]). Each subtopic represents a specialisation of the initial term. Querying those terms into the repository's search engine, we are able to retrieve resources corresponding to that specialisation. Considering each topic as a new query to the search engine, the user is able to browse the available resources in the same way as a directory service. In this manner, we complement the functionality of the keyword-based search engine but overcoming its main limitations (mentioned in the introduction), which derive from its lack of semantics.

In addition, for each new subtopic of the hierarchy (that at the same time, represents a new more specific domain of knowledge), the same process can be repeated recursively, obtaining a more detailed multi level taxonomy. Through this mechanism, the user can request further details (finer grained hierarchies) in the topics in which he is particularly interested.

As a final note, the characteristics that a particular electronic repository should fulfil in order to be able to apply our methodology are:
- It must have an internal search engine that allows standard query formulations. This is mandatory as it is a crucial part of the proposed methodology.

-   It should be possible to present the result in a summarized form, in terms of abstract, previews, *etc.*
-   It must allow external access to perform queries and retrieve result sets via a computer program.

7.2.2.2 Prototype

The proposed methodology has been implemented as a web interface that is placed on top of a particular digital library and provides a portal for accessing its resources in a taxonomic directory service fashion. The system controls the access to the library's search engine to retrieve resources according to the extracted topics transparently.

The interface (as shown in Figure 50) provides the main functionalities to manage searches, allowing to refine a particular subtopic or to specify different predefined settings for the mentioned selection and learning thresholds, controlling the behaviour of the system. Concretely, "*Search width*" controls several predefined learning thresholds (from 80% to 50% learning rates), resulting in *simple, medium* and *complex* searches (with better domain's coverage at the cost of increasing the processing time). On the other hand, "*Search precision*" controls the selection threshold (between 0.001 and 0.00001), allowing *high, medium* and *low* precision (with increasing recall). Results are presented as a hierarchy (on the left) in which each item represents an hyperlink to the results of the search associated to that automatically extracted subtopic into the electronic repository.

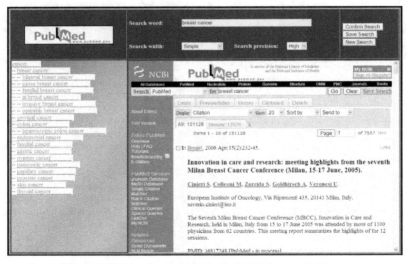

Figure 50. Web interface provided for the PubMed electronic library.

We have adapted the system to the following digital libraries (that fulfil the requisites exposed above):

- The Association for Computing Machinery[39] (ACM): ACM provides the computing field's premier Digital Library and serves its members and the computing profession with leading-edge publications, conferences, and career resources.
- PubMed[40]: PubMed is a service of the U.S. National Library of Medicine that includes over 16 million citations from MEDLINE and other life science journals for biomedical articles back to the 1950s.
- IEEE Computer Society[41]: With nearly 100,000 members, the IEEE Computer Society is the world's leading organization of computer professionals. Founded in 1946, it is the largest of the 39 societies of the IEEE.
- NASA Astrophysics Data System[42]: is a NASA-funded project which maintains three bibliographic databases containing more than 4.7 million records: Astronomy and Astrophysics, Physics, and ArXiv e-prints.

From the user's point of view, the process starts by specifying through the web interface a particular digital library from a list of supported ones. Then, a particular query and the search parameters can be specified in the top frame. Once the search is confirmed, the system executes the described taxonomy learning methodology. When the process is finished the resulting one level taxonomy is presented. By clicking over each topic the system automatically retrieves (by querying the library's search engine) the associated available resources, which are presented in the main frame. At this point the user has also the opportunity of refining a specific subtopic by selecting it and defining a new search (with the desired parameters), in order to obtain a multilevel hierarchy as shown in Figure 50. It is also possible to save and store in HTML format the taxonomies obtained through several recursive searches.

This results in a system that is able to return automatically, depending on the specific library and searching parameters, a hierarchy of topics for every possible domain from less than one minute (for small general searches useful for casual users) to half an hour (for enormously detailed searches useful for researchers or web managers).

7.2.2.3 Evaluation

The evaluation is performed in the same way as for the taxonomic case (described in §6.3). The list of subtopic candidates of the initial concept, which are finally selected or rejected, is manually evaluated. Checking the presence or absence of the extracted concepts in a domain's standard classification and comparing it to the decision of the selection procedure, we can compute the amount of correctly and incorrectly classified terms and measure the performance of the proposed algorithm.

---

[39] http://www.acm.org/

[40] http://www.ncbi.nlm.nih.gov/entrez/query .fcgi? DB=pubmed

[41] http://www.computer.org/ portal/site/ieeecs/index.jsp

[42] http://adswww.harvard.edu/

sensor
-- accelerate sensor
-- acoustic sensor
-- active sensor
-- adaptive sensor
-- air sensor
-- airborne sensor
-- amperometric sensor
-- angle sensor
-- aperture sensor
-- array sensor
-- bio sensor
-- biological sensor
-- boom sensor
-- cantilever sensor
-- capacitive sensor
-- ccd sensor
-- chemical sensor
-- chemochromic sensor
-- classification sensor
-- cmos sensor
-- common sensor
-- compact sensor
-- control sensor
-- cophasing sensor
-- current sensor
-- curvature sensor
-- detection sensor
-- disparate sensor
-- displacement sensor
-- disposable sensor
-- dual sensor
-- edge sensor
-- electrode sensor
-- elevation sensor
-- eo sensor
-- fiber sensor
-- fibre sensor
-- field sensor
-- flexible sensor
-- fluidic sensor
-- force sensor
-- gas sensor
-- glucose sensor
-- gmr sensor

-- gmti sensor
-- gpr sensor
-- gravitational sensor
-- ground sensor
-- guidance sensor
-- hall sensor
-- hartmann sensor
-- heterogeneous sensor
-- hoc sensor
-- humidity sensor
-- hybrid sensor
-- hyperspectral sensor
-- image sensor
-- inertial sensor
-- instrumentation sensor
-- ir sensor
-- ladar sensor
-- laser sensor
-- lidar sensor
-- lightweight sensor
-- loop sensor
-- lsst sensor
-- magnetic sensor
-- magnetostrictive sensor
-- mass sensor
-- measurement sensor
-- mechanical sensor
-- mems sensor
-- mesh sensor
-- metrology sensor
-- microcantilever sensor
-- micron sensor
-- microwave sensor
-- modal sensor
-- monitoring sensor
-- motion sensor
-- multifunctional sensor
-- multimodal sensor
-- multiple sensor
-- multispectral sensor
-- nanoribbon sensor
-- netted sensor
-- novel sensor
-- optical sensor

-- optoelectronic sensor
-- passive sensor
-- piezoresistive sensor
-- pixel sensor
-- pmmw sensor
-- position sensor
-- power sensor
-- predictive sensor
-- pressure sensor
-- prototype sensor
-- pulse sensor
-- radar sensor
-- radiometric sensor
-- remote sensor
-- resonator sensor
-- rf sensor
-- robotic sensor
-- satellite sensor
-- scale sensor
-- seismic sensor
-- silicon sensor
-- simulated sensor
-- single sensor
-- slope sensor
-- smart sensor
-- spectral sensor
-- spectroscopic sensor
-- static sensor
-- steerable sensor
-- tactile sensor
-- temperature sensor
-- tilt sensor
-- triangulation sensor
-- type sensor
-- typhimurium sensor
-- unattended sensor
-- undersea sensor
-- vacuum sensor
-- vector sensor
-- volumetric sensor
-- wavefront sensor
-- weather sensor
-- wireless sensor
-- zoom sensor

Figure 51. One level taxonomy of *Sensor* subtopics discovered in the NASA library with *Medium precision* and *Medium search*.

bacteria
-- acetogenic bacteria
-- acid bacteria
-- adherent bacteria
-- aerobic bacteria
-- aeruginosa bacteria
-- airborne bacteria
-- algicidal bacteria
-- ammonifying bacteria
-- anaerobic bacteria
-- anammox bacteria
-- atypical bacteria
-- avirulent bacteria
-- bacteroidales bacteria
-- beneficial bacteria
-- benthic bacteria
-- biofilm bacteria
-- bordetella bacteria
-- causative bacteria
-- cellulolytic bacteria
-- cfu bacteria
-- chimiolithoautotrophic bacteria
-- coli bacteria
-- coliform bacteria
-- colonic bacteria
-- commensal bacteria
-- culturable bacteria
-- degrading bacteria
-- ehrlichiae bacteria
-- endophytic bacteria
-- endosymbiontic bacteria
-- endosymbiotic bacteria
-- engulf bacteria
-- enteric bacteria
-- enteropathogenic bacteria
-- epiphytic bacteria
-- faecal bacteria
-- faecalis bacteria

-- fecal bacteria
-- fermentative bacteria
-- firmicutes bacteria
-- friendly bacteria
-- halophilic bacteria
-- halorespiring bacteria
-- harmful bacteria
-- heterotrophic bacteria
-- hindgut bacteria
-- hyperthermophilic bacteria
-- immobilized bacteria
-- inactivated bacteria
-- indicator bacteria
-- intestinal bacteria
-- intracellular bacteria
-- lactic bacteria
-- luminal bacteria
-- magnetotactic bacteria
-- malolactic bacteria
-- methanogene bacteria
-- methylotrophic bacteria
-- motile bacteria
-- multiresistent bacteria
-- negative bacteria
-- noncultivated bacteria
-- noncutaneous bacteria
-- nonpathogenic bacteria
-- nucleating bacteria
-- opportunistic bacteria
-- oropharyngeal bacteria
-- oxalotrophic bacteria
-- pallidum bacteria
-- pathogenic bacteria
-- periodontal bacteria
-- periodontopathic bacteria
-- periodontopathogenic bacteria
-- pfabr bacteria
-- photosynthetic bacteria

-- phototrophic bacteria
-- phytopathogenic bacteria
-- planktonic bacteria
-- pneumophila bacteria
-- positive bacteria
-- probiotic bacteria
-- pseudomonas bacteria
-- pseudotuberculosis bacteria
-- psychrophilic bacteria
-- putida bacteria
-- pylori bacteria
-- recombinant bacteria
-- resistant bacteria
-- rhizobial bacteria
-- rhizobium bacteria
-- rhizospheric bacteria
-- rumen bacteria
-- salmonella bacteria
-- shigella bacteria
-- soil bacteria
-- spoilage bacteria
-- staphylococcal bacteria
-- sulfur bacteria
-- susceptible bacteria
-- symbiotic bacteria
-- syntrophic bacteria
-- transformable bacteria
-- uncultured bacteria
-- unicellular bacteria
-- unopsonized bacteria
-- uropathogenic bacteria
-- vacuolate bacteria
-- vegetative bacteria
-- viable bacteria
-- virulent bacteria
-- wolbachia bacteria
-- yogurt bacteria

Figure 52. One level taxonomy of *Bacteria* subtopic discovered in the PudMed library with *High precision* and *Complex search*.

As an example, we present the results obtained in two well distinguished domains over their more adequate repositories: a technological one (*Sensor*) for the NASA repository, included in Figure 51, and a medical one (*Bacteria*) for the PubMed library, shown in Figure 52. Following the same concept per concept expert-based evaluation guidelines presented in §6.3, we obtain measures about *precision* and *local recall* shown in Table 48 and Table 49. The evaluation is performed for different search sizes, including other statistics such as the number of extracted topics or the runtime.

Table 48. Evaluation results and statistics for several search sizes for the *Bacteria* domain in the PudMed digital library with *High* search precision and one level search.

Bacteria Search size	Precision	Local Recall	Local F-measure	#Correct topics	#Analyzed resources	Run time
Simple	83 %	100 %	90.7%	10	20	12 sec.
Medium	87.5 %	87.5 %	87.5%	14	60	45 sec.
Complex	91.4 %	82.3 %	86.6%	107	1260	6 min.

Table 49. Evaluation results and statistics for several search sizes for the *Sensor* domain in the NASA Astrophysics digital library with *Medium* search precision and one level search.

Sensor Search size	Precision	Local Recall	Local F-measure	#Correct topics	#Analyzed resources	Run time
Simple	90 %	96.6%	93.18%	29	40	1 min
Medium	87.7%	93%	90.27%	93	240	4.5 min
Complex	77.4%	88.8%	82.7%	429	3700	33 min

Observing the results, we can see that, following the same tendency observed in the previous taxonomic evaluations (see §6.3 and §7.2.1.1), the correctness of the candidate selection procedure is high as the number of mistakes (incorrectly selected and rejected concepts from the candidate list), is maintained around a 10-20%. In this case, it is curious to see that for the *Bacteria* domain, the precision grows up in relation to the search size. However, observing the number of topics that we are able to extract for *simple* and *medium* search sizes, one can see that the number is too low (in comparison to the *Sensor* domain) to obtain trustworthy measures.

Concerning the number of correct extracted topics, as expected, it grows in relation to the number of explored resources that, at the same time, requires more runtime. Here we can see how the system adapts its behaviour to the domain generality, analysing more or less resources according to the search parameters and the feedback provided by learning rates.

As a final test, we compare these results to the ones obtained by our general taxonomy learning methodology from the whole Web (introduced in §6.3.2) using the same domain of knowledge (*Sensor,* which is characterized by the proliferation of noun phrase-based hyponyms). We have set the search precision and search size to Medium as those thresholds are the same used as default for the Web taxonomy learning process. The results of this evaluation are presented in Table 50.

Table 50. Comparison of the result quality (*precision* and *local recall*) and learning performance (*correct topics vs. runtime*) for the first level of the *Sensor* taxonomy using a NASA Astrophysics digital library search (with *Medium* search precision and *Medium* search size) against the full Web search using the default thresholds.

Sensor Search	Precision	Local Recall	Local F-measure	#Correct topics	Run-time	Topics per min.
NASA *Medium*	87.7 %	93 %	90.27%	93	4.5min.	20.6
Web *Default*	80.6%	88.2%	82.7%	106	17 min.	6.2

One can see that, as expected, using a high quality source such as a digital library against the full Web using similar executing conditions, brings better quality results (90,27% against 82,7% *local F-measures*). In addition, the especially designed analytical procedure results in a higher learning performance (20,6 *vs.* 6,2 *correct topics extracted per minute*). Even though, the general Web learning approach is not that far in terms of result quality and represents a more general approach (due to the heterogeneity of the Web) with potentially higher domain coverage (thanks to the use of Hearst patterns and the amount of available resources). The conclusion is that both approaches seem valid enough for achieving their respective goals (efficient structuring of digital libraries *vs.* learning domain ontologies).

As a summary, the presented methodology for structuring digital libraries can bring benefits for the users of a particular electronic repository. On the one hand, it allows normal users to browse and access the library's electronic resources in a directory fashion in a very immediate way (performing short searches). On the other hand, it can also represent a valuable tool for web masters or domain experts that can automatically generate indexes for structuring large digital libraries (executing exhaustive searches).

7.2.3 Ontology-based web search

In the last years it has been argued that the performance of a web search engine can be improved by using ontologies [Fensel, 2001]. They provide a semantic ground that can help to sort out web pages with relevant information about a concept from those containing data with just syntactic similarities to the concept.

In order to demonstrate the suitability of our domain ontologies in guiding semantic web searches, we have designed an integrated approach for web information retrieval and filtering. The domain ontologies needed for this process are the hierarchical tree structure containing classes (concepts) and main features (attributes) that we are able to obtain.

The system uses two previously developed tools for knowledge acquisition and information retrieval. The first one is the domain ontology learning prototype system presented in §7.1. Its results can be used as input for the system described in [Moreno *et al.*, 2004], which implements methods and techniques that allow the use of the information contained in the domain ontology in order to move from a purely syntactic keyword-based web search to a semantically grounded search. The final result is a set of filtered, ranked and classified web resources according to the concepts contained in the domain ontology. As the processing required to treat with a huge repository like the Web is a very time consuming task, the full system is presented in a distributed approach. Again, in order to provide a scalable solution, we have used the agent paradigm [Wooldridge, 2002] as the implementation approach.

Following the same philosophy that characterizes our research, the full system (described ontology learning and ontology-based web retrieval) operates in a fully unsupervised, automatic and domain independent way.

7.2.3.1 Ontology-driven web information retrieval

In this section, the ontology-based Web information retrieval system [Moreno *et al.*, 2004; Bocio *et al.*, 2005] is introduced. Its aim is to find the web pages which are relevant to a given domain of interest using a *domain ontology* as input (manually or automatically composed). It is required that the ontology contains concepts of the search domain and features of each one. It should represent concepts as classes in a hierarchical class-subclass structure, and the features as slots of the classes. A class and all its ancestors define a *class path*. Each class contains its own slots and it inherits all those which are defined in the ancestors.

For instance, Figure 53 depicts a manually composed domain ontology about a subset of machine learning technologies where the classes are labelled as C and the slots as S. The names of the classes are used to find the web pages which are related to the search domain, and the names of the slots in a class are used to evaluate to what extent the retrieved pages have interesting information. The main idea is that the retrieved web pages are textual instances of the concepts, but conditioned to the meaning of the concept in the whole ontology. That means that the same concept in a different ontology would produce different results because it is in a different context.

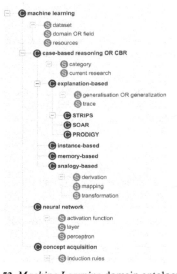

Figure 53. *Machine Learning* domain ontology.

The ontology-based web retriever is designed as an autonomous multi-agent system that can be deployed as a complement of the ontology learning multi-agent system described in §7.1. In that case, the first one receives the output of the second one in the form of a domain ontology that fulfils the requirements described above. According to the available knowledge, different types of agents are created and managed dynamically (created, configured and finalized) in function of the execution requirements at each moment.

In more detail, the search process is composed by several stages: *splitting* the domain ontology, *retrieving* the web pages, *rating* the retrieved pages, and *joining* the results. Those tasks are performed co-ordinately, as shown in Figure 54, by three types of agents: a *Coordinator Agent* (CA), a *Weight Agent* (WA) and some *Internet Agents* (IA).

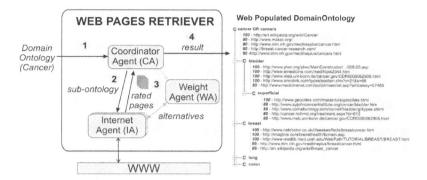

Figure 54. Agent-based ontology driven web retriever platform. The example results correspond to the *Cancer* domain.

The process starts when the automatically acquired domain ontology is received by CA (step 1). Then, it performs the *splitting* stage, in which the ontology is divided in smaller parts. Concretely, each class of the domain ontology defines a smaller ontology which contains not only the class itself but also its class path; this sort of ontology is called *query ontology*. The CA distributes those sub-ontologies among the available IAs (step 2).

Each IA uses the names of the classes in the query ontology as keywords to define a *query* into a standard keyword-based search engine. For each of these queries, a set of web pages is *retrieved*.

If the number of web pages does not reach an expected value (if the particular query is excessively restrictive), the system raises an additional process to increase the number of pages. In this case, IAs can request the help of the WA. This agent is able to find less constrained sets of keywords that can be used by IAs to find more pages. This process is based in a weighted expansion tree that is built up from the initial query, as Figure 55 depicts for the class STRIPS. The building process is as it follows: each node of the tree is expanded with sub-nodes representing queries where one of the keywords in the parent query has been removed, except the keyword that represents the name of the current class.

For instance, the right bottom side of Figure 55 shows the list of the keywords that are in the query related to the class STRIPS. Observe that only the initial letters of the keywords are displayed in the figure. When one of the antecedents of STRIPS (i.e. *"machine learning"*, *"case-based reasoning"*, or *"explanation-based"*) is removed from the initial query, the nodes A, B, C are respectively expanded. The figure also shows how the keyword *"STRIPS"*, represented by the letter S, is in all three sub-nodes. Finally, the numbers in the nodes indicate the amount of web pages that the search system can find using all the keywords in the node.

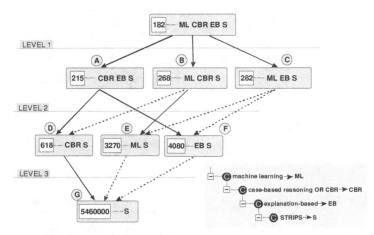

Figure 55. Best First search implemented by the Weight Agent to retrieve additional web sites.

Once the required amount of web resources have been obtained, the IA uses the semantic information of its subontology (class attributes) to *rank* these pages. Concretely, all the obtained web sites are rated according to their relevance within the query ontology (20).

$$R_c(p, A) = \frac{number\,of\,attributes\,found\,(p, A)*100}{total\,number\,of\,attributes(A)} \tag{20}$$

If p stands for the recovered web page for a class C whose rate is being calculated, and A is the set of attributes (inherited or not) of C, the *attributes found* are the ones in A that appear in the page p. $R_C(p,A)$ defines the relevance of the web page p with respect to the class C and, after normalising it in the range [0,1], it is used to rank the retrieved pages.

Once the process is finished, the IA sends the rated and ranked list of web pages to the CA (step 3). Then, the CA incorporates them into the domain ontology. When all the IAs have returned their partial results, all the pages obtained for all the classes in the domain ontology are *joined* in a single structure. It contains each single page as an instance of the class in the ontology. This is presented to the user as the final result (step 4). Concretely, for each automatically acquired concept, a set of 2-tuple formed by an URL and a rate is presented. This last value indicates the degree of relevance of the particular URL and its associated concept according to the ranking measure employed during the retrieval and ranking process. Note that due to a specificity policy implemented, no redundant results between classes and subclasses are presented.

7.2.3.2 Evaluation

As the present proposal is an integration of two previously developed tools, the quality of the final results depends on the performance of each methodology. Regarding the evaluation of the taxonomies obtained by the first module, a discussion is offered in §6.3. With respect to the second module, in [Moreno *et al.*, 2004] several evaluations are presented in different technological domains, starting from ontologies composed manually by experts.

The full platform has been tested in technical domains such as medicine, biotechnology and computer science. The evaluation has been performed by comparing the results against the web search engine used during the analysis (Google). More concretely, for the list of web sites retrieved for each automatically discovered concept, two users were requested to rate each web site according to their degree of interest for the particular domain with a value between 0 and 100. The same process was repeated for the first web sites returned by Google when manually querying the same acquired concept. These ratings indicate which approach returns, in average, the most interesting set of web resources for the particular domain.

As an example, in Figure 57 and Figure 56, expert's rating for our results against Google for a pair of concepts of the cancer domain is presented.

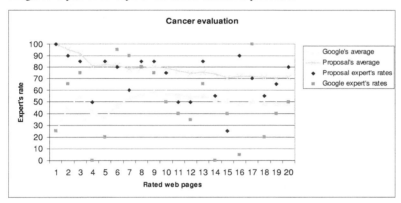

Figure 56. User's ratings for the first 20 web pages returned by our approach against the ones retrieved by Google for the *Cancer* concepts.

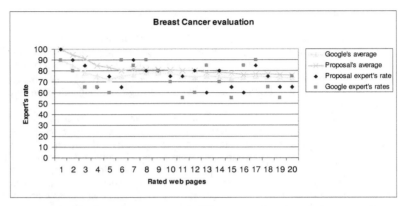

Figure 57. User's ratings for the first 20 web pages returned by our approach against the ones retrieved by Google for the *Breast Cancer* concept.

One can see that, for the most general concept (*cancer*), the quality of our results overpasses significantly, in average, the ones presented by Google. This behaviour has been observed for several tested domains and it is caused by the higher contextualization that the presented approach can apply to the web sites analysis thanks to the automatically acquired knowledge for the domain. Observing the average rating for a more concrete concept (*breast cancer*), we can see that the quality of the returned web sites by each system is very similar. In this case, the search is, in both cases, contextualized enough to retrieve high quality resources.

As a conclusion, as other authors has previously argued [Fensel, 2001], the use of knowledge (domain ontologies) can improve the classical web search, especially for general queries. In addition, the nature of our ontologies makes them adequate for those purposes as they have been directly extracted from the Web content.

7.3 Summary

In this chapter we have offered a detailed overview on how our different knowledge acquisition methodologies have been implemented in a distributed fashion. The employed programming paradigm based on agents is suitable to define the highly flexible and scalable system that our approach requires. Studying the computation complexity, one can see how a parallel approach is very suitable –and necessary- to obtain a good performance in wide domains. We have shown how our system is able to scale well when enough computational resources (in function on the number of tasks to execute) are provided.

Moreover, several applications of the proposed methodologies and their potential results have been presented. In addition to the concrete applications introduced up to this moment, other interesting aspects can be mentioned.

On the one hand, the domain ontology provides a structured representation of the knowledge associated to a certain domain. In this sense it can be used in several knowledge-demanding tasks that require interoperability such us electronic commerce, distributed information systems such us multi-agent systems, Web Services and the mentioned Semantic Web [Berners-lee *et al.*, 2001]. Moreover, intelligent knowledge guided methodologies for searching information from unstructured sources [Magnin *et al.*, 2002; Alani *et al.*, 2003; Sheth, 2003] can also use the results as the knowledge base for performing semantic searches.

On the other hand, topic hierarchies of the web resources considered according to the extracted knowledge represent an improvement over the classical searching for web resources [Lawrie and Croft, 2003]. This allows the user to access the desired information in a much direct way even if he is not an expert on the concrete domain. In this sense, it can be used as a tool for e-learning tasks where a student without specific knowledge in a certain domain can explore it in an interactive way, selecting new concepts, discovering important terms and how they are related and, finally, accessing concrete websites that contain specific information.

Aside from improving the access to web resources, the semantic structure extracted from the Web can help to improve the classical searching process by allowing query refinements according to the discovered concept hierarchy [Pasca, 2005].

Chapter 8

Conclusions and future work

Up to this moment, we have described in detail all the developed learning methodologies, the evaluation tests performed, the implementation and the possible applications of the methods and results. In this final chapter, we provide a final summary of the work and present the conclusions from the general knowledge acquisition point of view and from the concrete perspective of each ontology learning method. In the last section, we suggest several lines of future research about different open issues presented in previous chapters and give some ideas on how they can be tackled.

8.1 Summary

The main aim of the present work has been to develop methods for acquiring knowledge from the Web in order to compose a domain ontology. The most important and novel point is the complete integration with this environment, offering an especially adapted, automatic, unsupervised and domain independent approach that covers the main aspects of the ontology learning process (concepts, taxonomies, instances and labelled non-taxonomic relationships).

Many learning methodologies from different information repositories have been developed in the past, but it is not until now that authors are starting to focus their efforts on the Web. This environment adds new troubles to the information processing, derived from the *untrustworhiness*, *size*, *noise* and *lack of structure* of web resources. However, other characteristics as the *redundancy* and the existence of *web search engines* may help to tackle this environment. Regarding the first point, redundancy can allow us to infer information relevance, manage untrustworthiness and develop lightweight analytical approaches that can be adequate and scalable for the size of the Web. In relation to the second point, web searchers classically conceived as a final user interface for accessing web resources hide lots of potential regarding the inference of information distribution. Valuable web scale statistics can be extracted efficiently if adequate queries are performed. This can save us from analysing large amounts of resources and help us to obtain scalable learning methodologies. Moreover, their lack of any semantic content makes them suitable for any domain of knowledge. This is especially interesting in dynamic technological domains.

In addition, as we want to obtain results for these specific and concrete domains, in many situations, we will not be able to start from any predefined knowledge that many methodologies employ. This is why we have developed a completely unsupervised and automatic methodology that makes the minimum assumptions about previous knowledge or information structure. In order to achieve good results and learning performance following those premises, we have opted for an incremental learning methodology: several learning procedures are performed iteratively and potentially concurrently, using the knowledge acquired up to a moment as a bootstrap. Introduced feedback mechanisms allow a certain degree of self-control, including a dynamic adaptation of the size of the analysed corpus in function of the domain's productiveness and a management of the finalisation of the learning process.

Finally, manual and automatic evaluation procedures for each learning step have been designed. They provide encouraging results on the suitability of our approach for learning ontological entities in several well distinguished domains.

Taking all of these characteristics into consideration, we believe that our proposal can represent a new and interesting addition over the current state of the art of the technology in the ontology learning area.

8.2 Conclusions

Considering the performed research, the developed methodologies and the obtained and evaluated results, we have extracted the following general conclusions:

- As other authors have enounced in the past [Brill, 2003; Cilibrasi and Vitanyi, 2004; Etzioni *et al.*, 2005], we expect to have contributed in considering the Web as a valid repository for performing knowledge acquisition tasks. In fact, we have developed learning methods covering the main steps of the ontology construction process especially adapted to this environment, obtaining reliable results.

- Available web IR tools (web search engines) can be extensively exploited to aid the ontology learning process. Through the development, we have presented ideas and methods for constructing suitable queries in function of the knowledge already acquired and the specific learning stage. As a result, we can dynamically obtain a corpus of resources to analyse at each moment and very robust web scale statistics about Web information distribution.

- Several knowledge acquisition techniques can be adapted to the Web. Considering the characteristics introduced in chapter 3 and our goals, the employed techniques should be simple and lightweight. Concretely, the use of linguistic patterns fits very well with the unsupervised nature of our learning approach and can be adapted to the limited query expressiveness offered by web search engines (our massive and automatic IR tools). Statistical analyses used to infer semantics (such as taxonomic relationships or concepts' relatedness) are very suitable as we have an enormous and heterogeneous repository of information and a way to obtain robust measures in a very immediate way. Finally, lightweight natural language analytical procedures are needed in order to *i)* maintain the domain independence of our learning approach (even limited to English written texts) and *ii)* scale well when dealing with huge amounts of noisy information resources.

- When developing automatic and unsupervised approaches, self-control mechanisms are required. We have included feedback about how the learning process evolves and bootstrapping techniques applied over fine grained learning steps. Both can improve the learning performance.

  Other conclusions related with our developed methodologies are:
- In relation to the taxonomy learning, widely used Hearst's and noun phrase-based patterns can be combined to improve the final results. Concretely, on the one hand, Hearst's based extractions *precision* can be improved with noun phrase-based extractions by minimizing the semantic ambiguity. On the other hand, noun phrase-based extractions *recall* can be improved by incorporating the more general Hearst's extractions.
- The classical approach for taxonomy learning using linguistic patterns and statistical analyses can be also applied to the much less studied non-taxonomic learning. In this case, verb phrases can be considered as domain related patterns used to compose IR queries and compute statistical measures. The semantics of the relationships between concepts are expressed by the particular verb phrase.
- Almost any stage of the knowledge acquisition process (taxonomic and non-taxonomic learning and semantic disambiguation) requiring an estimation of the information distribution, can be addressed in an unsupervised way with a carefully designed and tuned statistical score, computed directly by querying a web search engine, as those presented in chapter 5.
- Regarding the evaluation, the use of WordNet as the base from which to develop automatic procedures can be a valid approach. However, it has been observed during the evaluation that its coverage for certain domains (in relation to glosses, synsets, semantic links, *etc.*) can be too limited to extract reliable conclusions.
- When developing highly distributed systems with requirements of flexibility and dynamicity, the use of multi-agent systems can be a suitable high level implementation paradigm. They certainly offer some advantages over other approaches such as the dynamic management of working threads or the highly elaborated execution framework, including mobility and communication capabilities that ease the development of complex distributed systems.

8.3 Future work

In this section, we describe several future lines of research and present some preliminary ideas on how they can be tackled. Regarding the learning process, some issues can be addressed in order to improve the final results:
- The recall of the taxonomy learning process may be improved if additional linguistic patterns for hyponymy detection are applied. Concretely, some authors [Agichtein and Gravano, 2000; Iwanska *et al.*, 2000; Pasca, 2004; Snow *et al.*, 2004] have been working in refining Heart's patterns. However, many of the new regular expressions define very subtle variations or specific forms rarely used. In consequence, it should be studied if including additional concrete patterns to the taxonomic learning results in a final improvement or it only overheads the learn-

ing process. In our opinion, the basic but general pattern set used until this moment (introduced in §4.1) is enough for obtaining good coverage (in function of the established learning thresholds) thanks to the size and redundancy of information in the Web (as observed during the learning rates analysis in §5.6.2).

- If one is particularly interested in the retrieval of instances used for ontology population, the proposed method for detecting named entities based on linguistic patterns and capitalization heuristics can be more widely developed. Concretely, it can be executed a posteriori of the ontology learning process over the different taxonomically and non-taxonomically related classes and in conjunction with a search engine that properly distinguishes capitalized terms in order to retrieve additional named entities. Moreover, at this moment, the identification of the full entity name (in those cases in which it is composed by several terms) is left to the named entity detection package used during the evaluation (see §6.4). Contributions to solve this last issue can be developed with novel algorithms [Downey *et al.*, 2007]. In any case, the particular instance semantic should be taken into consideration by, for example, analysing named-entity's context for the particular ontology, in order to make a contribution to the ontology population field.

- The non-taxonomic learning can be improved if verb phrases (used as domain dependent pattern) are further processed. Concretely, due to the diversity of ways of expressing a particular verb phrase (in function of the verbal tense or subject number), some valid candidate extractions may be omitted due to the too restrictive matching policy implemented by keyword-based search engines. In this case, a procedure to properly conjugate verb phrases in common forms, applying each of them to the retrieval of candidates by constructing different queries, may aid to increase the quantity of extracted knowledge.

- The information extracted from VerbNet and associated to the verb phrases during the non-taxonomic learning can be used to infer the semantics of the relations [Gómez and Segami, 2007]. We may detect verbs that have a similar "meaning" or express the same "kind" of relationship. In addition, thematic roles may be exploited to interpret in which way the subject or the object of the relationships is affected. All that information can then be modeled in the ontology using more advanced ontological formalisms such as property characteristics or class restrictions. However this is certainly an intricate task and may require the use of more complex analyses to achieve the proper natural language understanding.

- As has been commented in previous sections, the semantic disambiguation methods can be integrated in the full learning process. On the one hand, synonym sets can be used to expand the search to other web resources that were not potentially retrieved by the keyword-based search engine and a specific domain keyword. This could improve the *recall* of the final results when dealing with narrow domains where a limited amount of resources is retrieved (see in Figure 58 an example of taxonomies retrieved for synonyms discovered for the *cancer* domain). On the other hand, polysemy disambiguation may aid to improve the *precision* of the final taxonomy in polysemic domains by presenting a more structured hierarchy with clustered classes according to superclass senses. However the final impact on the results of those extra processing stages should be considered carefully. On the one hand, for the first case, even though the final recall can be higher, the noise introduced by not truly equivalent terms can affect negatively to the precision. On the other hand, for the second case, the precision improvement may be questionable when dealing with non well-differentiated senses.

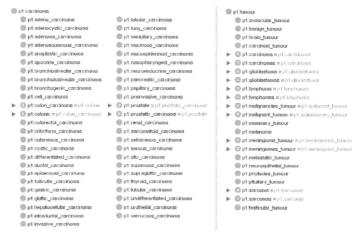

Figure 58. Results obtained for the first level of the taxonomy of the *Cancer* domain using two of its automatically discovered synonyms (*carcinoma* on the left, *tumour* on the right) with the same execution conditions.

- Even though we are able to extract some domain features from the redundancies observed in the taxonomy of classes, this is only a first approach for detecting class attributes. Class attributes are rarely considered in ontology learning techniques due to their potential complexity [Gómez-Pérez *et al.*, 2004] even though they can certainly enrich the semantics of the corresponding class. Attribute detection can be addressed by developing especially adapted Web methodologies in order to exploit semi-structured data associated to domain classes such as itemizes, lists, tables or indexes [Popescu and Etzioni, 2005].

- More efforts can be put in the future regarding the evaluation of results. More expert opinions can be requested to further evaluate the results, including other domains or verb labels. Other tests over standard reduced repositories can be performed in order to compare the learning performance with other approaches.

- The implemented multi-agent system can be improved. On the one hand, more fine grained tasks may be defined (*e.g.* one for each phase of the learning process) and modeled over different agents, improving the parallelism. On the other hand, we can exploit agent communication capabilities. In this last case, in addition to the task coordination, they may exchange partial results or retrieved web resources in order to avoid redundant analyses or repeat web requests already performed. Even though this may represent an improvement in relation to the runtime spent in accessing, retrieving and analyzing web resources, the overhead introduced by the inter-agent communication should be considered.

Regarding the applications of the proposed methodologies and results, some interesting cases can be researched:

- One of the most important applications of domain ontologies consists on bringing machine readable semantic content that web documents lack by employing annotation. This will help to achieve the paradigm of semantic web search proposed by the Semantic Web [Berners-Lee *et al*, 2001]. However, even if representative semantic structures can be obtained in an automatic and efficient way, the labor of annotating web documents is usually performed manually [Kahan *et al.*, 2001]. In our case, as domain ontologies are obtained directly from the analysis of web documents, a certain degree of automatic annotation could be performed directly during at the construction stage. For example, if we have discovered instances (as named entities) for a specific class, we can annotate the web resources from which those instances have been extracted according to the specific class to which they belong. Methodologies for annotating automatically web content (the web resources analysed) can be studied. In addition, once the semantic structure is obtained and the annotation methodology developed, it should not be difficult to extend the annotation to other web resources.

- From a more general point of view, results obtained from web annotation can be used to bring a further understanding of the domain by means of reasoning. On the one hand, a domain ontology can be populated using discovered annotated entities. On the other hand, ontology semantics can be used to perform inference over those individuals, resulting in additional knowledge not directly discovered.

- Once the reliability of our learning methodologies has been evaluated in bringing structure to electronic repositories such as digital libraries, and in comparison with other available approaches (such as taxonomic search engines), it could be also interesting to apply them to wider environments such as the automatic composition of web directory services.

- It could be interesting to test from the final user point of view the advantages of structured representation of web resources that we are able to obtain in relation to the classical way of presenting results by a web search engine. For example, we can measure the efficiency of the user's searching for information of a specific domain using those two different approaches.

- In order to test the real performance of our learning approaches and applications, it would be very interesting to have direct access to a web search engine IR database without limitations. This will minimize the delays and overheads introduced by the web queries requested during the learning (that represent a time interval several orders of magnitude higher than the time required to perform the analysis of the web content). Even though we try to minimize active waits using a distributed parallel approach, they still represent an important waste of time.

- From another point of view, detecting named-entities can be a useful tool for performing market studies, retrieving important companies and organisations and their associated web resources, which are related to a certain aspect of the knowledge domain. Moreover, those instances are selected without classical restrictions (*e.g.* "organisations", "persons"...) allowing to detect all kinds of entities and events.

- Several executions in different moments for the same domain using the same parameters, can allow us to study the evolution of the information in that domain, and detect for example that a new concept has potentially appeared. This aspect can support a certain degree of high level question answering of the kind of "which items have appeared in the domain?", "which ones are now more relevant than before?", "which seem to be obsolete?", *etc.*

Bibliography

[Abecker *et al.*, 1999] Abecker, A., Bernardi, A., and Sintek, M.: Proactive knowledge delivery for enterprise knowledge management. In Proceedings of the 11th Conference on Software Engineering and Knowledge Engineering. Kaiserslautern, Germany, June 17-19 1999. 103-117.

[Adelberg, 1998] Adelverg, B.: NoDoSE: A tool for semi-automatically extracting semistructured data from text documents. In Proceedings of SIGMOD'98 Conference. 1998. 283-294.

[Agichtein and Gravano, 2000] Agichtein, E. and Gravano, L.: Snowball: Extracting relations from large plaintext collections. In Proceedings of the 5th ACM International Conference on Digital Libraries (DL-00), San Antonio, Texas, 2000. 85-94.

[Agirre and Rigau, 1995] Agirre, E. and Rigau, G.: A Proposal for Word Sense Disambiguation using Conceptual Distance. In: Proceedings of the International Conference on Recent Advances in NLP. RANLP'95. 1995. 16-22.

[Agirre *et al.*, 2000] Agirre, E., Ansa, O., Hovy, E., and Martinez, D.: Enriching very large ontologies using the WWW. In Proceedings of the Workshop on Ontology Construction of the European Conference of AI (ECAI-00). Berlin, Germany, 2000.

[Agrawal *et al.*, 1993] Agrawal, R., Imielinksi, T. and Swami, A.: Mining association rules between sets of items in large databases. In Proceedings of the ACM SIGMOD Conference on Management of Data. 1993. 207-216.

[Ahmad *et al.*, 2003] Ahmad, K., Tariq, M., Vrusias, B. and Handy, C.: Corpus-based thesaurus construction for image retrieval in specialist domains. In Proceedings of the 25th European Conference on Advances in Information Retrieval (ECIR). 2003. 502-510.

[Alani *et al.*, 2003] Alani, H., Kim, S., Millard, D., Eal, M., Hall, W., Lewis, H, and Shadbolt, N.: Automatic Ontology-Based Knowledge Extraction from Web Documents. IEEE Intelligent Systems, IEEE Computer Society, 2003. 14-21.

[Alfonseca and Manandhar, 2002] Alfonseca, E. and Manandhar, S.: An unsupervised method for general named entity recognition and automated concept discovery. In Proceedings of the 1st International Conference on General WordNet, Mysore, India. 2002.

[Alfonseca and Rodríguez, 2002] Alfonseca, E., and Rodríguez, P.: Automatically Generating Hypermedia Documents depending on User Goals, Workshop on Document Compression and Synthesis in Adaptive Hypermedia Systems, AH-2002, Málaga, Spain. 2002.

[Arocena and Mendelzon, 1998] Arocena A. and Mendelzon A.O.: Restructuring documents, databases, and Webs. In Proceedings of ICDE'98 Conference. 1998. 24-33.

[Aussenac-Gilles and Seguela, 2000] Aussenac-Gilles, N. and Seguela, P.: Les relations séman-
tiques: du linguistique au formel. Cahiers de grammaire, N° spécial sur la linguistique de corpus, 25. Toulouse : Presse de l'UTM. 2000. 175-198.

[Aussenac-Gilles et al., 2000] Aussenac-Gilles, N., Biébow, B. and Szulman, S.: Corpus
Analysis for Conceptual Modelling. Workshop on Ontologies and Text, Knowledge Engineering and Knowledge Management: Methods, Models and Tools, 12th International Conference EKAW'2000, Juan-les-pins, France, Springer-Verlag. 2000. 13-20.

[Bachimont et al., 2002] Bachimont, B., Isaac, A. and Troncy, R.: Semantic commitment for
designing ontologies: a proposal. In A. Gomez-Perez and V.R. Benjamins (Eds.): EKAW
2002, LNAI 2473. 2002. 114–121.

[Bachimont, 2000] Bachimont, B.: Engagement sémantique et engagement ontologique: con-
ception et réalisation d'ontologies en ingénierie des connaissances. In Ingénierie des Connias-
sances: Evolutions récentes et nouveaux défis, Eyrolles, 2000.

[Banko et al., 2007] Banko, M., Cafarella, M., Soderlan, S., Broadhead, M. and Etzioni, O.:
Open Information Extraction from the Web. In proceedings of IJCAI 2007. 2007. 2670-2676.

[Baugartner et al., 2001] Baugartner, R., Flesca S. and Gottlob, G.: Visual Web information
extraction with Lixto. In Proceedings of VLDB'01 Conference. 2001. 119-128.

[Berners-lee et al., 2001] Berners-lee, T., Hendler, J. and Lassila, O.: The semantic web. Scientific American. 2001.

[Berry et al., 1995] Berry, M.W., Dumais, S.T. and Letsche, T.A.: Computational Methods for
Intelligent Information Access. Proceedings of Supercomputing '95, San Diego, California,
1995.

[Bhat et al., 2004] Bhat, V., Oates, T., Shanbhag, V. and Nicholas, C.: Finding aliases on the
web using latent semantic analysis. Data Knowledge & Engineering 49. 2004. 129-143.

[Bisson et al., 2000] Bisson, G., Nedellec, C. and Cañamero, D.: Designing Clustering Methods for Ontology Building. The Mo'K Workbench. In S. Staab, A. Maedche, C. Nedellec, P.
WiemerHasting (eds.), Proceedings of the Workshop on Ontology Learning, 14th European
Conference on Artificial Intelligence, ECAI'00, Berlin, Germany. August 20-25, 2000. 13-
19.

[Bocio et al., 2005] Bocio, J., Isern, D., Moreno, A., Riaño, D.: Semantically Grounded Information Search on the WWW. In: Artificial Intelligence Research and Development, Vol. 100.
IOS Press. 2005. 349–356.

[Borst, 1997] Borst, W.N.: Construction of Engineering Ontologies. Centre for Telemática and
Information Technology, University of Tweety. Enschede, The Netherlands. 1997.

[Borthwick, 1999] Borthwick, A.: A Maximum Entropy Approach to Named Entity Recognition. Phd. thesis. New York University. 1999.

[Brewster et al., 2001] Brewster, C., Ciravegna, F. and Wilks, Y.: Knowledge Acquisition for
Knowledge Management: Position Paper. In Proceeding of the IJCAI-2001 Workshop on
Ontology Learning held in conjunction with the 17th International Conference on Artificial
Intelligence (IJCAI-01), Seattle, August, 2001.

[Brewster, 2002] Brewster, C.: Techniques for Automated Taxonomy Building: Towards Ontologies for Knowledge Management. In Proceedings of the 5th Annual CLUK Research Col-
loquium. Leeds, 2002.

[Brewster et al., 2004] Brewster, C., Alani, H, Dasmahapatra, S and Wilks, Y.: Data-driven Ontology Evaluation. In Proceedings of the 4th International Conference on Language Resources and Evaluation. 2004.

[Brill *et al.*, 2001] Brill, E., Lin, J., Banko, M. and Dumais, S.: Data-intensive Question Answering. In Proceedings of the Tenth Text Retrieval Conference TREC-2001. 2001. 393-400.

[Brill, 2003] Brill, E.: Processing Natural Language without Natural Language Processing. In Proceedings of CICLing 2003, LNCS 2588. 2003. 360–369.

[Budanitsky and Hirst, 2001] Budanitsky, A. and Hirst, G: Semantic distance in WordNet: An experimental, application-oriented evaluation of five measures. NAACL01. 2001.

[Buitelaar, et al., 2003] Buitelaar, P., Olejnik, D. And Sintek, M.: A protégé plug-in for ontology extraction from text based on linguistic analysis. In Proceedings of the International Semantic Web Conference (ISWC). 2003.

[Buitelaar *et al.*, 2005] Buitelaar, P., Cimiano, P., Magnini, B. (eds): Ontology Learning from Text: Methods, Evaluation and Applications Frontiers in Artificial Intelligence and Applications Series, Vol. 123, IOS Press, July 2005.

[Buitelaar *et al.*, 2005b] Buitelaar, P., Cimiano, P., Grobelnik, M. and Sintek, M.: Ontology Learning from Text. Tutorial at ECML/PKDD, Oct. 2005, Porto, Portugal.

[Buitelaar *et al.*, 2006] Buitelaar, P., Cimiano, P., Racioppa, S., Siegel, M.: Ontology-based information extraction with SOBA. In Proceedings of LREC 2006. 2006. 2321-2324.

[Bunescu, 2003] Bunescu, R.: Associative Anaphora Resolution: A Web-Based Approach. In Proceedings of the EACL-2003 Workshop on the Computational Treatment of Anaphora, Budapest, Hungary, April, 2003. 47-52.

[Burton-Jones *et al.*, 2003] Burton-Jones, A., Storey, V.C., Sugumaran, V. and Purao, S.: A Heuristic-based methodology for Semantic Augmentation of User Queries on the Web. In Proceedings of Conceptual modelling- ER 2003. LNCS 2813. Chicago, USA. 2003. 476-489.

[Byrd and Ravin, 1999] Byrd, R. and Ravin, Y.: Identifying and extracting relations from text. In NLDB'99 - 4th International Conference on Applications of Natural Language to Information Systems. 1999.

[CACM, 2002] CACM, Special issue on ontology. Communications of ACM, 45(2). 2002.

[Califf and Mooney, 1999] Califf M.E. and Mooney, R.J.: Relational learning of pattern-match rules for information extraction. In Proceedings of AAAI'99. 1999. 328-334.

[Calvo and Gelbukh, 2003] Calvo, H. and Gelbukh, A.: Improving Prepositional Phrase Attachment Disambiguation Using the Web as Corpus. LNCS 2905. 2003. 604–610.

[Cameron, 2002] Cameron, I.: Web-based cape systems -now and the future-. In CAPE Forum, Tarragona, Spain, 2002.

[Caraballo, 1999] Caraballo, S.A.: Automatic construction of a hypernym-labeled noun hierarchy from text. In Proceedings of the 37th Annual Meeting of the Association for Computational Linguistics. 1999. 120-126.

[Chaelandar and Grau, 2000] Chaelandar, G. and Grau, B.: SVETLAN' - A System to Classify Words in Context. In S. Staab, A. Maedche, C. Nedellec, P. Wiemer-Hastings (eds.) Proceedings of the Workshop on Ontology Learning, 14th European Conference on Artificial Intelligence ECAI'00, Berlin, Germany, August 20-25. 2000. 19-24.

[Charniak, 1999] Charniak, E. and Berland, M.: Finding parts in very large corpora. In Proceedings of the 37th Annual Meeting of the ACL. 1999. 57-64.

[Church et al, 1991] Church, K.W., Gale, W., Hanks, P. and Hindle, D.: Using Statistics in Lexical Analysis. In: Uri Zernik (ed.), Lexical Acquisition: Exploiting On-Line Resources to Build a Lexicon. New Jersey: Lawrence Erlbaum. 1991. 115-164.

[Cilibrasi and Vitanyi, 2004] Cilibrasi, R. and Vitanyi, P.M.B.: Automatic meaning discovery using Google. Available at: http://xxx.lanl.gov/abs/cs.CL/0412098. 2004.

[Cilibrasi and Vitanyi, 2006] Cilibrasi, R. and Vitanyi, P.M.B.: The Google Similarity Distance. IEEE Transaction on Knowledge and Data Engineering. 19(3). 2006. 370-383.

[Cimiano et al., 2004] Cimiano, P., Pick, A., Schmidt, L. and Staab, S.: Learning Taxonomic Relations from Heterogeneous Sources of Evidence. In Procedings of the ECAI 2004 Ontology Learning Workshop. 2004.

[Cimiano and Staab, 2004] Cimiano, P. and Staab, S.: Learning by Googling. SIGKDD Explorations, 6(2). 2004. 24-33.

[Cimiano and Wenderoth, 2005] Cimiano, P. and Wenderoth, J.: Automatically Learning Qualia Structure from the Web. In Proceedings of the ACL Workshop on Deep Lexical Acquisition. 2005. 28-37.

[Cimiano, 2006] Cimiano, P.: Text Analysis and Ontologies. Summer School on Multimedia Semantics. 2006.

[Ciravegna 2001] Ciravegna, F.: Adaptive Information Extraction from Text by Rule Induction and Generalisation. In Proceedings of the 17th International Joint Conference on Artificial Intelligence (IJCAI), 2001.

[Ciravegna et al., 2003] Ciravegna, F., Dingli, A., Guthrie, D. and Wilks, Y: Integrating Information to Bootstrap Information Extraction from Web Sites. In Proceedings of the IJCAI Workshop on Information Integration on the Web. 2003. 9-14.

[Collins and Singer, 1999] Collins, M. and Singer, Y.: Unsupervised models for named entity classification. In Proceedings of the 1999 Conference on Empirical Methods in Natural Language Processing and Very Large Corpora (EMNLP/VLC-99), College Park, Maryland, 1999. 189–196.

[Corcho et al., 2006] Corcho, O., Fernández-López, M. and Gómez-Pérez, A.: Ontologies for Sofware Engineering and Software Technology. Calero, C., Ruiz, F. and Piattini, M. (eds). 2006.

[Crescenzi and Mecca, 1998] Crescenzi, V. and Mecca, G.: Grammars have exception. Information Systems 23(8). 1998. 539-565.

[Crescenzi et al., 2001] Crescenzi, V., Mecca G. and Merialdo P.: RoadRunner: towards automatic data extraction from large Web sites. In Proceedings of VLDB'01 Conference, 2001. 109-118.

[Cucerzan and Yarowsky, 1999] Cucerzan, S. and Yarowsky D.: Language independent named entity recognition combining morphological and contextual evidence. In Proceedings of the Conference on Empirical Methods in Natural Language Processing and Very Large Corpora (EMNLP/VLC-99). College Park, Maryland, 1999. 90–99.

[Cui et al., 2004] Cui, H., Kan, M. and Chua, T.: Unsupervised learning of soft patterns for generating definitions from online news. In Proceedings of the 13th World Wide Web Conference. 2004. 90-99.

[Cutting, 1992] Cutting, D., Karger, D., Pedersen, J. and Tukey, J.W.: Scatter/Gather: A Cluster-based Approach to Browsing Large Document Collections. In Proceedings of the 15th Annual International ACM/SIGIR Conference, Copenhagen. 1992. 318-329.

[Daudé et al., 2003] Daudé J., Padró L. and Rigau G.: Validation and Tuning of WordNet Mapping Techniques. In Proceedings of the International Conference on Recent Advances in Natural Language Processing (RANLP'03). Borovets, Bulgaria, 2003.

[de Lima, 1999] de Lima, E.F. and Pedersen, J.O.: Phrase Recognition and Expansion for Short, Precision biased Queries based on a Query Log. In Proceedings of the 22nd Annual International ACM SIGIR Conference on Research and Development in Information Retrieval. 1999. 145-152.

[Decker et al., 1999] Decker, S., Erdmann, M., Fensel, D. and Suder, R.: Ontobroker: Ontology Based Access to Distributed and Semi-Structured Information. In Proceedings of Semantic Issues in Multimedia Systems (DS-8). Rotorua, New Zealand. 1999. 351-369.

[Deerwester et al., 1990] Deerwester, S., Dumais, S., Landauer, T., Furnas, G. and Harshman, R.: Indexing by latent semantic analysis. Journal of the American Society of Information Science 41(6). 1990. 391-407.

[Dellschaft and Staab, 2006] Dellschaft, K, and Staab, S.: On How to Perform a Gold Standard Based Evaluation of Ontology Learning. In proceedings of The Semantic Web - ISWC 2006 LNAI 4273. 2006. 228-241.

[Ding et al., 2004] Ding, L., Finin, T., Joshi, A., Pan, R., Cost, R.S., Peng, Y., Reddivari, P., Doshi, V.C., Sachs, J.: Swoogle: A Search and Metadata Engine for the Semantic Web. In Proceedings of the Thirteenth ACM Conference on Information and Knowledge Management, ACM Press. 2004. 652-659.

[Doorenbos et al., 1997] Doorenbos, R., Etzioni, O. and Weld, D.S.: A Scalable Comparison-Shopping Agent for the World-Wide Web. In Proceeding of the AGENTS '97 Conference. 1997. 39-48.

[Downey et al., 2007] Downey, D., Broadhead, M. and Etzioni, O.: Locating Complex Named Entities in Web text. In Proceedings of ICJAI 2007. 2007.

[Dujmovic and Bai, 2006] Dujmovic, J. and Bai, H.: Evaluation and Comparison of Search Engines Using the LSP Method. ComSIS 3(2). 2006. 711-722.

[Economist, 2005] Economist: Corpus collosal: How well does the world wide web represent human language? The Economist, January 20, 2005. Available at: http://www.economist.com/science/displayStory.cfm?story id=3576374. 2005.

[Eikvil, 1999] Eikvil, L.: Information extraction from World Wide Web – a survey, Technical report 945. Norweigan computing Center, 1999.

[Embley et al., 1999] Embley, D.W, Campbell, D.M., Jiang, Y.S., Liddle, S.W., Lonsdale, D.W., Ng, Y. and Smith R.D.: Conceptual-model-based data extraction from multiple-record Web Pages, Data Knowledge Engineering 31(3). 1999. 226-251.

[Engels, 2001] Engels, R.: CORPORUM-OntoExtract. Ontology Extraction Tool. Deliverable 6. Ontoknowledge. http://www.ontonowledge.org/del.shtml. 2001.

[Etzioni *et al.*, 2004] Etzioni, O., Cafarella, M., Downey, D., Kok, S., Popescu, A., Shaked, T., Soderland, S. and Weld, D.S.: WebScale Information Extraction in KnowItAll. In Proceedings of WWW2004, New York, USA. 2004.

[Etzioni *et al.*, 2005] Etzioni, O., Cafarella, M., Downey, D., Popescu, A.M., Shaked, T., Soderland, S., Weld, D.S. and Yates, A.: Unsupervised named-entity extraction form the Web: An experimental study. Artificial Intelligence 165. 2005. 91-134.

[Faatz and Steinmetz, 2002] Faatz, A. and Steinmetz, R.: Ontology enrichment with texts from the WWW. In Proceedings of Semantic Web Mining 2nd Workshop at ECML/PKDD-2002. Helsinki, Finland. 20th August 2002.

[Farreres *et al.*, 2004] Farreres, J., Gibert, K. and Rodríguez, H.: Towards Binding Spanish Senses to WordNet Senses through Taxonomy Alignment. In Proceedings of GWC 2004. Masaryk University. 2004. 259-264.

[Faure and Nedellec, 1998] Faure, D. and Nedellec, C.: A corpus-based conceptual clustering method for verb frames and ontology acquisition. In Proceedings of LREC-98 Workshop on Adapting Lexical and Corpus Resources to Sublanguages and Applications, Granada, Spain. 1998. 1-8.

[Faure and Poibeau, 2000] Faure, D. and Poibeau, T.: First experiments of using semantic knowledge learned by ASIUM for information extraction task using INTEX. In: S. Staab, A. Maedche, C. Nedellec, P. Wiemer- Hastings (eds.), Proceedings of the Workshop on Ontology Learning, 14th European Conference on Artificial Intelligence ECAI'00, Berlin, Germany. 2000. 7-12.

[Fellbaum, 1998] Fellbaum, C.: WordNet: An Electronic Lexical Database. Cambridge, Massachusetts: MIT Press. More information: http://www.cogsci.princeton.edu/~wn/. 1998.

[Fensel *et al.*, 2001] Fensel, D., van Hermelen, F., Horrocks, I., McGuiness, D.L. and Patel-Schneider, P.F.: OIL: An Ontology Infrastructure for the Semantic Web. IEEE Intelligent Systems (16). 2001. 38-44.

[Fensel, 2001] Fensel, D.: Ontologies: A Silver Bullet for Knowledge Management and Electronic Commerce. Springer Verlag. 2001.

[Fernández-López *et al.*, 1997] Fernández-López, M., Gómez-Pérez, A. and Juristo, N.: METHONTOLOGY: From Ontological Art Towards Ontological Engineering. In Proceedings of the Spring Symposium on Ontological Engineering of AAAI. Stanford University. USA, 1997. 33-40.

[Finkelstein-Landau and Morin, 1999] Finkelstein-Landau, M. and Morin, E.: Extracting Semantic Relationships between Terms: Supervised vs. Unsupervised Methods. In Proceedings of the International Workshop on Ontological Engineering on the Global Information Infrastructure, Dagstuhl. 1999. 71-80.

[Fleischman and Hovy, 2002] Fleischman, M. and Hovy, E.: Fine grained classification of named entities. In Proceedings of the 19th Conference on Computational Linguistics (COLING), 2002. 1-7.

[Flesca *et al.*, 2004] Flesca, S., Manco, G., Masciari, E., Rande, E. and Tagarelli, A.: Web wrapper induction: a brief survey. AI Communications 17. IOS Press. 2004. 57-61.

[Fortuna *et al.*, 2005] Fortuna, B., Grobelnik, M., Mladenic, D.: Visualization of Text Document Corpus. Informatica, 29. 2005. 497-502.

[Fox, 1992] Fox, M.S.: The TOVE Project: A Common-sense Model of the Enterprise. In Proceedings of the Industrial and Engineering Applications of Artificial Intelligence and Expert Systems. LNAI 604. 1992. 25-34.

[Freitag and MacCallun, 1999] Freitag, D. and McCallum, A.: Information extraction with HMMs and shrinkage. In Proceedings of the AAAI-99 Workshop on Machine Learning for Information Extraction, 1999. 31-36.

[Freitag, 2000] Freitag, D.: Machine learning for information extraction in informal domains, Machine Learning 39(2-3). 2000. 233-272.

[Gal et al., 2004] Gal, A., Modica, G. and Jamil, H.: OntoBuilder: Fully Automatic Extraction and Consolidation of Ontologies from Web Sources. In Proceedings of the 20th International Conference on Data Engineering (ICDE'04). 2004. 853-860.

[Gibbins et al., 2003] Gibbins, N., Harris, S. and Shadbolt, N.: Agent-based semantic web services. In Proceedings of the Twelfth International World Wide Conference (WWW2003), ACM Press. Hungary, 2003.

[Girju and Moldovan, 2002] Girju, R. and Moldovan, D.: Text Mining for Causal Relations. In Proceedings of the FLAIRS Conference. 2002. 360-364.

[Gluschko et al., 1999] Gluschko, R., Tenenebaum, J., and Meltzer, B.: An XML Framework for Agent-based E-Commerce. Communications of the ACM 42(3). 1999. 106-114.

[Gómez and Semagi, 2007] Gómez, F. and Segami, C.: Semantic interpretation and knowledge extraction. Knowledge-Based systems, 20. 2007. 51-60.

[Gómez-Perez and Manzano-Macho, 2003] Gómez-Pérez, A., Manzano-Macho, D.: A survey of ontology learning methods and techniques. Deliverable 1.5. OntoWeb. 2003.

[Gómez-Pérez et al., 2004] Gómez-Pérez, A., Fernández-López, M. and Corcho, O.: Ontological Engineering, 2nd printing. Springer Verlag.. ISBN: 1-85233-551-3. 2004

[Grefenstette, 1992] Grefenstette, G.: Finding Semantic Similarity in Raw Text: The Deese Antonyms. In: R. Goldman, P. Norvig, E. Charniak and B. Gale (eds.), Working Notes of the AAAI Fall Symposium on Probabilistic Approaches to Natural Language. AAAI Press. 1992. 61-65.

[Grefenstette, 1997] Grefenstette, G.: SQLET: Short Query Linguistic Expansion Techniques: Palliating One-Word Queries by Providing Intermediate Structure to Text. In Proceedings of Information Extraction: A Multidisciplinary Approach to an Emerging Information Technology. LNAI 1299. International Summer School, SCIE-97. Italy, 1997. 97-114.

[Greffenstette, 1999] Grefenstette, G.: The World Wide Web as a resource for example-based Machine Translation Tasks. In Proceedings of Aslib Conference on Translating and the Computer. London. 1999.

[Gruber and Olsen, 1994] Gruber, T.R. and Olsen, F.: An ontology for Engineering Mathematics. In Proceedings of the Fourth International Conference on Principles of Knowledge Representation and Reasoning. Bonn, Germany. 1994. 258-269.

[Gruber, 1993] Gruber, T.R.: Toward principles for the design of ontologies used for knowledge sharing. In Guarino, N., Poli, R. (eds) International Workshop on Formal Ontology in Conceptual Analysis and Knowledge Representation. Padova, Italy. 1993. 907-928.

[Guarino et al., 1999] Guarino, N., Masolo, C., Vetere, G.: OntoSeek: Content-Based Access to the Web. IEEE Intelligent Systems, 14(3). 1999. 70-80.

[Guarino, 1998] Guarino, N.: Formal Ontology in Information Systems. In Guarino N. (ed) 1st International Conference on Formal Ontology in Information Systems (FOIS'98). IOS Press. Trento, Italy. 1998. 3-15.

[Gupta et al., 2002] Gupta, K.M., Aha, D.W., Marsh, E. and Maney, T.: An architecture for engineering sublanguage WordNets. In Proceedings of the First International Conference On Global WordNet. Mysore, India. 2002. 207-215.

[Haase, 2000] Haase, K.: Interlingual BRICO. IBM Systems Journal, 39. 2000. 589-596.

[Hahn and Schnattinger, 1998] Hahn, U. and Schnattinger, K.: Towards text knowledge engineering. In Proceedings of the 15th National Conference on Artificial Intelligence & 10th Conference on Innovative Applications of Artificial Intelligence. AAAI Press / MIT Press. Madison, Wisconsin, Menlo Park, CA; Cambridge, MA. 1998. 524-531.

[Hahn and Schulz, 2000] Hahn, U. and Schulz, S.: Towards Very Large Terminological Knowledge Bases: A Case Study from Medicine. In Proceedings of the Canadian Conference on AI 2000. 2000. 176-186.

[Hammer et al., 1997] Hammer, J. McHugh, J. and Garcia-Molina, H.: Semistructured data: The TSIMMIS experience. In Proceedings of the 1st East-European Symposium on Advances in Databases and Information Systems. 1997. 1-8.

[Hearst, 1992] Hearst, M.A.: Automatic acquisition of hyponyms from large text corpora. In Proceedings of the 14th International Conference on Computational Linguistics (COLING-92). Nantes, France, 1992. 539–545.

[Hearst, 1996] Hearst, M.A.: Improving Full-Text Precision on Short Queries using Simple Constraints. In Proceedings of the Symposium on Document Analysis and Information Retrieval. Las Vegas, NV. 1996.

[Hearst, 1998] Hearst, M.A.: Automated Discovery of WordNet Relations. In Christiane Fellbaum (Ed.) WordNet: An Electronic Lexical Database, MIT Press. 1998. 132-152.

[Helflin and Hendler, 2000] Heflin, J. and Hendler, J.: Searching the Web with SHOE, In: Papers from the AAAI Workshop on Artificial Intelligence for Web Search, pp. 35-40, 2000.

[Hirst and St-Onge, 1998] Hirst, G. and St-Onge D.: Lexical chains as representations of context for the detection and correction of malapropisms. In Fellbaum C, editor. WordNet: An electronic lexical database. Cambridge, MA: MIT Press. 1998. 305–321.

[Hotho et al., 2001] Hotho, A., Maedche, A., and Staab, S.: Ontology-based text clustering. In Proceedings of the IJCAI-2001 Workshop Text Learning: Beyond Supervision. Seattle. 2001.

[Hsu and Dung, 1998] Hsu, C.N. and Dung, M.T.: Wrapping semistructured Web pages with finite-state transducers. In Proceedings of the Conference on Automatic Learning and Discovery, 1998. 66-73.

[Hwang, 1999] Hwang, C.H.: Incompletely and imprecisely speaking: Using dynamic ontologies for representing and retrieving information. In Proceedings of the 6th International Workshop on Knowledge Representation meets Databases (KRDB'99), Linköping, Sweden. July 29-30, 1999. 14-20.

[Ide and Veronis, 1998] Ide, N. and Veronis, J.: Introduction to the Special Issue on Word Sense Disambiguation: The State of the Art. Computational Linguistics. 24(1). 1998. 1–40.

[IEEE, 2001] IEEE, Special issue on the Semantic Web. IEEE Intelligent Systems. 2001.

[Iria, 2006] Iria, J., Brewster, C., Ciravegna, F. and Wilks, Y.: An Incremental Tri-Partite Approach to Ontology Learning. In Proceedings of the International Conference on Language Resources and Evaluation. Genoa, 22-28 May, 2006.

[Iwanska et al., 2000] Iwanska, L.M., Mata, N. and Kruger, K.: Fully automatic acquisition of taxonomic knowledge from large corpora of texts. In L.M. Iwanksa and S.C. Shapiro, editors, Natural Language Processing and Knowledge Processing. MIT/AAAI Press. 2000. 335-345.

[Jans, 2000] Jans, T.B.: The effect of query complexity on Web searching results. Information Research, 6(1). October 2000.

[Jennings, 2000] Jennings, N.: On agent-based software engineering. Artificial Intelligence 117. 2000. 277-296

[Jiang and Conrath, 1997] Jiang, J. and Conrath, D.: Semantic Similarity Based on Corpus Statistics and Lexical Taxonomy. In Proceedings of the 10th International Conference on Research on Computational Linguistics. Taiwan. 1997.

[Jones and Paynter, 2002] Jones, S. and Paynter, G.W.: Automatic extraction of document keyphrases for use in digital libraries: evaluation and applications. Journal of the American Society for Information Science and Technology 53(8). 2002. 653-677.

[Kahan et al., 2001] Kahan, J., Koivunen, M., Hommeaux, E. and Swick, R.: Annotea: an open rdf infrastructure for shared web annotations. In Proceedings of the WWW10 Conference. Hong Kong. May 1-5, 2001. 623-632.

[Kashyap, 1999] Kashyap, V.: Design and Creation of Ontologies for Environmental Information Retrieval. In Proceedings of the 11th European Workshop on Knowledge Acquisition, Modelling and Management (EKAW). 1999.

[Kavalec and Svatek, 2005] Kavalec, M. and Svatek, V.: A Study on Automated Relation Labelling in Ontology Learning. In P.Buitelaar, P. Cimiano, B. Magnini (eds.), Ontology Learning and Population from Text: Methods, Evaluation and Applications, IOS Press, 2005. 44-58.

[Kavalec et al., 2004] Kavalec, M., Maedche, A. and Skátek, V.: Discovery of Lexical Entries for Non-taxonomic Relations in Ontology Learning. In Proceedings of SOFSEM 2004, LNCS 2932. 2004. 249-256.

[Keller et al., 2002] Keller, F., Lapata, M. and Ourioupina, O.: Using the web to overcome data sparseness. In Proceedings of EMNLP-02. 2002. 230-237.

[Kesseler 1996] Kesseler, M.: A Schema Based Approach to HTML Authoring. World Wide Web Journal 96(1). O'Reilly, 1996.

[Khan and Luo, 2002] Khan, L. and Luo, F.: Ontology Construction for Information Selection In Proceedings of 14th IEEE International Conference on Tools with Artificial Intelligence. Washington DC. November 2002. 122-127.

[Kietz et al., 2000] Kietz, J.U., Maedche, A. and Volz, R.: A Method for Semi-Automatic Ontology Acquisition from a Corporate Intranet. In Aussenac-Gilles N, Biébow B, Szulman S (eds) EKAW'00 Workshop on Ontologies and Texts. Juan-Les-Pins, France. October, 2000. 37-50.

[Kipper et al., 2000] Kipper, K., Dang, H.T. and Palmer, M.: Class-based construction of a verb lexicon. In Proceedings of the 7th National Conference on Artificial Intelligence AAAI 2000. Austin, USA. 2000. 691-696.

[Kobayashi and Takeda, 2000] Kobayashi, M. and Takeda, K.: Information Retrieval on the Web. ACM Computing Surveys, 32(2). 2000. 144–173.

[Krupka and Hausman, 1998] Krupka, G. and Hausman, K.: IsoQuest, Inc.: Description of the NetOwl extractor system as used for MUC-7. In Proceedings of the 7th Message Understanding Conference (MUC-7), Fairfax, Virginia. 1998.

[Kusmerick 2000] Kusmerick, N.: Wrapper induction: efficiency and expressiveness. Artificial Intelligence Journal 118(1-2). 2000. 15-68.

[Kwok et al., 2001] Kwok, C.T., Etzioni, O. and Weld, D.S.: Scaling question answering to the web. ACM Transactions on Information Systems. 2001. 150-161.

[Laender et al., 2002] Laender, A.H.F., Ribeiro-Neto, B.A., da Silva, A.S. and Teixeira, J.S.: A brief survey of Web data extraction Tools. SIGMOD Records 31(2). 2002. 84-93.

[Lamparter et al., 2004] Lamparter, S., Ehrig, M. and Tempich, C.: Knowledge Extraction from Classification Schemas. In Proceedings of the CoopIS/DOA/ODBASE 2004. LNCS 3290. 2004. 618-636.

[Landauer and Dumais, 1997] Landauer, T.K. and Dumais, S.T.: A Solution to Plato's Problem: The Latent Semantic Analysis Theory of the Acquisition, Induction, and Representation of Knowledge. Psychological Review, 104. 1997. 211-240.

[Lassila and McGuinness, 2001] Lassila, O., McGuinness, D.: The Role of Frame-Based Representation on the Semantic Web. Technical Report KSL-01-02. Knowledge Systems Laboratory. Stanford University. Standford, California. 2001.

[Lawrence, 2000] Lawrence, S.: Context in Web Search. IEEE Data Engineering Bulletin 23(3). 2000. 25–32.

[Lawrie and Croft, 2003] Lawrie, D.J. and Croft, B.: Generating Hierarchical Summaries for Web Searches. In Proceedings of SIGIR'03. Toronto Canada. 2003. 457-458.

[Leacock and Chodorow, 1998] Leacock, C. and Chodorow, M.: Combining local context and WordNet similarity for word sense identification. In C. Fellbaum, editor, WordNet: An electronic lexical database. MIT Press.1998. 265–283.

[Lee et al., 1993] Lee, J.H., Kim, M.H. and Lee, Y.J.: Information Retrieval Based on Conceptual Distance in ISA Hierarchies. Journal of Documentation, 49. 1993. 188-207.

[Lee et al., 2003] Lee, C., Na, J. and Khoo C.: Ontology Learning for Medical Digital Libraries. In Proceedings of ICADL 2003. LNCS 2911. 2003. 302-305.

[Lenat and Guha, 1990] Lenat, D.B. and Guha, R.V.: Building Large Knowledge-based Systems: Representation and Inference in the Cyc Project. Addision-Wesley, Boston, Massachusetts. 1990.

[Levin, 1993] Levin, B.: English verb classes and alternations. PhD Thesis. Chicago University Press. 1993.

[Lin, 1998] Lin, D.: Automatic Retrieval and Clustering of Similar Words. In Proceedings of the 17th International Conference on Computational Linguistics and 36th Annual Meeting of the Association for Computational Linguistics. Montreal. 1998. 768-773.

[Lonsdale *et al.*, 2002] Lonsdale, D., Ding, Y., Embley, D.W. and Melby A.: Peppering Knowledge Sources with SALT; Boosting Conceptual Content for Ontology Generation. Proceedings of the AAAI Workshop on Semantic Web Meets Language Resources, Edmonton, Alberta, Canada. July 2002. 30-36.

[Lopez and Motta 2004] Lopez, V. and Motta, E.: Ontology-Driven Question Answering in AquaLog. In Proceedings of NLDB. 2004. 89-102.

[Maarek *et al.*, 2000] Maarek, Y.S., Fagin, R., Ben-Shaul I.Z. and Pelleg, D.: Ephemeral document clustering for web applications. Technical Report RJ 10186. IBM Research. 2000.

[Maedche and Staab, 2000] Maedche, A. and Staab S.: Discovering Conceptual Relations from Text. In Proceedings of the 14th European Conference on Artificial Intelligence. IOS Press, Amsterdam. 2000. 321-325.

[Maedche and Staab, 2001] Maedche, A. and Staab, S.: Ontology Learning for the Semantic Web. IEEE Intelligent Systems, Special Issue on the Semantic Web, 16(2). 2001.

[Maedche and Staab, 2003] Maedche, A. and Staab, S.: Ontology Learning. In S. Staab & R. Studer (eds.) Handbook on Ontologies in Information Systems. Springer. 2003.

[Maedche *et al.*, 2003] Maedche, A., Neumann, G. and Staab, S.: Bootstrapping an Ontology-Based Information Extraction System, Studies in Fuzziness and Soft Computing. Intelligent Exploration of the Web, Springer, 2003. 245-259.

[Maedche, 2002] Maedche, A.: Ontology Learning for the Semantic Web. Kluwer Academic Publishers. 2002.

[Magnin *et al.*, 2002] Magnin, L., Snoussi, H., Nie, J.: Toward an Ontology–based Web Extraction. In Proceedings of the Fifteenth Canadian Conference on Artificial Intelligence, 2002.

[Magnini *et al.*, 2003] Magnini, B., Serafini. L. and Speranza, M.: Making explicit the hidden Semantics of hierarchical classifications. ITC-first Technical report 0306-09. June 2003.

[Manning and Schütze, 1999] Manning, C.D. and Schütze, H.: Foundations of Statistical Natural Language Processing. Cambridge, Massachusetts: MIT Press. 1999.

[Markert *et al.*, 2003] Markert, K., Modjeska, N. and Nissim, M.: Using the web for nominal anaphora resolution. In Proceedings of the EACL Workshop on the Computational Treatment of Anaphora. 2003.

[Martin and Eklund, 2000] Martin, P. and Eklund, P: Knowledge Indexation and Retrieval and the Word Wide Web. IEEE Intelligent Systems, Special Issue "Knowledge Management and Knowledge Distribution over the Internet". 2000.

[McCallum, 2003] McCallum, A.: Efficiently inducing features or conditional random fields. In Proceedings of the Nineteenth Conference on Uncertainty in Artificial Intelligence, 2003.

[Meaning, 2005] Meaning Project: Developing Multilinguial Web Scale Technologies. IST-2001-34460. http://nipadio.lsi.upc.edu/wei4/doc/mcr/meaning.html. 2005.

[Mihalcea and Edmonds, 2004] Mihalcea, R. and Edmonds, P.: Proceedings of Senseval-3: The 3rd Int. Workshop on the Evaluation of Systems for the Semantic Analysis of Text. Barcelona, Spain. 2004.

[Mikheev and Finch, 1997] Mikheev, A. and Finch, S.: A Workbench for Finding Structure in Texts. In Proceedings of ANLP-97. Washington D.C. 1997. 8-16.

[Mikheev et al., 1999] Mikheev, A., Moens, M. and Grover, C.: Named entity recognition without gazetteers. In Proceedings of the 10th Conference of the European Chapter of the Association for Computational Linguistics (EACL-99). Bergen, Norway. 1999. 1–8.

[Miller, 1996] Miller, G.A.: Contextuality, in Mental Models in Cognitive Science. J. Oakhill and A. Garnham, Editors. Psychology Press: East Sussex, UK. 1996. 1–18.

[Missikoff et al., 2002] Missikoff, M., Navigli, R. and Velardi, P.: The Usable Ontology: An Environment for Building and Assessing a Domain Ontology. In Proceedings of the International Semantic Web Conference (ISWC) 2002. Sardinia, Italia. June 9-12th, 2002. 39-53.

[Moldovan and Girju, 2001] Moldovan, D.I. and Girju, R.C.: An interactive tool for the rapid development of knowledge Bases. International Journal on Artificial Intelligence Tools 10(1-2). March, 2001. 65-86.

[Montoyo, 2000] Montoyo, A: Método basado en Marcas de Especificidad para WSD. Procesamiento del Lenguaje Natural, 26. Septiembre, 2000.

[Moreno et al., 2004] Moreno, A., Riaño, D., Isern, D., Bocio, J., Sánchez, D., Jiménez, L.: Knowledge Exploitation from the Web. In Proceedings of the 5th International Conference on Practical Aspects of Knowledge Management (PAKM 2004). LNAI, 3336. Vienna. 2004. 175-185.

[Moreno et al., 2005] Moreno, A., Valls, A., Sánchez, D. and Isern, D.: Construcción automática de ontologies para la Web Semántica. In Proceedings of the Workshop in Ontologías y la Web Semántica, CAEPIA 2005. Santiago de Compostela. 2005.

[Moreno et al., 2006] Moreno, A., Valls, A., Isern, D. and Sánchez, D.: Applying Agent Technology to Healthcare: The GruSMA Experience. IEEE Intelligent Systems 21(6). 2006. 63-67.

[Morin, 1999] Morin E.: Automatic acquisition of semantic relations between terms from technical corpora. In Proceedings of the fifth international congress on terminology and knowledge engineering (TKE-99). Vienna. 1999. 268-278,

[Morita et al., 2004] Morita, T., Shigeta, Y., Sugiura, N., Fukuta, N., Izumi, N., Yamaguchi, T.: DODDLE-OWL: OWL-based Semi-Automatic Ontology Development Environment. In Proceedings of EON2004. 2004.

[Mulholland et al., 2001] Mulholland, P., Zdrahal, Z., Domingue, J., Hatala, M., Bernardi, A.: A Methodological Approach to Supporting Organizational Learning. International Journal of Human-Computer Studies, 55(3), 2001. 337-367.

[Muslea et al., 2001] Muslea, I., Minton, S. and Knoblock, C.: Hierarchical wrapper induction for semistructured information sources, Autonomous Agents and Multi-Agent Systems 4. 2001. 93-114.

[Navigli and Velardi, 2004] Navigli, R. and Velardi, P.: Learning Domain Ontologies from Document Warehouses and Dedicated Web Sites. In Computational Linguistics 30(2). June, 2004. 151-179.

[Neches et al., 1991] Neches, R., Fickes, R.E., Finin, T. Gruber, T.R., Senator, T. and Swartout W.R.: Enabling technology for knowledge sharing. AI Magazine 12(3). 1991. 36-56.

[Nirenburg and Raskin, 2004] Nirenburg, S. and Raskin, V.: Ontological Semantics SERIES: Language, Speech, and Communication, MIT Press, 2004.

[Nobécourt, 2000] Nobécourt, J.: A method to build formal ontologies from text. In Proceedings of the EKAW-2000 Workshop on ontologies and text. Juan-Les-Pins, France. 2000.

[Oliveira et al., 2001] Oliveira, A., Pereira, F.C. and Cardoso, A.: Automatic Reading and Learning from Text. In Proceedings of the International Symposium on Artificial Intelligence, ISAI'2001. December, 2001.

[OntoWeb, 2002] OntoWeb D.1.3: "Whitepaper: ontology evaluation tools". Available at: http://www.aifb.unikarlsruhe.de/WBX/ysu/publications/eon2002_whitepaper.pdf. 2002.

[Palmer et al., 1998] Palmer, M., Rosenzweig, J. and Schuler, W.: Capturing Motion Verb Generalizations with Synchronous TAGs. Predicative Forms in NLP. Kluwer Press. December, 1998.

[Pantel and Ravichandran, 2004] Pantel, P. and Ravichandran, D.: Automatically labelling semantic classes. In Proceedings of the 2004 Human Language Technology Conference (HLT-NAACL-04). Boston, Massachusetts. 2004. 321–328.

[Pasca and Harabagiu 2001] Pasca, M. and Harabagiu, S.: The Informative Role of WordNet in Open-Domain Question Answering. In Proceedings of the NAACL Workshop on WordNet and Other Lexical Resources: Applications, Extensions and Customizations. 2001. 138-143.

[Pasca, 2004] Pasca, M.: Acquisition of Categorized Named Entities for Web Search. In Proceedings of the thirteenth ACM International Conference on Information and Knowledge Management. USA. 2004. 137-145.

[Pasca, 2005] Pasca, M.: Finding Instance Names and Alternative Glosses on the Web: WordNet Reloaded. In Proceedings of CICLing 2005. LNCS 3406. 2005. 280-292.

[Patwardhan and Pedersen, 2006] Patwardhan S, Pedersen T.: Using WordNet-based context vectors to estimate the semantic relatedness of concepts. In: Proceedings of the EACL 2006 workshop, making sense of sense: Bringing computational linguistics and psycholinguistics together. Trento, Italy. 2006. 1–8.

[Patwardhan, 2003] Patwardhan, S.: Incorporating dictionary and corpus information into a context vector measure of semantic relatedness. Master of Science Thesis, Department of Computer Science, University of Utah. 2003.

[Pease and Niles, 2002] Pease, R.A. and Niles, I.: IEEE Standard Upper Ontology: A Progress Report. The Knowledge Engineering Review 17(1). 2002. 65-70.

[Pedersen et al., 2006] Pedersen, T., Serguei, Pakhomov, S., Patwardhan, S., Chute, C.: Measures of semantic similarity and relatedness in the biomedical domain. Journal of Biomedical Informatics. 2006.

[Pedersen, et al., 2004] Pedersen, T., Patwardhan, S. and Michelizzi, J.: WordNet::Similarity – Measuring the Relatedness of Concepts. http://search.cpan.org/dist/WordNet-Similarity. American Association for Artificial Intelligence. 2004.

[Petrie, 2001] Petrie, C.: Agent-based software engineering. Agent-Oriented Software Engineering. LNAI. 1957. Springer-Verlag, Berlin. 2001. 58-76.

[Phillips and Riloff, 2002] Phillips, W. and Riloff, E.: Exploiting strong syntactic heuristics and co-training to learn semantic lexicons. In Proceedings of the Conference on Empirical Methods in Natural Language Processing (EMNLP-02). Philadelphia, Pennsylvania. 2002. 125–132.

[Popescu and Etzioni, 2005] Popescu, A. and Etzioni, O.: Extracting Product Features and Opinions from Reviews. In Proceedings of HLT-EMNLP. 2005.

[Pustejovsky et al., 2002] Pustejovsky, J., Castano, J., Zhang, J., Cochran, B. and Kotecki, M.: Robust relational parsing over biomedical literature: Extracting inhibit relations. In Proceedings of the Pacific Symposium on Biocomputing. 2002. 362-373.

[Ravichandran and Hovy, 2002] Ravichandran, D. and Hovy, E.: Learning surface text patterns for a question answering system. In Proceedings of the 40th Annual Meeting of the Association of Computational Linguistics (ACL-02), Philadelphia, Pennsylvania. 2002. 41-47.

[Reinberger and Sypns, 2004] Reinberger, M.L., Spyns, P.: Discovering knowledge in texts for the learning of DOGMA inspired ontologies. In Proceedings of the ECAI 2004 Workshop on Ontology Learning and Population. 2004. 19-24.

[Reinberger et al., 2004] Reinberger, M.L., Spyns, P., Pretorius, A.J. and Daelemans, W.: Automatic initiation of an ontology. In R. Meersman, Z. Tari et al. (eds.), On the Move to Meaningful Internet Systems, LNCS 3290 , Springer. 2004. 600–617.

[Resnik and Smith, 2003] Resnik, P. and Smith, N.: The web as a parallel corpus. Computational Linguistics, 29(3). 2003. 349-380.

[Resnik, 1993] Resnik, P.: Selection and Information: A Class-based Approach to Lexical Relationships. PhD thesis, University of Pennsylvania. 1993.

[Resnik, 1998] Resnik, P.: Semantic Similarity in a Taxonomy: An Information-Based Measure and its Application to Problems of Ambiguity in Natural Language. Journal of Artificial Intelligence Research, 11. 1998. 95-130.

[Richardson et al., 1994] Richardson, R., Smeaton, A. and Murphy, J.: Using WordNet as a Knowledge Base for Measuring Semantic Similarity between Words. In Proceedings of the AICS Conference. Trinity College, Dublin. 1994.

[Ridings and Shishigin, 2002] Ridings, C. and Shishigin, M: PageRank Uncovered. Available at: http://www.voelspriet2.nl/PageRank.pdf. 2002.

[Rinaldi et al., 2005] Rinaldi, F., Yuste, E., Schneider, G., Hess, M. and Roussel, D.: Exploiting Technical Terminology for Knowledge Management. In P.Buitelaar, P. Cimiano, B. Magnini (eds.), Ontology Learning and Population, IOS Press, 2005.

[Rosso et al., 2003] Rosso, P., Masulli, F., Buscaldi, D., Pla, F. and Molina, A.: Automatic Noun Disambiguation. In Proceedings in Computational Linguistics and Intelligent Text Processing (CICLing-2003). LNCS, 2588. Springer-Verlag. 2003. 273–276.

[Rosso et al., 2005] Rosso P., Montes-y-Gomez, M., Buscaldi, D., Pancardo-Rodrıguez, A. and Villaseñor, L.: Two Web-Based Approaches for Noun Sense Disambiguation. In Proceedings of CICLing 2005. LNCS 3406. 2005. 267–279.

[Roux et al., 2000] Roux, C., Proux, D., Rechermann, F. and Julliard, L.: An ontology enrichment method for a pragmatic information extraction system gathering data on genetic interactions. In Proceedings of the ECAI2000 Workshop on Ontology Learning (OL2000). Berlin, Germany. August, 2000.

[Sabou, 2004] Sabou, M.: Extracting ontologies from software documentation: a semiautomatic method and its evaluation. In Proceedings of the ECAI-2004 Workshop on Ontology Learning and Population (ECAI-OLP). 2004.

[Sabou, 2005] Sabou, M.: Learning Web Service Ontologies: an Automatic Extraction Method and its Evaluation In Ontology Learning. In P.Buitelaar, P. Cimiano, B. Magnini (eds.), Ontology Learning and Population. IOS Press, 2005.

[Sabou, 2006] Sabou, M.: Building Web Service Ontologies. PhD Thesis. SIKS Dissertation Series. 2006.

[Sánchez and Moreno, 2004a] Sánchez, D. and Moreno, A.: Creating ontologies from Web documents. In Proceedings of the Setè Congrés Català d'Intel·ligència Artificial (CCIA'04) IOS Press. Barcelona. October 21-22, 2004. 11-18.

[Sánchez and Moreno, 2004b] Sánchez, D. and Moreno, A.: Automatic generation of taxonomies from the WWW. In Proceedings of the 5th International Conference on Practical Aspects of Knowledge Management (PAKM 2004). LNAI 3336. Vienna, Austria. December 2-3, 2004. 208-219.

[Sánchez and Moreno, 2005a] Sánchez, D. and Moreno A.: Development of new techniques to improve Web Search. In Proceedings of the 9th International Joint Conference on Artificial Intelligence (IJCAI'05) Edinburgh, Scotland. 30 July – 5 August 2005. 1632-1633.

[Sánchez and Moreno 2005b] Sánchez, D. and Moreno, A.: Web Mining Techniques for Automatic Discovery of Medical Knowledge. In Proceeding of the 10th Conference on Artificial Intelligence in Medicine (AIME 05). LNAI 3581. Aberdeen, Scotland. 23 - 27 July 2005. 409-413.

[Sánchez and Moreno 2005c] Sánchez, D. and Moreno, A.: Web-scale taxonomy learning. In Proceedings of the Workshop Learning and Extending Lexical Ontologies by using Machine Learning Methods. ICML 2005. Bonn, Germany, 7 - 11 August 2005.

[Sánchez and Moreno, 2005d] Sánchez, D. and Moreno, A.: Automatic discovery of synonyms and lexicalizations from the Web. In Proceedings of the Vuitè Congrés Català d'Intel·ligència Artificial (CCIA'05). Artificial Intelligence Research and Development 131. IOS Press. L'Alguer, Italy. 26-28 October 2005. 205-212.

[Sánchez and Moreno, 2005e] Sánchez, D. and Moreno, A.: A Multi-agent System for Distributed Ontology Learning. In Proceedings of the Third International Workshop on Multi-Agent systems, EUMAS 2005. Brussels, Belgium. 7-8 December 2005. 504-505.

[Sánchez and Moreno, 2006a] Sánchez, D. and Moreno, A.: A methodology for knowledge acquisition from the web. International Journal of Knowledge-Based and Intelligent Engineering Systems 10(6). 2006. 453-475.

[Sánchez and Moreno, 2006b] Sánchez, D. and Moreno, A.: Discovering Non-taxonomic Relations from the Web. In Proceedings of the 7th International Conference on Intelligent Data Engineering and Automated Learning (IDEAL 2006). E. Corchado et al. (Eds). LNCS 4224. Burgos, Spain. 20-23 September, 2006. 629-636.

[Sánchez and Moreno, 2007a] Sánchez, D. and Moreno, A.: Learning Medical Ontologies from the Web. In Proceedings of the Workshop From Knowledge to Global Care. 11th Conference on Artificial Intelligence in Medicine. 7 July, 2007.

[Sánchez and Moreno, 2007b] Sánchez, D. and Moreno, A.: Bringing taxonomic structure to large digital libraries. International Journal on Metadata, Semantics and Ontologies 2(2). 2007.

[Sánchez and Moreno, 2007c] Sánchez, D. and Moreno, A.: Semantic disambiguation of tax-onomies. In Proceedings of the Desè Congrés Internacional de l'Associació Catalana d'Intel·ligència Artificial (CCIA'07). IOSPress. Andorra. October 25-26, 2007.

[Sánchez and Moreno, 2008a] Sánchez, D. and Moreno, A.: Pattern-based automatic taxonomy learning from the Web. To be published in the European Journal on Artificial Intelligence (AI Communications). IOS Press. 2008.

[Sánchez and Moreno, 2008b] Sánchez, D. and Moreno, A.: Learning non taxonomic relation-ships from web documents for domain ontology construction. To be published Data & Knowledge Engineering. Elsevier. 2008.

[Sánchez et al., 2005] Sánchez, D., Isern, D. and Moreno, A.: An Agent-Based Knowledge Acquisition Platform. 9th International Workshop on Cooperative Information Agents. In Proceedings of the Third German Conference on Multiagent System Technologies (MATES/CIA 2005). LNAI 3550. Koblenz, Germany, 11-13 September 2005. 118-129.

[Sánchez et al., 2006] Sánchez, D., Isern, D. and Moreno, A.: Integrated Agent-Based Ap-proach for Ontology-Driven Web Filtering. In Proceedings of the 10th International Confer-ence on Knowledge-Based & Intelligent Information & Engineering System (KES 2006). LNAI 4253. Bournemouth, UK. 9-11 October, 2006. 758-765.

[Sánchez et al., 2007] Sánchez, D., Rodríguez, A. and Moreno, A.: Parallel execution of com-plex tasks using a distributed, robust and flexible agent-based platform. In Proceedings of the III Taller en Desarrollo de Sistema Multiagente. II Congreso Español de Informática. Setem-ber 11-14, 2007.

[Sanderson and Croft, 1999] Sanderson, M. and Croft, B.: Deriving concept hierarchies from text. In Proceedings of the 22nd Annual International ACM SIGIR Conference on Research and Development in Information Retrieval. Berkeley, USA. 1999. 206-213.

[Schlobach et al., 2004] Schlobach, S., Olsthoorn, M. and de Rijke, M.: Type checking in open-domain question answering. In Proceedings of the European Conference on Artificial Intelligence (ECAI). 2004.

[Schurr and Staab, 2000] Schnurr, H.P. and Staab, S.: A proactive inferencing agent for desk support. In Proceedings of the AAAI Symposium on Bringing Knowledge to Business Proc-esses. Stanford, CA, USA. AAAI Technical Report, Menlo Park. 2000.

[Schutz and Buitelaar, 2005] Schutz, A., Buitelaar, P.: RelExt: A Tool for Relation Extraction in Ontology Extension. In Proceedings of the 4th International Semantic Web Conference. 2005. 593-606.

[Schütze, 1993] Schütze, H.: Word Space. In: S.J. Hanson, J.D. Cowan, and C.L. Giles (eds.), Advances in Neural Information Processing Systems 5, San Mateo California: Morgan Kaufmann. 1993. 895-902.

[Senseval, 2004] Sens Eval: Evaluation exercises for Word Sense Disambiguation. http://www.senseval.org/publications/senseval.pdf. 2004.

[Shamsfard and Barforoush, 2002] Shamsfard, M. and Barforoush, A.: An introduction to Hasti: An Ontology Learning System. Artificial Intelligence Soft Computing. 2002.

[Sheth, 2003] Sheth, A.: Ontology-driven information search, integration and analysis. In Proceedings of MATES. 2003.

[Sidorov and Gelbukh, 2001] Sidorov, G. and Gelbukh, A.: Word Sense Disambiguation in a Spanish Explanatory Dictionary. In Proceedings of TALN-2001. France. 2001. 398-402.

[Sinha and Narayanan, 2005] Sinha, S. and Narayanan, S.: Model Based Answer Selection. In: Proceedings of the AAAI Workshop on Textual Inference in Question Answering. 2005.

[Sintek *et al.*, 2004] Sintek, M., Buitelaar, P. and Olejnik, D.: A Formalization of Ontology Learning From Text. In Proceedings of EON2004. 2004.

[Skounakis *et al.*, 2003] Skounakis, M., Craven, M. and Ray, S.: Hierarchical hidden markov models for information extraction. In Proceedings of the Eighteenth International Joint Conference on Artificial Intelligence. 2003. 427-433.

[Smith and Poulter, 1999] Smith, H. and Poulter, K.: Share the Ontology in XML-based Trading Architectures. Communications of the ACM 42(3). 1999. 110-111.

[Snow *et al.*, 2004] Snow, R., Jurafsky, D. and Ng, A.Y.: Learning syntactic patterns for automatic hypernym discovery. Advances in Neural Information Processing Systems 17. 2004. 1297-1304.

[Soderland *et al.*, 1995] Soderland, S., Fisher, D., Aseltine, J. and Lehnert, W.: CRYSTAL: Inducing a conceptual dictionary. In Proceedings of the Fourteenth International Joint Conference on Artificial Intelligence. 1995. 1314–1321.

[Soderland, 1999] Soderland, S.: Learning information extraction rules for semistructured and free text. Machine Learning, 34(1-3). 1999. 233-272.

[Solorio *et al.*, 2004] Solorio, T., Pérez, M., Montes, M., Villaseñor, L. and López, A.: A Language Independent Method for Question Classification. In Proceedings of the 20th International Conference on Computational Linguistics (COLING-04). Geneva, Switzerland. 2004. 1374-1380.

[Sowa, 1999] Sowa, J.F.: Knowledge Representation: Logical, Philosophical, and Computational Foundations. Brooks Cole Publishing Co., Pacific Grove, California. 1999.

[Spink, 2001] Spink, A., Wolfram, D., Jansen, B.J. and Saracevic, T.: Searching the Web: The Public and Their Queries. Journal of the American Society for Information Science. 52(3). 2001. 226–234.

[Staab and Schnurr 2000] Staab, S. and Schnurr, H.P.: Smart Task Support through Proactive Access to Organizational Memory. Journal of Knowledge-based Systems, Elsevier, 2000. 251-260.

[Stevenson and Gaizauskas, 2000] Stevenson, M. and Gaizauskas, R.: Using corpus-derived name lists for named entity recognition. In Proceedings of the 6th Conference on Applied Natural Language Processing (ANLP-00). Seattle, Washington. 2000. 290-295.

[Stevenson *et al.*, 2005] Stevenson, M., and Greenwood, M.: A Semantic Approach to IE Pattern Induction. In Proceedings of the 43rd Annual Meeting of the Association for Computational Linguistics, 2005. 379-386.

[Stokoe *et al.*, 2003] Stokoe, C., Oakes, M.P. and Tait, J: Word Sense Disambiguation in Information Retrieval Revisited. In Proceedings of the 26th ACM SIGIR. Canada. 2003. 159-166.

[Studer *et al.*, 1998] Studer, R., Benjamins, V.R. and Fensel., D.: Knowledge Engineering: Principles and Methods. IEEE Transactions on Knowledge and Data Engineering 25(1-2). 1998. 161-197.

[Stumme et al., 2003] Stumme, G., Ehrig, M., Handschuh, S., Hotho, A., Maedche, A., Motik, B., Oberle, D., Schmitz, C., Staab, S., Stojanovic, L., Stojanovic, N., Studer, R., Sure, Y., Volz, R., and Zacharias, V.: The Karlsruhe View on Ontologies. Technical Report University of Karlsruhe, Institute AIFB, 2003.

[Sure et al. 2000] Sure, Y., Maedche, A. and Staab, S.: Leveraging Corporate Skill Knowledge -- From ProPer to OntoProPer, In Proceedings of PAKM. 2000. 1-9.

[Surowiecky, 2004] Surowiecki, J.: The Wisdom of Crowds: Why the Many Are Smarter Than the Few and How Collective Wisdom Shapes Business, Economies, Societies and Nations. Doubleday Books, 2004.

[Szulman et al., 2002] Szulman, S., Biebow, B. and Aussenac-Gilles, N.: Structuration de Terminologies à l'aide d'outils d'analyse de textes avec TERMINAE. Traitement Automatique de la Langue (TAL) 43(1). 2002. 103-128.

[Thompson and Mooney, 1997] Thompson, C.A. and Mooney, R.J.: Semantic Lexicon Acquisition for Learning Parsers. Technical Note. January 1997.

[Turney, 2001] Turney, P.D.: Mining the Web for synonyms: PMI-IR versus LSA on TOEFL. In Proceedings of the Twelfth European Conference on Machine Learning. Freiburg, Germany 2001. 491-499.

[Uschold and Grunninger, 1996] Uschold, M. and Grunninger, M.: Ontologies. Principles, Methods and Applications. Knowledge Engineering Review 11(2), 1996. 93-155.

[Uschold et al. 1998] Uschold, M., King, M., Moralee, S. and Zorgios, Y.: The Enterprise Ontology, Knowledge Engineering Review, 13(1). 1998. 31-89.

[Valarakos et al., 2004] Valarakos, A.G., Paliouras G., Karkaletsis V. and Vouros, G.: Enhancing Ontological Knowledge Through Ontology Population and Enrichment. In Proceedings of EKAW 2004. LNAI 3257. 2004. 144-156.

[Van Heijst et al., 1997] Van Heijst, F., Schreiber A., and Wielinga, B.J.: Using explicit ontologies in KBS development. International Journal of Human-Computer Studies 45. 1997. 183-292.

[Velardi et al., 2002] Velardi, P., Navigli, R. and Missikoff, M.: Integrated approach for Web ontology learning and engineering. IEEE Computer 35. November, 2002. 60-63.

[Velardi et al., 2005] Velardi, P., Navigli, R., Cucchiarelli, A. and Neri, F.: Evaluation of OntoLearn, a methodology for automatic learning of domain ontologies. Paul Buitelaar Philipp Cimmiano and Bernardo Magnini Editors. IOS Press. 2005.

[Vintar et al., 2003] Vintar, S., Todorovski, L., Sonntag, D. and Buitelaar, P.: Evaluating context features for medical relation mining. In Proceedings of the ECML/PKDD Workshop on Data Mining and Text Mining for Bioinformatics. 2003.

[Volk, 2001] Volk, M.: Exploiting the WWW as a Corpus to Resolve PP Attachment Ambiguities. In Proceedings of Corpus Linguistics. Lancaster. 2001.

[Volk, 2002] Volk, M.: Using the Web as Corpus for Linguistic Research. Catcher of the Meaning. Pajusalu, R., Hennoste, T. (Eds.). Department of General Linguistics 3, University of Tartu, Germany. 2002.

[Voorhees, 1994] Voorhees, E.M.: Query Expansion Using Lexical-Semantic Relations. In Proceedings of the 17th Annual International ACM/SIGIR Conference on Research and Development in Information Retrieval. Dublin, Ireland. 1994. 61-69.

[Voorhess, 2001] Voorhees, E.M.: Overview of the TREC 2001 question answering track. In Proceedings of the Text REtrieval Conference, 2001. 42-51.

[Vossen, 1998] Vossen, P.: EuroWordNet: A Multilingual Database with Lexical Semantic Networks. Dordrecht, Netherlands: Kluwer. Available at: http://www.hum.uva.nl/~ewn/. 1998.

[Vossen, 2001] Vossen, P.: Extending, trimming and fusing WordNet for technical documents. In Proceedings of the NAACL Workshop on WordNet and Other Lexical Resources. Pittsburgh. 2001.

[Wagner, 2000] Wagner, A.: Enriching a lexical semantic net with selectional preferences by means of statistical corpus analysis. In Proceedings of the ECAI-2000 Workshop on Ontology Learning, Berlin. August, 2000. 37-42.

[Weiss, 1999] Weiss, G.: Mutliagent systems: a modern approach to distributed artificial intelligence. The MIT Press, Cambridge. 1999.

[Weng et al., 2006] Weng, S., Tsai, H., Liu, S. and Hsu, C.: Ontology construction for information classification. Expert Systems with Applications 31. 2006. 1–12.

[Widdows, 2003] Widdows, D.: Unsupervised methods for developing taxonomies by combining syntactic and statistical information. In Proceedings of the Human Language Technology / Conference of the North American Chapter of the Association for Computational Linguistics (HLT/NAACL). Canada, 2003. 276-283.

[Wiemer-Hastings et al., 1998] Wiemer-Hastings, P., Graesser, A.: Inferring the meaning of verbs from context. In Proceedings of the Twentieth Annual Conference of the Cognitive Science Society. 1998. 1142-1147.

[William, 2002] William, L.: Measuring Conceptual Distance Using WordNet: The Design of a Metric for Measuring Semantic Similarity. R. Hayes, W. Lewis, E. Obryan, and T. Zamuner (Eds.), The University of Arizona Working Papers in Linguistics. Tucson: University of Arizona. 2002.

[Wooldridge, 2002] Wooldridge, M.: An Introduction to multiagent systems. West Sussex, England: John Wiley and Sons, Ltd. 2002.

[Wu and Hsu, 2002] Wu, S.H and Hsu W.L.: SOAT: A Semi-Automatic Domain Ontology Acquisition Tool from Chinese Corpus. In Proceedings of the 19th International Conference on Computational Linguistics. Taipei, Taiwán. 2002. 1-5.

[Wu and Palmer, 1994] Wu Z. and Palmer M.: Verb semantics and lexical selection. In Proceedings of the 32nd annual meeting of the association for computational linguistics. Las Cruces. 1994. 133–8.

[Xu et al., 2002] Xu, F., Kurz, D., Piskorski, J. and Schmeier, S.: A Domain Adaptive Approach to Automatic Acquisition of Domain Relevant Terms and their Relations with Bootstrapping. In Proceedings of LREC 2002, the third international conference on language resources and evaluation. Las Palmas, Canary island, Spain. May 2002.

[Yarowsky, 1995] Yarowsky D.: Unsupervised Word-Sense Disambiguation Rivaling Supervised Methods. In Proceedings of the 33rd Annual Meeting of the Association for Computational Linguistics, Cambridge, MA. 1995. 189-196.

[Yeol and Hoffman, 2003] Yeol Yoo, S. and Hoffmann, A.: A New Approach for Concept-Based Web Search. In Proceedings of the Australian Conference on Artificial Intelligence. LNAI 2903. 2003. 65–76.

[Zamir and Etzioni, 1999] Zamir, O. and Etzioni, O.: Grouper: A dynamic clustering interface to web search results. Computer Networks 31. 1999. 1361–1374.

[Zhang and Dong, 2004] Zhang, D. and Dong, Y.: Semantic, Hierarchical, Online Clustering of Web Search Results. In Proceedings of the 6th Asia Pacific Web Conference (APWEB), Hangzhou, China. 2004.

www.ingramcontent.com/pod-product-compliance
Lightning Source LLC
LaVergne TN
LVHW062314060326
832902LV00013B/2218